"The most laudable purpose of autobiographical works is to help others reflect on the world in ways that are enlightening and motivating, and the best of those are written by thoughtful people based on lives of deep involvements and rich experiences. Rip Rapson has written a book that could only have been penned by a person of deep convictions, commitment to action, and a legacy of meaningful results. His consistent work across the decades has culminated in a new model for how America's interwoven system of government, business, and philanthropy can uplift individuals and entire cities."

HENRY CISNEROS, former mayor of San Antonio and secretary of Housing and Urban Development under President Bill Clinton

"This book is full of interesting tales told by a supremely talented leader who has managed to find himself at the center of some of the most intractable-seeming problems of his time, always with an eye toward creative solutions that others miss. In his self-effacing way, Rip Rapson draws compelling lessons from his adventures pioneering new approaches to protect the environment, authentically address racial injustice, transform a major philanthropy, and reinvigorate an iconic American city in crisis. His insights from challenges he has faced down over the decades are remarkable and deeply relevant. This book is a delight and a salve for our times."

CECILIA MUÑOZ, former director of the White House Domestic Policy Council under President Barack Obama

"Rip's mastery of the English language—and the drawing pen—is on full display with stories and lessons in civic engagement, strategic philanthropy, and groundbreaking partnerships. He does so with grace and humility. This book is a treasure, as is its author."

ELAINE ROSEN, former chair, the Kresge Foundation

"This is more than a memoir. Rip Rapson takes the reader on an engaging journey through some of the most recognizable challenges confronting cities and regions. What emerges is a powerful portrait of what's possible when residents engage, leaders collaborate, and coalitions share risk. Anyone who believes in the promise of local problem solving will be inspired by this collection of stories about leadership 'from all quarters.'"

AMY LIU, cofounder of Brookings Metro and former president of the Brookings Institution

DRAWN TO CHALLENGE

Stories of creative leadership in the public interest (with doodles)

By

This book is a memoir. It reflects the author's present recollections of experiences over time. Some dialogue has been recreated.

Published by Transect Press, Detroit

Design by Kristi Anderson, Two Spruce Design

Printed by Smart Set, Inc., Minneapolis, Minnesota
The typefaces are Adobe Caslon Pro and Futura PT.

Manufactured in the United States of America

ISBN: 978-1-956573-13-8

CONTENTS

I guess I shouldn't have been surprised when my mother and father were arrested in my junior year of high school.

Not embezzlement. Not drugs. Not even excessive unpaid parking tickets. But for protesting the demolition of our neighborhood's quirky, one-of-a-kind used bookstore to make way for a Red Barn fast food franchise.

But I *was*. Even though they had warned me about what to expect, it was shocking to see them on television being shepherded into a police van. And yet, there was a conventional—almost soft—edge to the disequilibrium. My father was, after all, dean of the University of Minnesota's School of Architecture, and my mother, a librarian with a passion for cataloging illustrated children's books. Principles of preservation and books blunted the sharpness. And to my relief, they wouldn't be held long—indeed might even be home for dinner.

I don't know that the Red Barn incident was as much formative as it was affirming. There were things large and small that were inevitable trip wires for one's decision to put himself or herself in a zone of discomfort and risk: in my parents' case, trip wires deeply grounded in a belief system about the value of balanced, healthy communities and one's responsibility to fight for them.

In what follows, I'll describe the catalysts to action that I've been privileged to witness, participate in, or help shape over five decades of life experiences. In many circumstances, there was unresolved tension—a disequilibrium that needed to be resolved by the value system of a lead protagonist. In others, there was simply an impetus to action or behavior that illuminates the way people I admire make decisions.

The result is less a treatise on principles of leadership and more a constellation of leadership moments.

It would be entirely reasonable to presume that stories scattered across a fifty-year landscape can be little more than nostalgic irrelevancies to the wickedly complex challenges of the present. And it would be folly to expect that solutions aged over decades could do adequate service if superimposed wholesale on our contemporary context. Too much has changed. Everything, in fact.

Or at least the presenting forms of problems have changed. The question is whether it is possible to discern, extract, and adapt patterns of thought and behavior underlying how successive generations pursue social change. The vast and varied scholarship of leadership suggests that it is: that cumulative and iterative knowledge morphs how decisions are made from generation to generation, while drawing on a taproot of enduring principles. That is the premise of what follows in these pages.

Because although the two dozen stories that follow are decidedly creatures of their time, many grew a long and practical tail:

- A high school student engagement process 54 years ago that reshaped public school policies in Minneapolis for more than two decades . . .
- A mediation that permanently changed decades of accepted management techniques of public forestlands . . .
- A battle for the fate of a national wilderness that still reverberates in debates over the area's future almost 50 years later . . .
- A neighborhood investment framework that shaped the form and vitality of a city's neighborhoods for a generation . . .
- A conflict to preserve an historical landmark in the 1990s that culminated decades later in a viable reuse of the building . . .
- A 20-year-old business engagement initiative that continues to define a metropolitan region's approach to civic health . . . .
- A decade-old suite of actions still reshaping the trajectory of Detroit.

Tail or no, the stories are intended to paint a picture of decision-making across the public, private, nonprofit, philanthropic, and civic realms. The sum constitutes leadership with a soft "l"—with some decisions precipitated by moments of self-contained personal uncertainty, some by circumstances of decidedly limited consequence, and some by inflection points of broad, enduring community importance.

The protagonist(s) in each of the stories could be a community organizer or a land-use planner . . . a superintendent of schools or a high school debate coach . . . an architect facing down a giant of Shakespearean theater or a mediator guiding a city's path out of bankruptcy . . . a gang leader or a city council member . . . a mayor or an adviser to the President of the United States.

The through line of each situation was the need to make a decision or pursue a path that was neither self-apparent nor easy: a decision that could only be made by balancing a gyroscopic tension between principle and pragmatism.

I was part of the mix in all but one of the stories—the exception involving my father. My engagement was far less a measure of my importance to the outcome than a reflection that I had a role to play. More often than not, that role was table-setting: to help frame the problem, to push toward an approach to solving it, and to make sure that there was indeed a protagonist who could use that process to enact the desired change.

I've proceeded in chronological sequence, but with some license.

The stories begin with my time from high school—normally neither the most formative nor intriguing period of one's problem-solving signature. In my case, though, I was drawn into two opportunities that underscored the methods that would serve me best in subsequent years.

I then jump to my first big job—as a legislative assistant from 1974-78 in the Washington,

D.C. office of U.S. Representative Donald Fraser—where I spent two years developing and shepherding a bill to protect the Boundary Waters Canoe Area in northern Minnesota.

Stepping out of the chronological queue, I describe the titanic battles between my father, the architect of the Guthrie Theater in Minneapolis, and the theater's founder, Sir Tyrone Guthrie. Their dueling visions of design became an indelible reminder of the importance of resolving creative tensions through principle, not expediency.

After leaving Fraser's congressional office and attending law school in New York, I signed on with the Minneapolis law firm of Leonard, Street and Deinard, where I was an associate from 1981-1987, and a partner from 1988-1989. The stories from this period center on using the firm's platform to provide legal services to organizations and causes that couldn't afford to pay for them.

A half-dozen years after I had become a partner in the law firm, Don Fraser approached me again. He had been elected mayor of Minneapolis after leaving the Congress in 1978 and asked me to replace his retiring deputy mayor. The next suite of five stories arises from my four years, from 1989 to 1993, in that position. Creating a comprehensive neighborhood revitalization program, preserving a WPA armory, seeking a solution to gang violence, designing a citywide arts initiative, helping a neighborhood create a pathbreaking center for environmental innovation.

When Fraser announced that he would retire as Mayor in 1993, I entered the race to succeed him. The next two stories chronicle that campaign and my subsequent efforts to champion, from outside city hall, the issues I'd sought to advance while inside it.

A few months after the mayor's race, I joined the University of Minnesota's Design Center for the American Urban Landscape, a unit of the College of Architecture and Landscape Architecture. Created and run by the brilliant husband-and-wife team of Bill Morrish and Catherine Brown, the Design Center became the home for an initiative I led called the Community Connections Project, which explored how aging first-ring suburban communities could draw lessons from their large urban neighbors. It also became the place I was tutored by Morrish in creating schematic depictions of ideas and projects, which I describe in the story entitled "Right Brain."

I moved from the Design Center to the Minneapolis-based McKnight Foundation in 1999, serving as president through 2006. Two stories emerge from that time: the first about preventing a road expansion project from undermining a growing Latinx culture that was taking root; the second about about the birth of the Itasca Project, an unprecedented effort to enlist the Twin Cities corporate community to collaborate with the public and nonprofit communities in steering toward a more equitable approach to regional growth.

I joined the Detroit-based Kresge Foundation in 2006. The final five stories derive from that period, with particular emphasis on helping the city of Detroit weather a series of existential crises and move toward economic stability.

Although I try to illuminate some patterns in the final chapter, that task is ultimately left to you. The stories come as a package, and not every one will resonate. My hope is that in their entirety, however, they suggest principles and problem-solving methods still relevant today—would that a half-century arc of being drawn to change leaves small doses of learning in its wake.

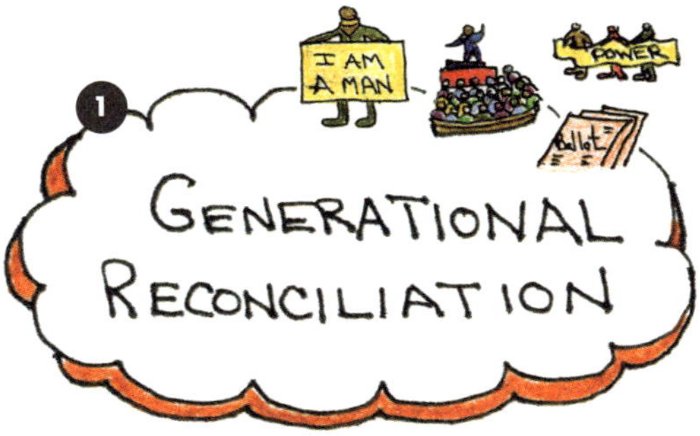

1 Generational Reconciliation

Trusting young people to lead

The last thing John B. Davis expected to see over breakfast was television images of a gang fight in the fast-food parking lot opposite Marshall-University High School.

As superintendent of the Minneapolis Public Schools, Davis had planned for months for what he knew would be a difficult opening day of school in the fall of 1969. It would mark the beginning of a court-ordered districtwide desegregation plan, and there was widespread anxiety that the epicenter of difficulty might be at Marshall-U, where two attendance areas would become one: the blue-collar working-class neighborhoods of Southeast Minneapolis and the largely African American neighborhoods of North Minneapolis. But scores of kids from both backgrounds, armed with knives and bats, squaring off before the very first bell wasn't part of the planning.

A rumble wasn't the only challenge on Davis's mind that fall. The fervor of anti-Vietnam War protests had played out that spring and summer—not only on high school and college campuses, but also on the streets of the city. Pain and fear were still simmering from street rebellions in North Minneapolis after the murders of Dr. Martin Luther King Jr. and Robert F. Kennedy. The city's politics had become deeply polarized between progressives and law-and-order advocates. And students had grown increasingly frustrated by what they perceived as faculty and administrative censorship of their rights to publish provocative articles in school newspapers, to invite social activist speakers, and to come and go from school campuses.

I had been elected the previous spring as president of the Minneapolis All-City Student Council, a largely ceremonial group of the student presidents of the system's 13 public high schools. Members of the council had traditionally met monthly, but had no real standing to do much of anything beyond discussing the things that irritated any normal high school student. But it dawned on Superintendent Davis that there was something to be said for seeing the city's tumult through the eyes of the students in his charge. The council seemed a ready made vehicle. So, he called its president—me—with an invitation to come to district headquarters the next day for a chat. He explained that he had arranged with my principal, Bryon Schneider, to excuse me from my first two periods of class.

Intimidated doesn't begin to do justice to what I felt. Davis was seen as a profoundly erudite, bow-tie-accessorized, progressive administrator who had been hired in 1967 after serving as superintendent of the Lincoln and Worchester Public School districts in

Massachusetts. He had marched with Coretta Scott King for civil rights and taken to the streets to protest the Vietnam War. He was larger than life.

When I entered the superintendent's offices at 807 Broadway, Davis and Schneider were engaged in a heated exchange and didn't even notice me. After a couple of moments, Davis realized I was there and sprinted out from behind his desk, stuck out his hand, and said, "We are so very glad you were willing to come see us." A geeky high school student "willing" to come see the superintendent? Disarming, to say the least.

Davis got right to the point. In his view, the schools had become a microcosm of the community's larger tensions. Many of those tensions had crystallized at my own high school, Marshall-University. He told me how distressed he had been when those dangerous group fights had erupted between Black and white students. He expressed concern about the School Board's denial of the student body's request to invite Dr. Angela Davis, a member of both the Communist and Black Panther parties, to speak at the school. He acknowledged the complexities of denying the student newspaper the ability to publish stories about anti-war protests or the difficulties of desegregation. Schneider chimed in that he had had no choice but to suspend scores of students for wandering off campus to nearby shops during lunch hour or for organizing unsanctioned protests.

Davis observed that the situation would only get worse—not just at my high school, but across the district—unless student voices took the lead in developing solutions. Schneider fidgeted and turned red, interjecting that that didn't mean that the administration was relinquishing its prerogatives to set policy and enforce rules. But Davis just smiled; he and Schneider had apparently been having exactly that conversation when I came in.

He turned to me and said: "Rip, what I want you to do as head of the all-city student council is to design and lead a process that will solicit student, parent, teacher, community, and administration input to develop policies for the issues you believe will be most important—and will have the greatest impact—in helping us move forward in such a difficult time."

Scores of kids from both backgrounds, armed with knives and bats, squaring off before the very first bell wasn't part of the planning.

Davis added that he would make his good offices available to ensure that the process was taken seriously. He anticipated that it would take the better part of the school year, but noted with a nod in Schneider's direction that he would make sure my principal didn't punish me too severely for taking time away from my classes.

The next year was a blur. I pulled together a steering committee of a half-dozen students from across the city to scope out what we might address. Particularly for a bunch of teenagers, it seemed overwhelming, even grandiose: forming recommendations about the rights of students to organize, assemble, and protest . . . championing due process rights for suspensions . . . instituting editorial controls for student newspapers . . . securing permission to leave the high school grounds . . . shouldering responsibilities associated with enlisting potentially controversial guest speakers . . . creating forums and processes for conversations about desegregation, integration, and racial reconciliation . . . and many others.

We met with all 13 student councils, convened open assemblies at each of the high schools, met until all hours of the night with parent groups, conducted interviews with teachers, and held numerous citywide public meetings. More than 60 meetings in all.

I was stunned to see and hear parents in working-class white neighborhoods vent their anger at a group of teenagers who could be so foolish as to push for reforms that were naïve, misguided, and just plain stupid. I was shaken to receive a bunch of really nasty, even threatening, personal notes from fellow students, some questioning why I was permitting myself to be co-opted by a cynical administration, and others mocking my grandiosity. And I was profoundly humbled to meet at the Phyllis Wheatly Center with more than 200 African American parents who wanted to know how I, together with a bunch of other well-heeled white teenagers, could presume to know what their sons and daughters needed when it was those Black students, not us, who were getting on buses each morning to attend all-white schools, and who were putting their safety on the line every time they walked into a school building.

In every case, the best I could do was to bear witness. Because each of these encounters conveyed substantial and painful truths. Reform is a complicated thing, and what we might propose could well turn out to be every bit as misguided as some predicted it would be. It was entirely possible that the view of many students was correct: that I was part of a predetermined Kabuki performance choreographed by the administration, a stylized exercise that could only end up discrediting student voices. And the Black families who shared their skepticism and anger had every reason to believe that nothing in my lived experience could be relevant to theirs.

So, we listened . . . and listened . . . and listened. But we also pressed on, revising the work endlessly, and ultimately developing a document suitable for delivery to Davis in the spring of 1970. It was called the Minneapolis Public Schools Student Bill of Rights and Responsibilities. Despite my—our—doubts about the legitimacy of our role, the wisdom of our ideas, and the political feasibility of the entire process, the document got an audience with Davis. He took it seriously. Indeed, very seriously.

I was shaken to receive a bunch of nasty, threatening personal notes from fellow students, some questioning why I was permitting myself to be co-opted by a cynical administration, and others mocking my grandiosity.

He wasn't about window dressing. He asked my team and me to brief his cabinet—twice. He assigned his head of public information to help us format the document and get it printed. He dedicated the entire agenda of a school board meeting to the report.

Davis warned me that the board would be every bit as rigorous with the student group as they'd be with a suite of controversial policy recommendations coming from his office. The only difference, he explained, was that it would be up to us, not him, to defend it. Making matters slightly trickier, he reminded me in an aside, was that the Minneapolis Federation of Teachers was threatening to strike over entirely different issues, so the board might be predisposed to crabbiness.

It crossed my mind as I stepped to the table facing the seven-person board that we might well have been set up. It certainly started that way, with two or three board members asking dismissive, antagonistic questions as we moved through each of the roughly dozen key sections. It was clear that some board members weren't about to turn over their policy prerogatives and responsibilities to a group of kids, no matter how well intentioned those kids might be.

But the tone changed when board member Judy Farmer took the microphone to remind her colleagues that what Davis had sought to do was to draw those most affected by district policy into the process of setting that policy. She went on to observe that in dedicating hundreds of hours soliciting ideas and feedback from every part of the community, we had done what the board members themselves—or Davis—probably could not have done. The room got quiet, and the previously belittling line of questions didn't resurface.

Farmer clearly had counted the votes. She moved to adopt the document, as proposed, as official Minneapolis Public School district policy. The motion passed.

I was so dazed, I don't remember whether it was a split vote or unanimous. But I do know that document remained official district policy for at least twenty years. Amendments emerged along the way, but the policy stayed virtually intact for decades.

It crossed my mind as I stepped to the table facing the seven-person Board that we might well have been set up.

The Student Bill of Rights and Responsibilities was not the U.S. Constitution. It didn't prevent the teachers' strike. It didn't make racial disparities go away. It didn't even succeed in getting Angela Davis to visit Marshall-U High School; she was preoccupied with fighting off federal felony charges. But it mattered to a lot of students, and it helped the district navigate a tumultuous time.

And it showed that young people can make a difference. That they can blend idealism with incremental, but meaningful, change. That they can arrive at solutions that reach beyond immediate self-interest. That they can bridge across generations and ideologies. That they can translate early leadership opportunity into constructive long-term patterns of civic engagement.

A 50-year-old lesson with potency today.

We saw it manifest with crystalline clarity after the George Floyd murder in spring 2020, during the March for Justice commemorating the 57th anniversary of Martin Luther King's "I Have a Dream" speech. In the energies of a crowd of all colors, all parts of the nation, all walks of life, and all ages, the optimism of a new generation gave new meaning to Dr. King's observation that "the whirlwinds of revolt will continue to shake the foundations of our nation until the bright day of justice emerges."

One young attendee said, "We are here so they can stop shooting us." Another offered "The law is that you can't attack an innocent Black man. They know that, but they're still doing it." And Yolanda King, the 13-year-old great granddaughter of Dr. King, said her generation would not be left out of the move toward justice: "My generation has already taken to the streets—peacefully and with masks and social distancing—to protest racism. And I want to ask the young people here to join me in pledging that we have only just begun to fight, and that we will be the generation that moves from me to we."

I so hope that Ms. King is right: that within her lifetime, we will have seen the long arc of the moral universe bending truly and meaningfully toward justice.

A similar phrase was invoked by a Unitarian minister named Theodore Parker almost a century earlier. Parker was an abolitionist pastor preaching at a time when he wasn't sure slavery would be abolished, and he didn't have the same level of certitude that Dr. King would convey a century later. He wrote: "I do not pretend to understand the moral universe. The arc is a long one. My eye reaches but little ways. I cannot calculate the curve and complete the figure by experience of sight. I can divine it by conscience. And from what I see I am sure it bends toward justice."

The engagement of the young people in this march and so many other protests over the past decade remind us that young people have a unique ability to speak truth to power with courage. But they also underscore that the emotions of faith must be rekindled generation by generation, expressed in the unique voices that each generation claims.

It is the voice of Greta Thunberg calling adults to account on the climate crisis . . . the students of Stoneman Douglas High School organizing nationwide student walkouts over gun violence . . . the young people of the Mikva Challenge reaching out to under-resourced communities and schools in Chicago, D.C., and southern California to envision a stronger, inclusive democracy that values the contributions of youth . . . the energies of CoCo, the Community Coalition in Los Angeles, training young activists and organizers of color.

> **We have so much to learn—not only from these and countless other young people, but also from the always-young voices within ourselves: the activated memories of our own impatience, bold audacity, and uncompromising conviction.**

In all cases, passion, courage, and profoundly sophisticated problem diagnosis and policy prescription; a recognition that change cannot be accomplished without an accounting and remediation of the deeply encoded racism that permeates every dimension of 21st century life; and a measured patience that is prepared to give structural change the necessary time to gestate, expand, and take root.

We have so much to learn—not only from these and countless other young people, but also from the always-young voices within ourselves: the activated memories of our own appropriate impatience, bold audacity, and uncompromising conviction. A place beyond pragmatism and caution, beyond the dulling effects of disappointment, beyond the inertia that complexity can engender.

2 Beyond Debate

Leading by listening

He didn't have the look of someone who was the indisputable master of his domain.

It was difficult to imagine that the same person who resembled your distant, slightly eccentric uncle—with a bushy beard, thick glasses, dancing eyes, and laugh erupting from his more-than-ample belly—could instill in high school students the sometimes blunt-force, sometimes nuanced, sometimes downright underhanded tricks of high school debate that would enable them to mercilessly dismantle the most meticulous logic paths of opposing teams. But James Seeden did exactly that, year after year, for some twenty years, at another high school before joining the faculty of Marshall-University High School in Minneapolis. Nobody had ever come close to approximating his success in producing high school debate champions.

He was also our junior year social studies teacher, his office in the corner of the building overlooking the school's side lawn. That became important because I was developing a bad habit of skipping third period—Seeden's social studies class—to organize a touch football game on Fridays. After the third Friday, Seeden took me aside and said, "Look, you're a good student and are keeping up. And you're a good quarterback. But neither of those things justifies your cutting class regularly. I'll make a deal with you, though: if you'll participate in my debate team, I'll treat that as makeup for the Fridays you're missing."

That seemed a small price to pay, so I agreed. And for a couple of weeks, I participated in all the research, skill trainings, and other preparations for our first debate . . . against Southwest High School, where Seeden had built his debate dynasty. It was a nightmare. Although I had walked into the debate room with a general sense of how to justify the United States bombings in Cambodia, the other side had stacks of index cards anticipating every possible argument. My partner and I, despite the Seeden touch, got trounced.

I screwed up my courage to tell Seeden that I just didn't have what it took to do the kind of intensive, formal preparation that debate required. I even made peace with the apparent inevitability of having to give up my Friday football sessions. I stayed after class to face the music. Seeden listened carefully before observing, "You didn't really want to learn the system, Rip. You thought that this was an exercise in spontaneous creativity. But it's not. It's all about preparation and practice and disciplined delivery."

I started to protest, but he held up a hand and said, "That's OK. Between your tennis after school and your football during lunch, I can see that that kind of regimen isn't in the cards." "So, no more Friday football?" I asked. "No, you can still do Friday football," he replied. "But I'm going to ask you to try something else. Every fall, the Minnesota State High School League conducts competitions in a variety of oral categories—extemporaneous speaking, creative expression, humorous interpretation, storytelling, and others. I think you would do well in a format called Discussion, which is essentially debate without having to do hours of research and memorization."

He went on to explain that the Discussion format put seven students into a 30-minute conversation about a topic that was revealed only when the group sat down. Participants were graded by judges who evaluated the quality of the contribution of each of the participants: less who talked the most, or who was most forceful, and more who helped shape and guide the conversation most effectively.

"I can't just walk in cold, can I?" I asked. "Not cold," he replied, "but armed with some techniques that can contribute to guiding a conversation toward resolution. If you're willing, you and I will go through some of those."

The district competition was in less than a week. Seeden spent a couple of hours with me walking through how to think about my role—not my point of view, because we wouldn't know what the topic was until the session began. He explained that I should give everyone else a chance to speak before I did . . . that I should strive to identify and elevate threads of consistency and seek to reconcile divergence . . . that I should suggest the outlines, if not the details, of what it might take to move an issue to different ground.

"What the judges will remember is that there was one person at the table looking to weave coherence while six or seven people seek to show they're smarter, or more insightful, or more polished than everyone else."

"What the judges will remember," he advised, "is that there was one person at the table looking to weave coherence while six people seek to show they're smarter, or more insightful, or more polished than everyone else. Those six cuts at the question are unlikely to be sufficiently powerful or distinct to sway the conversation. This isn't debate where you're trying to score a knockout punch. It's a conversation that is intended to clarify, or illuminate, or suggest shared agreement."

When I arrived at South High School for the competition, hundreds of students were gathering around signs for the dozen-or-so competition categories. I was stunned that an activity that flew under most students' radar—or, at least, under mine—was so popular. "Discussion" was in the Spanish classroom, with seven chairs arranged around a round table; I learned that ours would be one of seven tables, with the seven "winners" of each proceeding to a second, final stage.

Our group was assigned the question of how to reconcile the costs and benefits of protecting lake quality. Not so bad, I thought. But then one by one, each of my six tablemates made incisive, clearly prerehearsed, three-minute statements (Seeden later told me that most coaches had their students memorize broad themes in each of a dozen areas of current public affairs), each with forceful, almost defiant certitude. Cold panic: because I had taken

Seeden's advice and waited to the end to enter the conversation, I was now utterly intimidated by how good these six mini-lectures had been.

The good news was that the statements were both general and in conflict. So, I tried to distill the essence of each and push them toward some kind of convergent path that could be applied in the real world of Minneapolis lakes (which were, in fact, struggling with pollution). We then went around the table for another round. My frame held, with everyone feeling a need to bend their comments toward it, giving me a lot to work with when I was up again.

Synthesizing and reframing can themselves be acts of originality.

Ten minutes after we ended, the judges announced that I would advance to the second round. The same script played out; this time on the theme of whether the voting age should be lowered to 16. Same result: I was declared the district speech champion and told I would represent Minneapolis at the state championship.

I was in a daze at the statewide championship. I don't remember the topics or how many rounds I had to pass through. And whether I won—I did not—seemed less important than knowing that Seeden had taught me an approach to participating in complex conversations with applications well beyond a stylized high school competition.

The Seeden approach suited my temperament. It was easier for me to let others jockey for first voice. I felt more comfortable taking the temperature of a conversation before deciding whether to provoke it to greater heat or modulate it to greater calm. I preferred acknowledging the contributions of others to pretending I somehow had deeper or more creative insight. And it elevated my sense that synthesizing and reframing can themselves be acts of originality.

Over the ensuing years, I would come to see that sometimes this approach has distinct disadvantages. Anticipating the mood of a room was hard when making opening remarks to a conference. Holding back until others had put their positions on the table put me at a distinct disadvantage when vying for airtime at a mayoral candidate debate. Searching out middle ground could come across as wishy-washy to employees seeking an unambiguous, definitive point of view.

I've also found that this style of engagement can readily become a safe haven for reticence: providing cover for a form of introversion that risks letting others run a conversation—that tilts toward capitulating to the fear that my contribution won't measure up to the standards of the group.

Although I still struggle with that reticence, I've stuck to the Seeden style. Finding the through line—even if not in the moment, then over time—is worthwhile. Assessing the possibilities of synthesis, both as a bridging mechanism and as a prompt to coherence-making, has become second nature. Carrying a bias that a conversation should never leave the possibility of action on the table. A bit like jazz, I suppose: take something and riff on it, even if it's not yours to begin with.

3 MODULATED INVIOLABILITY

Preserving a national wilderness

Myron "Bud" Heinselman wasn't about to let petty politics destroy the forests, lakes, and streams that he'd spent the final chapters of his professional life protecting.

Heinselman had resigned from the United States Forest Service in 1974 solely to apply his 40 years of training and research to challenging his former employer's penchant for commercializing the great pine forests of Northern Minnesota. Heinselman was the nation's leading expert on the role of naturally occurring fire in regenerating softwood forests, with particular expertise in the red, white, and jack-pine expanses of the one-million-acre Boundary Waters Canoe Area, which stretches along the Minnesota-Ontario border.

A labyrinth of crystalline lakes, interconnecting rivers and streams, cliffs, and forests, the BWCA had been designated for wilderness management practices starting in 1926. But competing claims by loggers and fishermen, resort owners and wilderness seekers, mining prospectors and snowmobilers, had roiled the area for the last half-century. By the early 1960s, it had become a patchwork of management regimens: parts protected as wilderness, parts open to recreational motorboating and snowmobiling, and parts leased out for commercial timber harvesting.

Aiming to put to rest endless regulatory challenges, lawsuits, and political confrontations over these different claims on the land, Minnesota Senator Hubert Humphrey had engineered the inclusion of the BWCA when the national wilderness system was created in 1964. As a concession to the logging and recreational motorboating industries, however, Humphrey had carved out exceptions for the BWCA, making it the only unit of the wilderness system that grandfathered in preexisting motorboat routes, snowmobiling trails, and commercial uses.

In the early 1970s, a group called Friends of the BWCA formed to explore ways of eliminating those uses. Heinselman was among the founding members. With the help of their attorney, Charles Dayton, the Friends drafted legislation they hoped that members of the Minnesota congressional delegation would introduce and champion. It was a "pure wilderness" bill: no clear-cutting of untouched forests, no bulldozed logging roads, no motorized travel on the area's 1,000 lakes, no mining shafts for the region's copper and nickel deposits.

It was a strategy born of urgency. The Friends had sought legal injunctions to block a half-dozen active Forest Service timber sales of some 10,000 acres of "first-growth," or "virgin," stands. Despite Heinselman's testimony that this form of clearcut harvesting would do irreparable damage to the forest, inalterably changing the mix of trees away from the softwoods, the challenges were dismissed. The clear-cutting was poised to begin.

Hence, the legislative strategy. Even in a more collaborative era of congressional history, it was a long shot. Particularly so because congressional prerogatives required that in a matter of "localized interest," a bill's sponsor should be the member in whose district the matter was located. That would be John Blatnik, who had represented Minnesota's Eighth Congressional District for almost 30 years.

Blatnik had only six months before his declared retirement at the end of 1974. He heard the Friends out, even suggesting a compromise bill—but the clock ran out, and nothing was done. The Friends had to start over in the 1975 Congress with Blatnik's successor, his former chief of staff Jim Oberstar.

The Friends approached Oberstar to resuscitate the compromise Blatnik had appeared to favor. But Oberstar, wanting to put his own mark on the issue, developed his own compromise bill. By the end of 1975, he announced a plan to essentially bifurcate the BWCA, with half the area protected as wilderness and the other half designated as a national recreation area, open for motorboating, logging, and snowmobiling.

The proposal caught the environmental community off guard. They had sought to convince Oberstar that because millions of acres of lakes, trails, and forests lay outside the BWCA for motorboating, logging, and snowmobiling, protecting the BWCA would simply expand his constituents' options; they would be able to enjoy recreational experiences free from motors and chain saws.

Oberstar was unmoved. Things were working just fine, he told the Friends. He wasn't about to pull the plug on six pending timber sales of virgin timber. Nor did he endorse replanting miles of existing logging roads, closing 120 motorboat routes covering over 60 percent of the water surface area, or revoking the permit for an exploratory copper-nickel-mining shaft on the BWCA's southern border.

The Friends regrouped. Maybe protecting a unique natural resource should transcend congressional prerogative. This was a *national* wilderness area, after all; not a backyard playground belonging solely to the residents of a particular congressional district. They needed a legislative author with credibility who could see the national importance of the fight, and who'd have the courage and integrity to change the terms of the debate.

They found him in Representative Donald M. Fraser of Minnesota's Fifth District—most of which lay within Minneapolis. Fraser was a progressive with deep foreign policy bona fides serving his 14th year in the House. Although not known as an environmentalist, Fraser had a powerful national reputation. He'd worked with George McGovern to restructure the Democratic Party's rules at the 1972 convention, cofounded the House's Democratic Study Group, and was close to some of the body's most liberal members, including the chair of the powerful House Interior's Subcommittee on Parks and Recreation, Phil Burton of San Francisco.

Fraser was also my boss.

I had joined the Fraser Washington office as a legislative assistant in 1974 after graduating from college. My first two years had been spent largely as a liaison between the Washington and Minneapolis offices, working with education, community, and nonprofit organizations. That was about to change: in the late fall of 1975, Fraser called me into his office.

He said he intended to run for Hubert Humphrey's Senate seat. Humphrey was ailing and not expected to run for another term in 1978. Fraser knew he would need a clear suite of issues of statewide significance to complement his record on foreign policy and his accomplishments in Democratic Party reform. "That's one advantage of being an unapologetic liberal," he said with a smile. "The issues fall right into place: gun control, a woman's right to choose, civil rights—and environmentalism. I've been clear about the first three; looks like it's now time to be clear about the last."

He described his meeting with the Friends. "The good news is that this is the right thing to do," Fraser said. "The bad news is that we're about to throw oil on an incendiary situation: the locals will be livid if I get involved. A Minneapolis do-gooder siding with the environmentalists against the good working-class people of the Iron Range? We'll have to do our homework with particular care . . . and be respectful to people who see this as a way of life that they've fought hard to protect. And by 'us,' I mean you and me. I'm going to need you to step into this full time."

A labyrinth of crystalline lakes, interconnecting rivers and streams, cliffs, and forests, the BWCA had been designated for wilderness management practices starting in 1926. But competing claims by loggers and fishermen, resort owners and wilderness seekers, mining prospectors and snowmobilers, had roiled the area for the last half-century.

I was surprised: why not one of our more senior staff members? Fraser replied that he needed someone who understood Minnesota and its politics. "You can rely on our other staff as you get up to speed on the process of moving environmental legislation through the committees. They can also help you find the right legislative counsel to draft the bill. But this is yours."

Bud Heinselman was delighted to have someone dedicated full time to the cause. He told Fraser that he would stick like glue to me as I learned the issues, the people, and the geography. Another key figure was the Friends' attorney and lobbyist Charles Dayton, who had drafted the initial bill and would be key in developing legislative strategy. Between the two of them, and with the growing coalition of advocates the Friends was building, I would be in the best possible hands.

Fraser told me Representative Phil Burton from San Francisco would be a central player. A member of the Interior Committee, Burton chaired the subcommittee to which a bill would be referred. Except for House Speaker Jim Wright, Burton was arguably the House's most powerful member. "Burton is a friend. He's a die-hard liberal with a strong environmental constituency and the best horse-trader and vote-counter in the House. He'll likely remember, and not forgive, Oberstar's vote for Wright as Speaker—a contest Burton lost by a single vote. Get to know Burton; I've told him to make time for you."

My anxiety was rising with every sentence: quite an assignment for a 23-year-old legislative assistant with just two years of experience. But it got worse. As I turned to leave his office, Fraser tossed out a final piece of advice. "Rip, this isn't just about hard work and building relationships with a strong group of advocates; it's going to be a firestorm. John Blatnik was the chair of the Interior Committee, and Oberstar was Blatnik's chief of staff.

He knows all the members, he's smart, and he's a street fighter. He'll throw everything he has at us. He'll mobilize local residents to fight tooth and nail to keep soft-headed, big-city liberals from telling them how to live their lives.

"I'll take the political heat," Fraser continued. "That's my job, not yours. And we'll find allies who can buffer some of the blowback. But I fully expect that the bill's opponents will not only try to damage me politically, but also cut the legs out from under you—it will be you, after all, who will be running strategy and logistics day to day. This fight will test both of us."

Indeed it did.

For the next two years, I spent virtually all my waking hours on the issue. Heinselman and I became inseparable—professionally, personally. He and his wife Fran took a long-term rental across from the Longworth Office Building to be on the case 24 hours a day, seven days a week.

Charles (who quickly became "Chuck") Dayton, who shared Heinselman's passion, worked with congressional legislative counsel to draft the "Fraser bill," which eliminated all the "adverse uses" in the wilderness.

Heinselman and I had multiple conversations with Oberstar, hoping that he would back away from his proposal to split the area in two. We tried to convince him that the Fraser bill's all-of-it approach would be in the area's best interest... no luck, to put it mildly. Oberstar was categorically dismissive, to put it less mildly.

He did, however, arrange for Heinselman and me to visit with local residents and business owners to present our ideas. We met at the Gunflint Lodge, a gorgeous fishing resort owned by the Kerfoot family on a lake immediately outside the BWCA border.

My anxiety was rising with every sentence: quite an assignment for a 23-year-old legislative assistant with just two years of experience. But it got worse.

The group's first reaction was bemusement and incredulity: we couldn't be serious. When it became clear that we were, that reaction morphed into fury. It was like putting a match to dry timber.

No sooner had Heinselman and I returned to D.C. than residents of Ely, Grand Marais, and the towns in between began organizing protests, writing angry commentaries in local papers, and swamping the phones of the entire Minnesota congressional delegation. Seeing that Fraser wasn't about to back down in the face of the outrage, they started a steady stream of visits to D.C. to convince lawmakers that Fraser had launched an attack on the local way of life.

Heinselman and I stepped up our efforts as well, meeting with scores of lawmakers trying to line up cosponsors—and quiet supporters—for our bill. We brought testimonials from each member's constituents about their use of the BWCA, issue briefs, and above all, "Bud's maps."

Heinselman had printed a standard U.S. Forest Service map of the existing BWCA on a poster-sized foam core board. He then prepared clear mylar sheets that could be superimposed on the base, flipped one at a time, each falling on top of the preceding one. The first mylar showed all the timber sales colored in brown. The second depicted the road system in black. The third traced the motorboat routes in red. And the fourth illustrated the snowmobile trails in purple.

The cumulative image was a stew of colors covering the entire one million acres. It underscored the point more effectively than any issue brief could have. The wilderness area was blanketed by uses utterly inconsistent with—indeed anathema to—any reasoned conception of wilderness. The device seized the attention of busy Congress members and enabled them to hold the issues in memory.

But the real show was Representative Phil Burton.

Burton was a bear of a man, six-foot-something, built like the longshoremen who populated his district. He had a prodigious memory for political detail, the liberal sensibilities of his hometown San Francisco, and legislative infighting skills honed over a decade. Burton had run to succeed Tip O'Neill as Speaker of the House in 1976, losing by a single vote to Jim Wright of Texas after three rounds of voting: 148-147. Burton committed to memory every member who voted for him . . . and every member who hadn't. Fraser fell into the first category, Oberstar into the second.

At the packed Ely field hearings, Heinselman and Fraser were hung in effigy from the booms of logging trucks, and I received a death threat requiring a state trooper to stand watch at my room.

Officially, Burton was the Chair of the House Interior Committee's Subcommittee on National Parks and Recreation. Unofficially, he was the king of the nation's public lands. In 1977, he used the authority of his domain to shape and shepherd several historic pieces of legislation: the Alaska National Interest Lands Conservation Act, better known as the Alaska Lands bill, which was the largest expansion of protected lands in the nation's history; legislation to double the size of Redwoods National Park; and the omnibus parks bill, a bundle of 100 parks and preservation projects in 44 states with a pricetag of $1.2 billion.

He used his influence to get the Fraser and Oberstar BWCA bills referred to his subcommittee for primary jurisdiction—convincing House leadership that the Agriculture Committee should relinquish what Burton called "technically marginal" jurisdiction derived from the BWCA being located in a National Forest, overseen by the Department of Agriculture.

Burton's subcommittee meetings were masterworks of command and control, every detail choreographed to the last nod of the head. He recited key legislative language from memory and had a precise timetable for moving each bill to the full Interior Committee. Burton knew how every member of his subcommittee would vote, and what needed to be brokered in order to lock those votes down.

Burton would summon staff, other committee members, lobbyists, and anyone else who might impact the subcommittee's deliberations to his office for private "consultations," listening politely to convey interest, but then letting people know in no uncertain terms just how matters would unfold. Sometimes those conversations lasted just a few minutes, but for those requiring more jujitsu, the sessions could stretch into hours.

As the Fraser bill began its path, with subcommittee hearings in Washington and field hearings in the Twin Cities and Ely, Burton understood that the fight would be just as complex, heated, and protracted as the higher-profile Alaska, Redwoods, and omnibus bill debates. Indeed, at the packed Ely field hearings, Heinselman and Fraser were hung in effigy from the booms of logging trucks, the gymnasium with a 450-person occupancy capacity was filled with 1,200 residents eager to vent their displeasure, and I received a death threat requiring a state trooper to stand watch at my room.

Burton began inviting Heinselman and me to sit with him after dinner so he could extract every molecule of history, politics, or personality that might help him move the bill. His capacity for detail was supernatural: Burton learned the names of every contested lake and trail, studied the century-long logging and motorboating conflicts, and hatched theories about how different approaches might play to both Fraser and Oberstar's constituencies.

Our first couple of sessions with Burton stuck to the BWCA script. But as we joined him more frequently, they became free-wheeling, four- or five-hour political master classes. Holding a cigar in his left hand and a perpetually full glass of vodka in his right, Burton would ruminate about the evolution of the nation's progressive movement, dish on his political enemies, and plot about how to coax those members who needed further persuasion.

At one late-evening session, Burton announced that he'd canvassed the votes, and we needed to compromise.

Not about the logging: Heinselman had provided such air-tight testimony in the D.C. hearing about the harms of logging in the BWCA that the timber industry had quietly conveyed to Burton that they would acquiesce to a termination of logging in exchange for expanded access to contiguous stands of timber outside the BWCA.

Not about the mining: the actors seeking exploratory shafts were small fish, and Burton had invented the idea of "a Mineral Protection Zone" a ring on the perimeter of the wilderness in which mineral exploration would be banned.

But motorboating was another matter.

Residents of the area were canvassing congressional offices, making a convincing case that preventing the use of motorboats on large lakes at the area's perimeter would put resorts out of business, crush the local fishing economy, and force longtime residents to use a canoe just to enjoy the water. "We have to show some give," Burton said. "There must be some lakes that wouldn't be so bad to keep open. Can you identify some of those, Bud?"

Heinselman was quiet. "I don't think so, Mr. Chairman. We either treat this as a wilderness or we don't. If you want to zoom around with a 100-horsepower boat, there are hundreds of lakes within ten miles of the area. You don't need the BWCA for that."

"I respect that, Bud," Burton replied. "But we've got to give up something to appease some of the members who believe Oberstar's getting run over. He's a freshman and he's trying to protect his constituents. They are sympathetic to that, and they'll support him on the floor when he offers up a compromise . . . one neither you nor I will like.

"I need you to work with me to develop a third bill—my bill," Burton continued. "It will be just the two of you and me. So can you get me started by identifying a few lakes we could open up?" Heinselman slowly pointed to four lakes. "Will that be all?" he asked. Burton put a big hand on Heinselman's shoulder and said, "It's a good start."

Heinselman was despondent for days. But his respect for Burton was enormous, and he knew we were in the hands of a master tactician. Over the next two months, the three of us met regularly to frame "the Burton bill," with Burton occasionally consulting Forest Service staff to ensure we weren't getting sideways with the agency that would oversee the changes.

By December 1977, the Burton bill had taken shape to the chair's satisfaction. It expanded the BWCA's boundaries. It banned logging and snowmobiling. It ringed the area with a mining buffer zone. It permitted the continued use of ten-horsepower motorboats on a handful of perimeter lakes where resorts were located.

One agonizing delay after another set in, though. Finally, in April, Burton moved the bill through both the subcommittee and Morris Udall's full Interior Committee. When it came to the House floor in June, Oberstar laid exactly the ambush Burton had predicted, offering a substitute to the committee bill. But Burton offered a substitute to the substitute, containing concessions that he'd held in reserve, knowing he'd need to neutralize Oberstar further. The stratagem worked, and the Burton bill passed.

Next up: the Senate.

The norm of honoring the local representative's prerogative may have been overridden in the House, but that wasn't about to happen in the Senate. There would be complete deference to Senators Muriel Humphrey (Hubert Humphrey's widow, who'd been appointed to fill the seat when her husband died from cancer in January) and Wendell Anderson. It was now an election year—1978—and although Muriel Humphrey wouldn't be running (for the seat Fraser was seeking), Anderson would.

Anderson, the former Governor with a powerful statewide constituency, stepped in immediately. He made clear that no bill would pass the Senate without the support of the "people of Northern Minnesota." And the only way to fashion such a bill would be for him and his Senate colleagues to visit the area, talk to local residents, and come to their own view of what would be necessary. It seemed a death knell for the Friends—a return to the likelihood that the original Oberstar bill, or something much like it, would prevail.

Anderson convinced South Dakota Senator Jim Abourezk, chair of the Parks and Recreation Subcommittee of the Senate's Energy and Natural Resources Committee, to take the subcommittee to Ely. Anderson and Abourezk would be joined by Senators Metzenbaum of Ohio, Bumpers of Arkansas, and Humphrey. They would fly to Ely on July 16 on Vice President Walter Mondale's plane, Air Force 2.

It was a crafty and potent show of force, conveying unequivocally that the fate of the BWCA was now squarely in Anderson's hands. Ely had never seen anything like it. Air Force 2 circling the airport twice before landing at tiny Ely Municipal Airport. Staff, security, and media from all across the U.S. All choreographed to stoke local outrage and to pressure the environmental community to make deeper compromises.

"We either treat this as a wilderness or we don't. If you want to zoom around with a 100-horsepower boat, there are hundreds of lakes within ten miles. You don't need the BWCA for that."

Lost in the hoopla, however, was a small detail: it was Senator Abourezk who was really in charge. Abourezk was a shrewd and seasoned maverick who would not be cowed by the political and media extravaganza Anderson had set in motion. He was also a close friend of both Burton and Fraser. When Burton had earlier sounded him out about picking up the legislation in a timely way when it got to the Senate, Abourezk made his attitude clear: "Oberstar is screwing over Fraser. Fraser would be a damn good senator, and Oberstar's trying to ruin him. I don't like it."

After a day-and-a-half of touring and meetings, Abourezk announced that he wanted a debriefing session among the principals, without the politicians present. I was asked to coordinate a short presentation from the Friends. We made a few technical arguments, but then called on Sigurd Olson—the preeminent living wilderness writer—to make the moral case.

Olson was passionate, yet measured; poetic, yet succinct. He said there was no place on earth like the lake-land canoe wilderness of the Minnesota-Ontario border. To compromise its integrity in the name of short-term expediency would betray future generations. We hold the land in trust for our grandchildren and they for theirs. After he closed nobody spoke for what seemed an eternity.

Abourezk broke the silence. He noted that the two sides simply were talking different languages, leaving him and his colleagues with too little to work with. "Look, I'm not going to be able to figure out, and Congress isn't going to figure out, which of these lakes should be motorized and which of them should not be motorized. You simply have to work it out." And time was running out: if identical pieces of legislation weren't adopted by both houses by September, two years of legislative trench warfare would be for naught; the next Congress wouldn't likely revisit the issue.

Ely had never seen anything like it. Air Force 2 circling the airport twice before landing at tiny Ely Municipal Airport; staff, security, and media from across the U.S. All choreographed to stoke local outrage and to pressure the environmental community to make deeper compromises.

Abourezk then pulled Anderson into a sidebar to make the same point. Each side had identified a leading legal advisor—the Friends had chosen Dayton, the alliance representing the local residents, Ron Hotaling. Abourezk suggested to Anderson that Dayton and Hotaling be given the authority to work out a mutually acceptable compromise through a formal mediation process supported by the subcommittee. Anderson agreed.

Dayton would represent the Friends, with Heinselman and me serving as advisers. And Hotaling, who wasn't an attorney, would be replaced by Ron Walls, who was; Walls would be supported by a small delegation representing both the Ely area and the Gunflint Trail to the east. The mediator would be Tom Williams, a senior staffer for the Senate Energy and Natural Resources Committee and a trusted adviser to its chair, Henry "Scoop" Jackson. The sessions would continue in a conference room in the basement of the Russell Senate Building until the sides reached consensus.

No one talked about what might happen if that consensus didn't materialize.

The negotiations stretched over three interminable days. Early agreement emerged on a logging ban and a removal of access roads, on a mining ban, and on additional funding for hiking trails. Then came accord on buyouts for resort owners who didn't believe they could transition to a new form of management, and on continued motorboat use on the four perimeter lakes Bud had identified for Burton.

But Walls was pushing for motorized access to scores of additional lakes, enabling motors to penetrate deep into the heart of the wilderness. Dayton resisted. They finally narrowed the disputed areas to a half-dozen of the largest, most pristine lakes.

At about three in the morning of the third day, Dayton came out of the conference room with a grim look on his face. "This is it, Bud—you have to make the call. Nobody else can, or should." Dayton outlined a proposal to keep open the six contested lakes, but phase out motorized use over twenty years. He explained that that would permit local business owners enough time to make adjustments to their business model, increasingly emphasizing canoeing, hiking, snowshoeing, and cross-country skiing. "But I need your agreement," he continued. "If you can't do that, we'll pack up and look for another legislative opportunity in the future."

Heinselman sat down, ran his hands through his wispy hair, and began to cry. "I can't do it, Chuck. It's an abomination. It will destroy, for an entire generation, the idea of true wilderness. I'm 75 years old. And it's not about me, but at a personal level it means that I'll never see what I've worked my entire professional career to see." Dayton looked at me and shook his head. "Then we're done. I can't do anything more." I asked him to give Heinselman and me a minute.

We then called on Sigurd Olson—the preeminent living wilderness writer—to make the moral case. . . . After he closed, nobody spoke for what seemed an eternity.

It was the most painful minute of my young life. This strong, profoundly principled, heroically committed man broken down by what to many might seem a modest compromise. We talked for 45 minutes in the depressing darkness of that little room where we'd spent the past three days. We revisited all the ups and downs, all the acts of integrity and decency from people like Fraser and Burton, all the tactical turns that broke in our direction, all the progress that Dayton and Walls had made when nobody expected them to.

Finally, Heinselman looked up and said, "OK, Rip. We'll do it. But please don't ask me to defend it as the right thing to do." I walked down the hall, took Dayton outside the negotiation room, and told him that Bud had agreed. Dayton nodded, "Make sure Bud's OK."

The deal stuck. Anderson agreed to bring it to the Senate floor without the possibility of amendment. Burton agreed to the same on the House side. Despite some last-minute drama (in which the bill that was passed over to the House was "lost" underneath a stack of irrelevant paper), the bill was approved within minutes of the close of the 94th Congress. President Carter subsequently signed into law Public Law 95-495, The Boundary Waters Canoe Area Wilderness Act of 1978.

Up until that final negotiation, Heinselman had made an uncomfortable personal peace with pursuing the kind of incremental, iterative give-and-take required in a change process determined by politics. He had witnessed a long string of conflagrations and compromises, each threatening to undermine his long-term vision of a precious natural treasure. He struggled each time to ensure that its tradeoffs wouldn't be lethal.

But in those agonizing final moments in the Russell Building basement, that process became a bridge too far. At some point, reasoned compromises cross into forced capitulation. Heinselman's heart told him that that point had been reached. He was incapable, in that moment, of seeing a long-term triumph within reach—casting it instead as an accretive weight of harm that he would not in his lifetime see lifted.

What a poignant, intensely human leadership moment. On one hand, here was a man who had taught the world that the limited and short-term damage of natural fires was essential to the long-term preservation and health of entire forests. On the other hand, he was struggling with the tradeoff between a 20-year compromise on a handful of lakes and the assurance of a wilderness's long-term protection.

Heinselman ultimately made a principled modulation in the interest of the long-term common good. When the 20-year phase-out on the lakes expired, he wasn't there to witness the purity of wilderness management to which he had dedicated his life. But his children were—and theirs will be as well.

Defending design integrity in the face of theatrical passion

Sir Tyrone Guthrie had never had his artistic vision challenged—nobody would dare.

In 1959, Guthrie, the premier living director of Elizabethan theater and the founder of the Stratford Festival in Canada, announced his intention to create the first professional regional repertory theater in the U.S. heartland, where it would be free to experiment and flourish without the constraints of East Coast pressures and traditions.

After inviting submissions from interested cities, Guthrie narrowed the finalists to Detroit, Milwaukee, and Minneapolis. The Minneapolis business community mobilized immediately. Led by John Cowles Jr., the publisher of the *Minneapolis Star* and *Tribune* newspapers, the community had secured a site next to, and owned by, the Walker Art Center; designated an architect; and raised $400,000—a huge sum in those days. The architect was a nationally respected designer who was also the dean of the University of Minnesota's College of Architecture and head of the Minneapolis Planning Commission.

It worked: Guthrie chose Minneapolis. In doing so, he also wedded his fate to that architect—Ralph Rapson, my father.

At six feet, eight inches tall, Guthrie moved and spoke with a dramatic flair becoming of a Shakespearian actor. He enveloped any room, always accompanied by an entourage of assistants. His imperious ego ignited easily into squalls of temper—which is what happened when he learned the business community would not back off their choice of architect. Being assigned an architect not of his choosing guaranteed that Guthrie and Rapson would start off at dagger-point.

Guthrie had never met my father. He was confident that he could make the terms of engagement sufficiently unpleasant to ensure that a middle-of-the-continent architectural educator would opt for dignified withdrawal. He accordingly summoned my father for an introductory "meeting" at New York's swank Algonquin Hotel.

Rapson entered the dining room to see Guthrie seated with a large entourage selected to test every dimension of Rapson's qualifications: the producer Oliver Rhea, technical theater expert Peter Zeisler, assistant director Douglas Campbell, lighting specialist Jean Rosenthal, and set and costume designer Tanya Moiseiwitsch. Without a smile, Guthrie rose to his full height and said before my father could even sit down, "Young man, I want you to know that you would not have been my first choice to do this building." *En garde.* To which my father sat, nodded, and calmly replied, "Thank you for your confidence."

The rest of the meeting wasn't much better. For Guthrie, the architect was simply a draftsman for the execution of the artist's ideas. For my father, the architect was in equal parts an artist and craftsman, translating a client's needs into physical form through independent judgment, experience, and skill.

Guthrie asked Rapson whether he had ever designed a theater. Rapson answered that he and Eero Saarinen had jointly entered and won numerous theater competitions in the 1930s, but that he had never been the primary architect for a built theater. Guthrie gave a knowing look to his associates. Rapson caught it and said: "Mr. Guthrie, through my own work and through the projects of my students, I've probably designed more theaters than even you have been in. I can tell you more about theaters than you think." He then began to do exactly that.

Guthrie cut him short, telling him in turn about the theaters he most admired and wanted to emulate. He then handed Rapson a copy of his autobiography, *A Lifetime in the Theater*, taking his leave with a toss-off: "This will teach you more about theater than we can cover over tea. I'll see you in Minneapolis."

It was a revealing meeting—each man taking the measure of the other through the lens of certitude that his professional experiences and sensibilities would not be bent toward compromise.

And yet, whatever dynamic lay ahead, a project needed to be conceptualized, planned, and executed. The parrying and riposte of wills began immediately, and would persist through opening night three years later.

In the first round, Guthrie's prodigious experiences with the nuts and bolts of theater-craft shaped and drove the dynamics between the two men.

First was the nature, form, and size of the stage. The local organizers had joined with Guthrie's team to create a design team. They advocated for a flexible stage, which could accommodate either productions suited to a proscenium or those suited to an Elizabethan open, or "thrust," stage. Guthrie was infuriated by the possibility. He insisted that the stage be a thrust—a stage open on three sides. Guthrie argued that the 17th century plays he intended to mount had been written for an open stage, which provided far more production flexibility than a proscenium, and enabled greater intimacy by seating the audience as close to the action as possible.

Guthrie rose to his full height and said before dad could even sit down, "Young man, I want you to know that you would not have been my first choice to do this building." *En garde.* To which my father sat, nodded, and calmly replied, "Thank you for your confidence."

Here, Rapson sided with Guthrie; he'd already prepared preliminary studies envisioning exactly that configuration. But Guthrie took it a step further, saying that the stage dimensions had to be precise to the inch if the stage was going to accommodate Elizabethan plays. To demonstrate, Guthrie had Rapson measure the distances he traveled as he recited passages from *Richard III.* They repeated the exercise over and over with passages from different plays until they had determined the perfect depth and length of the stage.

That was stage logistics, squarely within Guthrie's domain. There was still the matter of stage design—Rapson's purview.

Whereas Guthrie wanted the simple semicircle of the Stratford stage, with the entire audience on one level, Rapson instead proposed an asymmetrical stage jutting into a 200-degree arc of seating, with a dramatic overhanging "alpine-slope" on stage-left: a long, continuous bank of seating that would blur the separation of the orchestra and balcony sections. Rapson also suggested "floating" acoustical clouds reaching down from the ceiling, mimicking the asymmetries of the stage and seating configuration, and cleverly concealing and accommodating the intricate systems of lighting, catwalks, ventilation, and heating.

"He was trying to pull the best concepts out of me. He forced me to defend every idea and to improve on a great many of them. He was an SOB right from the word go, but . . . when all was said and done, it was a strangely balanced give and take."

Guthrie argued that the scheme violated his principle of keeping matters simple, unembellished. Raked seating, padded seats, distracting stage structure—Rapson's ideas amounted to sheer blasphemy. They debated week after week, with the design committee caught in the middle.

Guthrie finally arranged for the group to fly to Stratford to see what he had in mind—and would insist on. Rapson was decidedly unimpressed, remarking years later: "There was a certain monotony [in] having every seat be identical. There was no variation whatsoever in the experience of one viewer to the next . . . or from one performance to the next, if one sat somewhere else in the hall. Just one large, undifferentiated, static mass, like any other auditorium."

Rapson sought to loosen Guthrie's preconceptions of what a theater should look like by drawing scheme after scheme, each incorporating a different combination of elements. Rapson noted, again later: "I think Guthrie was being quite calculating in this . . . . waging fights—really beautiful fights. He was trying to pull the best concepts out of me. He forced me to defend every idea and to improve on a great many of them. He was an SOB right from the word go, but . . . when all was said and done, it was a strangely balanced give and take."

Rapson slowly gained ground. An asymmetrical stage injected into the seating in a zig-zag pattern—with all the elements that followed from that design—would create greater audience intimacy, he argued. It would improve sightlines. It would enhance acoustics. It would facilitate actors' entrances and exits.

But then, it all threatened to fall apart over the design of the exterior.

Things started innocently enough. Guthrie told my father to present concept drawings for something "that looked like a theater." My father offered three; Guthrie liked none. Rapson tried five more, and Guthrie dismissed them with a perfunctory "That's not it." Rapson was flummoxed: "What is it that you're looking for?" he asked. To which Guthrie retorted, "Keep drawing. I'll let you know when you get it right."

Rapson focused on an exterior that would echo the dynamism of the interior. He suggested creating an abstractly patterned screen that would wrap around three sides of the building's glass core. The screen's irregular, open geometric shapes could serve like a mask, Rapson argued, with people on the outside able to look first through the façade's openings and then through the glass to the house itself.

Guthrie hated the idea, not understanding why the exterior couldn't be a simple plain envelope, as every other Elizabethan theater was. His agitation with Rapson's inability to give him what he wanted finally boiled over. He asked the board of the newly created Guthrie Theater Foundation to give him an audience about the problem.

In the presence of the judge and jury, Guthrie praised Rapson's work on the interior, but told the group that he was dissatisfied with the exterior. Rapson was about to defend his ideas when Guthrie plowed forward. "I'm going to make a recommendation that our architect won't like, but that is necessary under the circumstances. I want to call in a second architect to design the theater's exterior."

Nobody had expected that. Rapson rose from his chair and slammed a ruler on the walnut conference room table. "That is unacceptable and insufferable. If I hear *anyone* in this room express support for this ham-handed maneuver, I'll leave right now. And I'll take my drawings—all of them, including the construction documents—with me and you can start over." He rolled up the drawings and began heading toward the door.

John Cowles, the board's chair, called him back. "Let's not be hasty," he said. "Show us what you have, Ralph." Rapson unrolled his latest plans, saying, "We've developed some exciting schemes under the pressure of serious time restrictions, substantial budgetary constraints, and other unfavorable circumstances. We will work from these, and from nothing else."

The issue of the façade never came up again.

But one final battle remained to be waged. Ostensibly trivial, but ultimately titanic.

Guthrie had initially wanted to replicate Stratford's tightly bunched wooden seats. He reasoned that they needed to be sufficiently uncomfortable to make the audience sit up straight and pay attention. Rapson proposed, well, something quite different.

Rapson rose from his chair and slammed a ruler on the walnut conference room table. "That is unacceptable and insufferable. If I hear anyone in this room express support for this ham-handed maneuver, I'll leave right now.

He urged that the seats be upholstered, with enough knee room that people could sit comfortably. Guthrie relented—but insisted that they be brown so as to blend in, not compete with, the production. Rapson disagreed, suggesting that a spirited palette of ten different seat colors would enliven the interior and be no more distracting than the colors of the audience's collective wardrobe.

That was a bridge too far for Guthrie. Beige maybe, but not colors. Rapson offered a second option that toned the color palette down a bit. Still unacceptable for Guthrie. Beige, and not a hue more. Rapson muted it a bit more. Still a no-go.

Finally, there was no more time to ping-pong the issue. Guthrie had made his decision. Opening night was in just six weeks, and it promised to be a very big deal. Every major newspaper in North America and western Europe would be there to see the first two productions: George Grizzard and Jessica Tandy in *Hamlet*, and Hume Cronyn in Moliere's *The Miser*. The audience needed something to sit on; the order for the seats had to be called in. So Rapson did.

Three weeks out, the seats hadn't arrived. Two weeks out, still no seats. By this time, Guthrie was hauling Rapson into the office every morning to ask whether they had arrived;

every day, the same reply: "We're working on some production issues; they'll be here in time."

On the Monday morning before Wednesday's grand opening, as Guthrie was threatening to personally construct and install the wooden benches that had started the conversation, three huge delivery vans rolled up to the front of the theater.

Guthrie flew down the stairs and signed the bill of lading. But . . .

As the seats rolled down the ramp, Guthrie turned purple, began shaking violently, and then became apoplectic—homicidal would probably be more apt.

He saw a parade of 1,432 seats of red and green, blue and yellow, and the other six colors Rapson had proposed. As the seats streamed into the building, Guthrie yelled at his assistants, "Find that bast**d Rapson. I'm going to make sure he never draws again." When Rapson emerged, it took two stagehands and a delivery guy to restrain Guthrie. Rapson smiled and gave the workers instructions about how the seats were to be installed. Their confetti of colors became one of the theater's signatures.

Guthrie eventually settled down and made his peace—not just with the seats, but with all the dimensions of the theater's innovation and daring. And why shouldn't he? He'd accomplished his dream of creating a repertory company of international caliber in the nation's heartland. The intellectual, emotional, and creative swordsmanship with Rapson had taken a toll on both men. But it had generated something of genuine magnificence. All's well that ends well.

Rapson didn't prevail in every instance. . . . When Guthrie's intractability stemmed from his expertise and experience, Rapson accommodated. But when it derived from more personal motivations, he held fast.

It might seem as if Bud Heinselman, the ardent BWCA advocate, had yielded to the need to compromise while my father had not; an unsurprising outcome given the widely divergent stakes implicated in the two situations. After all, pursuing a design ethic is not the same as protecting a cherished wilderness.

But Rapson didn't prevail in every instance, choosing instead to calibrate his behavior in the face of an immovable force by drawing on a taproot of professional training, personal values, and tested principles of excellence. He, in turn, respected those traits in Guthrie, yielding when in the wheelhouse of Guthrie's accumulated expertise, experience, and instincts in the theater.

When Guthrie's intractability stemmed from that expertise and experience, Rapson accommodated. But when it derived from more personal motivations, Rapson held fast, incrementally changing up the design solution to give Guthrie comfort that his predispositions were being honored—just in ways uninformed by his professional experiences.

Mutual principled intransigence.

5 Nonbillable Time

Forging an unorthodox legal practice

It seemed an act of self-sabotage to decline an employment offer from one of the most accomplished lawyers in New York City.

Stephen Lefkowitz had taught property and real estate law at Columbia Law School for the last six years and was my—indeed, every Columbia Law student's—favorite professor. He memorized the name and face of each of the 300 entering students before their first class, and would flummox us all by acknowledging our question with "Thank you, Mr. Rapson" or "Mr. Margulies" or "Ms. Nazareth." He injected illuminating real-life examples into otherwise mind-numbing discussions of eminent domain, adverse possession, fee simple, and other arcane concepts—animating them with the richness of insight derived from experience as general counsel to the New York State Urban Development Corporation, counsel to Governor Nelson A. Rockefeller, and son of a legendary attorney general for the state of New York, Louie Lefkowitz.

He was as kind and understated as he was brilliant.

Professor Lefkowitz had always intended to return to law practice after a short stint of teaching. He would rejoin his small, fifteen-person practice to resume work on some of the most complex and seminal real estate transactions that would shape the New York City landscape of the 1980s and '90s. So when he asked me to come for an office visit a few months before graduation, I assumed it was his characteristically thoughtful way of saying goodbye to some of the students who had taken every class he had offered, as I had.

That was part of it. He thanked me for sticking with him. But he then shifted gears and said that he would indeed stay true to his plan and return to private practice. I told him that that would be an immeasurable loss for Columbia Law School, but a wonderful gift to New York City. He nodded and smiled. "I'd like you to be part of that plan," he said.

Lefkowitz explained that he had been keeping an eye on me: not just in his classes, but through the law school's Housing Clinic and a municipal finance seminar taught by his friend Harrison Golden, comptroller of the city of New York. "I read the analysis you did for Golden about affordable housing tax incentives," he said. "Actually, it was the diagram you created to explain the decision flow that caught my attention. Golden showed it to me—quite impressive." I was flattered, but completely taken aback. I had no idea where this was going.

That became clear when he continued, "I'd like you to join my firm this fall. We're committed to remaining small; we take on only projects we believe to be in the public interest. No straight-up commercial deals." He paused before adding, "We give our associates immediate touch points with the public agency clients we represent, so it's important to have someone who's comfortable with people, with public sector processes, and with detail. You strike me as having those qualities."

I was frozen. It was midway through my final year, and I hadn't settled on what to do next. I'd done summer legal internships with two different Minneapolis law firms and assumed I would return there. But this was a concrete, compelling, and utterly audacious alternative. I had loved every minute of my time in New York, and the prospect of making it my home and my professional landing pad was head-spinningly attractive. Lefkowitz could see I was off balance.

"Think about it," he advised. "Let's talk again in a week or two. Thank you, Mr. Rapson."

The toolbox-development side of the equation largely consumed the first couple of years, with the attendant long hours, rookie mistakes, and personal sense of inadequacy.

I did indeed think about it—and little else—over the next week. I knew I wanted to learn a trade, and there would be no better opportunity than in a firm that would give me direct proximity to someone of Lefkowitz's talent and values. I was already gravitating toward public decision-making, another box the Lefkowitz firm checked. And I was intrigued by the possibility of immersing myself in the vitality and complexity of the world's greatest city. And yet . . .

I was intimidated. By Lefkowitz's brilliance and daunting expectations. By the likely demands of fourteen-hour days in the pressure cooker of highly visible public projects. By the prospect of navigating life in a place I really didn't know, and that seemed overwhelming in its civic and political complexity.

I dragged myself back to Lefkowitz's office the following week. He took one look at me, and in an unforgettably kind gesture, said, "I can see that you've made your decision. Please don't second-guess yourself. But I'd be curious to know your thinking." I explained my hesitations. He nodded and chose not to challenge them. Instead he asked, "Mr. Rapson, you have an incredible future in front of you. What do you imagine it will be?"

I said it would start by putting down roots. I had been away from my home for almost eleven years—four in Los Angeles, four in D.C., and now three in New York—and I wasn't yet willing to fully turn my back on it. Lefkowitz nodded, "But it would appear that there is more beyond that."

I replied that, unlike New York, Minneapolis struck me as a place I could figuratively get my arms and head around. The scale seemed so much more manageable. The possibilities of drawing on family and personal networks might help ground me. Congressman Fraser had become Mayor Fraser, so I might find ways of connecting with his agenda. My parents and brother lived there.

Even if he felt this less than compelling, Lefkowitz just smiled. "Sounds like the right decision to me," he offered. "But you must promise to call me if you ever consider a change of direction." As we shook hands, I was convinced I had made the wrong decision.

Parsing the Lefkowitz alternative had made it clear, however, that whatever landing pad

I chose in Minneapolis had to be fully, unequivocally compelling. One was.

The Minneapolis law firm of Leonard, Street and Deinard was founded in 1922 by the brothers Amos and Ben Deinard, together with George Leonard, a Russian immigrant, and Arthur Street, a legal scholar. Ben and Amos were the soul of the firm.

Ben Deinard had stepped out of private law practice to serve in the Department of Justice during World War II, and was one of four civilians to participate in the Nuremberg war crimes trials—during which he was the lead prosecutor for cases against German businesspeople who had profiteered off the Nazis, including Alfred Krupp, the head of the munitions company that armed Germany for war.

Amos Deinard had been blind from early childhood, but earned both his law degree and his Ph.D. from Harvard with the help of Ben, who read all their lessons and cases aloud to his brother. Amos would be instrumental in launching a host of organizations serving the Minneapolis Jewish community, including the Minneapolis Jewish Federation, and worked throughout his career to eradicate employment discrimination.

By the time I interviewed with the firm, Leonard Street and Deinard had grown to some forty attorneys. Many had come from public service. All held deep pride in the firm's commitment to advancing issues and organizations central to community life. My questions about the ability of a junior attorney to balance paid work with public service were met with assurances that although my first priorities would be developing the toolbox of a corporate attorney and contributing to the business, the firm would welcome *pro bono* efforts to take on worthy causes.

The toolbox-development side of the equation largely consumed my first couple of years of practice, with the attendant long hours, rookie mistakes, and personal sense of inadequacy. None of these was unusual for a young attorney, but they were amplified by the unremitting attention of the partner who had been assigned to guide me along: the formidable Nancy Dreher, one of the first women to graduate from the University of Wisconsin law school and an unyielding stickler for preparation and follow-through. No sloppiness. No missed deadlines. No excuses.

As I moved through successive trials by fire, the door opened for me to represent small organizations that couldn't afford our services. It started with the arts.

As I moved through successive trials by fire, the door opened for me to represent small organizations that couldn't afford our services. It started with the arts. Helping the small letterpress Coffee House Press to incorporate and organize their early affairs. Managing the Fuller Young People's Theater transition from a Park Board program to a nonprofit dedicated to productions written, produced, and acted by young people. Advising authors of their intellectual property rights.

The requests started to snowball, though. I found myself representing the boards of a mental health organization and the city's largest domestic violence shelter . . . filing, on behalf of the Minnesota Civil Liberties Union, a challenge to the State of Minnesota's statute permitting involuntary mental health commitments of juveniles . . . challenging Hennepin County's denial of a permit for a group home for mentally impaired adults . . . appearing before local councils and commissions on behalf of environmental organizations seeking to prevent commercial development of an undeveloped lake or a native prairie.

On one hand, Dreher was exasperated; these non-paying cases were displacing the number of billable hours I could log in our little red time books. On the other hand, many of the firm's partners saw, in these cases, affirmation of the values on which the Deinards had built the firm. And they recognized that these examples of community support were powerful recruiting tools for young attorneys seeking a balanced legal practice.

Dreher hesitated when I asked whether I could apply to fill the remaining four-year term of an elected Minneapolis Public Library Board member, who'd had to resign. I suggested that it was the best of both worlds; it wasn't like sitting on the city council, with all the accompanying turbulence, huge time commitments, and potential political blowback for the firm. How controversial or onerous could it be, I asked, to sit on the governance board of the well-run, but sleepy, central library and its dozen branches? Rather, it would be a visible position that could only enhance the firm's reputation for civic-mindedness. Dreher, and the other partners, agreed.

The next four years weren't quite as sleepy as we anticipated.

The first jolt was a big one: we had to decide whether the library system should build a new central library to replace its cramped and technologically outdated 1961 building. The building had been a cornerstone of Minneapolis' downtown redevelopment in the 1960s, consuming an entire city block with a four-story collection, planetarium, auditorium, and a small museum—beloved by schoolchildren for its collection of Egyptian mummies—in its basement. But the library's chief, Joe Kimbrough, argued that the burgeoning digital information world and changing patterns of use necessitated a new, state-of-the art facility. I agreed to chair a special committee-of-the-whole to assess the possibilities.

Such a huge potential redevelopment project instantaneously became complex. Once our intentions became public, developers proposed ideas of every imaginable size and configuration. City hall was skeptical of the library board's ability to pull it off, but welcomed renewed energy on the relatively underdeveloped north end of the city's famous 1964 Lawrence Halperin-designed Nicollet Mall. The library board itself was divided about whether it was necessary, or wise.

How controversial or onerous could it be to sit on the governance board of the well-run, but sleepy, central library and its dozen branches?

Our first decision was to create a viable revenue model to support bond financing. After assessing multiple proposed concepts, we agreed to entertain ideas for a new facility that would occupy the first five floors, then rise up another dozen with residential housing.

The second was to select an architectural firm to create a conceptual design.

We landed on an American icon: Philip Johnson. Or at least, his firm. The lead designer would be the other named partner in the firm, John Burgee. Johnson and Burgee proposed a daring design that would arc over the Nicollet Mall in a quintessentially Johnson-like retro modernist statement. It created an immediate firestorm.

Questions intensified about whether the project was really needed. About whether the finances would pencil-out in a less robust economy—this was the 1980s, after all. About whether the planetarium should be preserved, replaced, or discarded. And countless others.

But mostly, about whether a central library building should cover the mall.

That question came to a head when Burgee came to an all-day library board meeting to present a comprehensive model that located the building in the surrounding six blocks of the project. In a moment of questionable judgment, I had invited an architectural consultant to provide objective input. He had just retired from thirty years as head of the University of Minnesota's School of Architecture, was Minnesota's most prominent architect, and was known for his fierce independence and outspokenness.

After Burgee walked the Board through the complexities of the site, the building program, and the proposed design, he stepped away from the scale model and nodded to the consultant. "Hello, Ralph," he said. "It's good to have someone of your stature helping the board. What do you think?" My father stood up from his seat in the audience and walked over to the model.

To my horror, he up picked the central piece of the model and turned it ninety degrees so that it no longer straddled the mall, but instead faced it. "You can't possibly think that blocking the mall's continuity from end-to-end is a good idea, John," my father said. "The mall is downtown's spine, connecting the full length of the central business district from Loring Park to the river. This design proposes that the mall stop for all intents and purposes at the library's property.

> **When the partners met to decide whether to elevate me from associate to partner, they were looking at an attorney who dedicated as many hours to nonbillable matters as he did to billable ones—and more than all the other associates combined.**

"But it doesn't—and it shouldn't," my father continued. "It needs to provide an open flow all the way to Yamasaki's building [the Northwestern Mutual Life Building] and the river. Dropping the building down this way would be architectural malpractice." He then sat down.

Burgee was white. Probably both from shock and anger. I thought this might be a good time to adjourn. We did.

We never fully regained our footing on the project. Burgee was not of a mind to compromise, the financial projections became increasingly tenuous, and the politics were growing increasingly divided. It seemed prudent to place it on the back burner—where it would stay until the early 2000s, when a brilliant design by Cesar Pelli was executed, with entrances on both the Nicollet and Hennepin Avenue sides, rather than closing off the mall.

The apparent death of the project was welcome news to Dreher. It was exactly the kind of public embroilment I had assured her that library board service would not entail. From then on, our board navigated only minor conflagrations. They included whether the library should exhibit Robert Mapplethorpe's works in our lobby and host a symposium on censorship and art (we did both)—a burning issue generated not only by Mapplethorpe's photographs, but also by the public display of Andres Serrano's "Piss Christ" photograph and by avant-garde performance artists at the Walker Arts Center. (We did both.) Whether we should close the Southeast Minneapolis branch library because of relatively low usage. (We did not.) Whether we should make a change in leadership of the system. (We did.)

When the members of the Leonard, Street and Deinard partnership met in 1987 to decide whether to elevate me from associate to partner, they were looking at an attorney who dedicated as many hours to nonbillable matters as he did to billable ones—and more than all the other associates combined. Several partners urged that the decision be deferred a year or two, to determine whether I could indeed become the kind of revenue generator the firm's future would require. Others countered that the firm had given the green light to my *pro bono* services and that that work was ultimately an asset to the firm.

It was a lengthy and heated meeting. In the end, the voice of the firm's then-senior litigator and one of the most respected attorneys in the state, Harold Field Jr., carried the day. Field had joined the firm in 1955 and had modeled what it meant to be of service to the community through scores of board service on public and nonprofit agencies. He'd also watched me "second-chair" him in several trials. Like Dreher, he was a consummate professional, but had taken me aside after some early mistakes—walking me through what had happened and how it could be avoided in the future. Firm, exacting, but with a commitment to patient and constructive mentoring.

Field reminded the assembled partners that although the firm now employed a hundred attorneys, it was still rooted in the ethic of community-mindedness that its founders had brought to legal practice a half century earlier. Being an attorney wasn't simply a question of generating revenue: it was a matter of serving the public, of perfecting a craft, of being a trusted colleague. Any candidate who possessed those qualities should be admitted to the partnership with open arms and gratitude.

I was.

Two years later, I would take a leave of absence from the firm to become deputy mayor of Minneapolis. Mayor Fraser wanted exactly what Field had articulated: someone whose legal training could be brought to bear on the sharp-edged social, economic, and political issues a mayor's office had to confront. Nonbillable hours weren't the only pathway to that end. But they sure helped.

Pioneering environmental mediation

An arcane environmental action being proposed by a soft-spoken, bespectacled, community organizer from rural Minnesota didn't seem all that inflammatory—at first.

Gary Payne was an amateur forester. He'd spent his life in the woods of Northern Minnesota and had come to believe that tree ecologies, left to their own devices, were far more effective than humans at regulating the life and death of forests. Payne was particularly disturbed by the practice of using planes and helicopters to apply herbicides to clear away the brush in old forest growth to make room for commercially valuable pine and fir timber stands.

Payne had tirelessly voiced his concern to state agencies over more than a half-dozen years, arguing that because herbicides sprayed from the air inevitably drifted beyond the target area—contaminating bodies of water and becoming ingested by game animals—the state should reconsider the practice. Forest management personnel were annoyed by Payne's persistence, and unmoved.

He'd approached multiple law firms to challenge the practice, but had had no takers. Somehow, though, he concluded that I might be willing to give him a hearing given the timber management issues we'd battled over during consideration of the Boundary Waters Canoe Area bill. When he came to talk with me in fall 1985, he had a fully formed strategy laid out. "We" would bring an administrative action under state environmental protection laws to block the practice.

It gave me pause. It would be a steep—perhaps impossibly steep—climb to take on a state agency over a well-established practice grounded in their interpretations of the science and the law. Getting a court to take a claim seriously would require highly technical (and costly) methods of proof of causation and damage, would provoke well-resourced defenses from the timber and herbicide industries, and would involve tangled issues of state administrative law.

My supervising partner, Nancy Dreher, was aghast: because of the degrees of difficulty, and because it was another call on my time that would not yield billable hours for the firm. Payne certainly couldn't afford our corporate rates, and there was no realistic provision for recovering fees under state administrative law. She agreed, however, to run the proposition by several other partners in the firm, particularly two who'd served as top aides to the state's attorney general. Gradually, the firm's partnership warmed to the idea that it could be a legitimate training vehicle for me, as well as a statement of the firm's commitment to environmental stewardship.

The condition was that we handle this exclusively through administrative law channels and not through the state court system. This route had the additional benefit of being required under state law. Were the administrative challenge to fail, my partners insisted, we would throw in the towel.

Step one was to lodge a petition with the state's Environmental Quality Board requesting that the Department of Natural Resources prepare an environmental assessment worksheet on the practice. We lined up the Sierra Club, a coalition of local environmental organizations dubbed People Against Chemical Contamination, and about fifty residents living adjacent to the forests being managed through aerially applied herbicides.

If the petition surprised the department, you would have never known it; their response was swift and decisive. Their practice was the only effective and economical way to manage commercially valuable timber stands. It had stood the test of time in accomplishing its purpose. They had never seen evidence of people, animals, or flora being harmed. In short: go away. Leonard Street and Deinard may be signing the papers, but Payne is behind this, and we've been swatting him away for years.

It would be a steep—perhaps impossibly steep—climb to take on a state agency over a well-established practice grounded in their interpretation of the science and the law.

The problem for the department was that this was a legally insufficient response. The department had failed to produce any documentation of why the practice was needed. It had declined to undertake any cost-benefit analysis comparing aerial application to hand-clearing of brush or other approaches. It had skated over any meaningful risk assessment.

Our response was equally swift. The department's reasoning was so incomplete that they should instead prepare a comprehensive Environmental Impact Statement—far more demanding than the environmental assessment worksheet we had initially requested.

The escalation was risky. If the agency wasn't willing or able to meet the burdens of a worksheet, it seemed unlikely that they would agree to do the more time consuming, labor intensive, and costly EIS. Even the Sierra Club disagreed with my taking this tack, opining that we should move the issue into the court system, where we'd have greater leverage.

That would be a complete break of faith with the law firm on my no-resort-to-the-courts pledge. I countered that the administrative path made sense if the State of Minnesota could be convinced that the issues should be—could be—resolved consensually.

My argument to Payne, his coalition, and the Sierra Club was that this was more than a pipe-dream; it was instead fundamentally in the state's interest to find a way to resolve this rather than fight to the death.

Democratic Governor Rudy Perpich, who had been governor during the profoundly contentious years of the BWCA battles, certainly didn't want to become embroiled in another environmental fight if he didn't have to. The top layers of his Department of Natural Resources were, moreover, filled with people with strong environmental credentials who, given a reasonable choice, would want to do the right thing. And the politics of fighting the Sierra Club and a blue-chip law firm—particularly given Payne's penchant for raising a ruckus—could turn out poorly for the state were the Perpich Administration painted as having knowingly, systematically poisoned rural Minnesotans, the game they hunted, and the crops they consumed.

I suggested that we try a form of mediation that could be accepted all around: by the state, the forest product industries, and environmentalists. A Minnesota Office of Dispute Resolution actually existed, although mediating a statewide environmental issue had never been tried. The situation seemed a good opportunity to break new ground.

I arranged a meeting with Deputy DNR Director Steve Thorne, who had been depicted to me as a dyed-in-the-wool conservationist of unusual thoughtfulness and honesty. He peppered me with questions about the scope of the issues, the good faith of my clients, the desirability of inviting private sector participants, and a host of others. As the questions continued, I began to fear that he was just leading me on.

But then, in a surprising turn, he grew quiet, leaning back in his chair and looking out the window. He nodded slowly, as if to himself. He refocused on me and said, "You know, Rip, this might be worth doing. This administration is sympathetic to so much of the environmental community's agenda, yet we're always fighting with them—with you—one way or another. I don't think there's a single division within my department that isn't in court somewhere with the Sierra Club, or the Izaak Walton League, or someone else. That's not the way to create good policy. We need to figure out better ways to resolve our differences, and identify places where agree more than we think. Mediation might be a good start."

As neither of us had participated in a mediated dispute resolution process, we agreed that we should lean on the state's Office of Dispute Resolution for guidance. Thorne called Roger Williams, the office's director, who readily agreed to design a suitable process and oversee its implementation. Thorne then informed the commercial parties that he wanted them in the mix.

The mediation would be led by a trained environmental mediator from outside Minnesota. It would be binding, with the participants forgoing legal action while the mediation proceeded. The department would refrain from issuing a final determination of the adequacy of their environmental assessment. In addition to environmental and DNR representatives, we would include representatives of the forest products, chemical manufacturing, and agricultural industries. And we would give ourselves no more than five months to resolve the issues.

The first step was to identify a mediator whose credentials and temperament would be acceptable to all three sides of the process. We had to go all the way to Seattle to find her.

Leah Patton had crafted an environmental mediation practice that was respected by both industry and environmentalists. The vice president of the Mediation Institute, Patton was known for meticulous technical preparation, expertise in environmental regulatory proceedings, and a track record of success. She agreed to fly to Minnesota to kick off the mediation. It was February of 1987.

Each of the three parties—the environmental coalition, the department, and the industry representatives—formed a working group and identified a lead representative. Patton hammered out an intricate set of rules governing attendance at the working sessions, confidentiality commitments, public communications, and funding. We agreed on a precise scope of the issues that would be put into play.

The process stretched out over four months, with eight daylong working sessions and countless exchanges of information, analysis, and debate. It's safe to say that neither the industry group nor the environmental group really believed at the outset that the other would act in good faith or ultimately compromise their positions. The early sessions evoked a small animal (Payne and me) standing in the way of a large bulldozer (industry and the DNR).

The industry representatives, who came from corporate headquarters motivated to hold the line against a ragtag group of local gadflies, gave every appearance of driving their bulldozer on full throttle: behaving civilly, but with a dismissive certainty that with patience, they could wait this one out and keep right on rolling. And indeed, Payne was scurrying around just like a small animal, bringing up this study on Roundup, that anecdote about a contaminated pond, and any other evidence he could serve up about herbicides being spread by wind, water, wildlife, or otherwise.

Patton was unfazed. She was titanium cloaked in velvet, unnervingly perceptive and resolute without ever losing her clarity, humility, and sense of balance. She let the first two sessions play out to each side's need to posture and its predisposition to distrust. It struck me that Patton was looking beyond the preliminary annoyances and discomforts, knowing that with each session, people would inch toward personal connections and away from reflexive defensiveness. As the veneers were peeled away, the substance underneath would become increasingly exposed.

Or at least so I thought. Because, abruptly and with unexpected force, Patton pivoted at the beginning of the third meeting.

She distilled the worst aspects of each side's position and confronted them in private caucusing sessions. It was brutal. I thought Payne was going to have a heart attack after Patton's conversation with our caucus. She pushed us on the absence of hard evidence, on the circumstantial nature of our case, on the speculative nature of the harm. "Don't worry," I tried to reassure him. "Can you imagine what she's doing to the state and industry folks? They have far less defensible positions."

"I'm not so sure," Payne replied, clearly in agony. "She's right. I can't really prove anything in a way the government and a huge corporation will accept. I think she's telling us we're going to get flattened, so should start finding a way to get comfortable with what they're doing."

Patton continued shuttling back and forth all day, with each conversation chipping away at the hardest edges of a particular argument. One element cracked and cast aside, she would return to the other two workgroups and do the same. Then back again to repeat the process with the next argument. On and on. She must have made five full cycles through the groups, leaving the distinct impression that nobody had a leg to stand on.

At the end of the third day, she sent each side away with homework. For the industry group, studies about the effects of certain chemicals on pregnancy. For the DNR, evaluations of the drift range of chemicals applied from helicopters and airplanes. For the environmentalists, actual documentation of water quality impairments or chemical residue found in deer or other forest creatures.

The homework became the predicate for the next meeting. And the next. Slowly, methodically, Patton removed certain allegations from the table, raising others in the process and sharpening the focus of the group. With growing clarity about what was really at issue, rigidities softened. We found ourselves on a complex and nuanced—but decidedly constructive—path toward a shared understanding of the risks, the costs, and the alternatives.

By the end of May, we realized that we might be able to translate that understanding into actionable agreement. We met on an overnight retreat in early June to see if we could.

Indeed, we could. In the state's first alternative dispute resolution of an environmental issue, we committed each of the parties to previously unimaginable steps.

The DNR would adopt "hand-management" of old-growth forests whenever possible, either by hand-spraying or removing brush and downed trees the old-fashioned way. The goal would be reducing aerial application of herbicides for forest management purposes by 50 percent over the next six years. Larger buffer zones would be created between sprayed areas and residences and surface water.

Only chemicals registered as safe by the Environmental Protection Agency could be used. The department would allocate $2 million for new roads and bridges, enabling crews using more labor-intensive techniques to control underbrush. A Forest Herbicide Committee under the direction of the Minnesota Office of Dispute Resolution would evaluate compliance and report to the parties annually. And the department would set aside $500,000 annually for six years for the University of Minnesota to develop non-chemical alternatives for vegetation management.

Payne had to be persuaded to settle for half the loaf. The industry representatives had to swallow an admission that their products were not above reproach. The DNR had to retrain its foresters to selectively pick, chop, saw, or otherwise clear deadwood and underbrush.

Dehumanizing and vilifying people who disagree with you may be emotionally satisfying at some level. But it's a poor problem-smashing tool compared with holding enough confidence in your perspective to submit it to the rigors of objective, multifaceted analysis.

The result enjoyed quite a bit of media coverage and praise for the state's willingness to pursue an innovative form of problem-solving. I had hoped that some of that positive aura might wash back onto my law firm, which had taken a substantial reputational risk by pursuing the matter. To some extent, it did. But it also reminded some of my partners that this was a boatload of time that could have been dedicated to generating fees. One more tension point in the coming decision about whether to elevate me to the firm's partnership.

The mediation process had lived up to its fundamental intent. Parties had agreed to the nature and scope of a problem, consented to a middle-ground suite of actions to redress it, and adopted an implementation path. This was a technique the state would now have in its toolbox for future controversies. And underneath the workmanlike success of this dispute-resolution machinery were a number of easily overlooked lessons.

In Gary Payne, we'd witnessed a person with little initial leverage, but an abiding moral mission, turn the tables on deep-pocketed, politically connected entities determined to preserve the status quo.

In Steve Thorne, we'd seen a public servant refuse to accede to well-established organizational default, embracing instead the possibility that an innovative problem-solving approach could loosen his agency's bureaucratic inertia.

In Leah Patton, we'd watched a dispute-resolution craftsperson of transcendent skill design a path in which issues were narrowed surgically, relationships built systematically, and insights surfaced incrementally until the unthinkable became not only possible, but compelling.

It became a powerful reminder that rigid predisposition across different hard-wired interests can be loosened by thoughtful analysis, balanced negotiation, and creative incrementalism. Although our current national political milieu seems incapable of embracing this kind of problem-solving machinery, it is nevertheless a machinery that offers potency when applied to the kind of challenges we confront in the ebbs and flows of local daily life.

Dehumanizing and vilifying people who disagree with you may be emotionally satisfying at some level. But it's a poor problem-smashing tool compared with holding enough confidence in your perspective to submit it to the rigors of objective, multifaceted analysis.

I've returned to that lesson repeatedly while navigating a path of public and philanthropic sector leadership: refraining from prematurely seeking resolution. Avoiding rigid adherence to the rectitude of a particular perspective. Pulling untested and unfamiliar data onto the table.

That doesn't mean one sacrifices a point of view; I wouldn't have taken on Payne's cause without believing in it. But I learned that one's sense of truth can be interrogated.

Few things are more difficult than reconciling one's own fiercely held moral conviction with the recognition that equally intense certitude may be felt on other sides of the question. Yet progress in the places and causes we hold dear requires exactly that muscle, discipline, and generosity of spirit.

Artistic Janus

Mistaking creative charisma for integrity

It was hard to imagine what could be objectionable about running a kids' theater program at small public park.

But Harvey Feldman had had enough.

Feldman was the assistant superintendent of the Minneapolis Park and Recreation Board, with responsibility for overseeing the scores of community parks in a municipal park system seen as one of the nation's finest. Not just the walking and bicycle pathways along the Mississippi River and around the city's ten lakes, but also neighborhood parks within a ten-minute walk of every city resident filled with ballfields, playgrounds, skating rinks, and community centers.

It was one of those community centers that was giving Feldman heartburn.

Normally soft spoken and even-keeled, Feldman sounded uncharacteristically exasperated when he called me at my law firm. "I know you represent lots of arts organizations, Rip. Could you do me a favor and help one more?" he asked. He explained that an extraordinarily talented, ambitious, and energetic young theater director named Steve DiMenna had been operating a theater company by and for young people out of Fuller Park, staging outdoor and indoor productions for several years.

"Haven't heard of them. Are they related to the Minneapolis Children's Theater?" I asked with trepidation, because that company hardly needed my help: they were a major cultural force in the community with their own state-of-the-art building, a large budget, and a national reputation for innovation.

"No, no," Feldman replied. "No relationship. They're teeny, operate on a shoestring, and limit their rehearsals and productions to after-school hours." So, what's the problem, I asked. Feldman explained that the theater, which had adopted the name the Fuller Young People's Theater, had just grown too big, too complicated, and too large a potential legal liability for the park system to continue supporting them as it had. The theater was demanding ever more in-kind support from park employees, overflowing storage space with sets and costumes, and pushing for more performance times in the evenings and on weekends.

I suggested that they might send Steve on his way and hope that he landed on his feet. "I just can't do that," Feldman replied. "He doesn't have any money to set up shop somewhere else as a nonprofit. I feel some obligation after having given him a launchpad. Plus," Feldman continued, "Steve wants to take the name with him. We can't let him do that—it would give the impression we were still sponsoring him."

The problem seemed relatively simple in the greater scheme of things. And Feldman was a terrific administrator and an utterly decent guy. So, I told him I'd meet with DiMenna to see what, if anything, might be done.

When I met DiMenna in the law firm's lobby the next week, he was every bit the vessel of combustible energy Feldman had described. All of twenty-four, he bounded across the room, and gripped my hand with both of his while giving a plaintive look. "You're my last hope," he said. "The Park Board is kicking me out in two weeks."

DiMenna spent the next two hours telling me how important it was to have a theater that focused on themes appropriate for young people. In addition to staging classics like *A Wrinkle in Time* and *Charlotte's Web*, they also staged original works. They engaged only young people as actors, which enabled them to work with seasoned (adult) set designers, lighting technicians, costume designers, stage managers, and directors. DiMenna explained that because they could reside rent free at the park, receive small community activity fees from the Park Board, and solicit donations, they'd been able to create four or five productions a year and build a loyal following of perhaps 100 students and parents.

The next two years were, in almost every respect, an upstart arts organization's dream.

"So, I need you—well, I'd like you—to help me form a nonprofit, create a board of directors, and convince the Park Board to let me keep the name," he concluded. "Oh, and I'd like you to be our chair."

A little bemused, I noted that I had known him all of ninety minutes. "But you have theater in your blood," he argued, referring to my father's design of the Guthrie Theatre and numerous other theaters. "And you've helped other arts organizations get off the ground," he continued, noting that I had incorporated and chaired a small literary nonprofit called Coffee House Press, represented the Mixed Blood Theater when it had been threatened with a water shutoff, and mediated a proposed merger of two film organizations, Intermedia Arts and Film in the Cities.

Before I could fully absorb this pretty impressive display of reconnaissance, he blurted, "Plus, you have a relationship with Harvey Feldman, and he isn't about to let me use the name. I have to have that and he's done negotiating with me." I cautioned him that although Feldman and I had worked together on a variety of projects, I certainly couldn't guarantee that the Park Board would come around. I also noted that I'd have to run the entire idea by my law partners since this would be yet another *pro bono* use of the firm's resources.

He again took my hand in both of his and thanked me. "Not a done deal," I said. He replied, "Maybe not, but I can hope, can't I?" I nodded. Force of nature was a phrase that came to mind.

Two weeks later, the pieces had fallen into place with remarkable speed. Leonard, Street and Deinard consented to taking on a new non-paying client. I had convinced Feldman that "Fuller" was a generic term that could just as readily refer to a "complete young person" as to a particular park in South Minneapolis. We filed for nonprofit status, with me agreeing to serve as the board chair and a couple of the theater's parents as board members. And we'd somehow identified a young pastor at United Methodist Church of Christ, Don Portwood, who was willing to let the theater not only mount its performances at the church, which was a just a few miles from the park, but also house its offices and technical workshop space there.

The next two years were, in almost every respect, an upstart arts organization's dream. DiMenna was utterly devoted to the kids, who worshipped him. He had a remarkable talent for creating memorable productions through donated materials, time, and creative inputs from scores of people. His work had begun to be covered by media critics. He had attracted young playwrights interested in writing for the theater, enabling him to address issues of teen mental health, pregnancy, and other topics of concern and interest to young people.

Money was tight, but the company began charging a nominal fee for the kids to participate, and its nonprofit status enabled it to raise small amounts of tax-deductible donations. The church was happy to provide space in kind, with contributions from the theater helping defray the electric and water bills. DiMenna was paid a very modest salary and, a couple of years in, hired a longtime friend to help manage the books and file taxes.

That latter move was, unfortunately, to be his undoing.

Two years into the theater's independence, I received a call from Melody, the bookkeeper. "Rip, I think we may have a problem, but I'm not sure. Could you meet to see if I'm imagining things?"

Melody spent the next two days poring over more than eighteen months of transactions with the bank. She had been right: money was unaccounted for. Many thousands of dollars.

Melody had noticed that the balances in the theater's checking account didn't seem to add up to the face value of the checks being deposited. DiMenna endorsed checks written to the organization, deposited them, and wrote the checks from the theater's account to pay his own salary. The absence of internal controls had made it difficult for Melody to detect the discrepancies earlier. She was chagrined that she hadn't. But she was now convinced that DiMenna was somehow skimming money off the top for his own use.

I asked her if she was comfortable doing a more thorough audit. She agreed; because it was still a small operation, she thought she could handle it. Melody spent the next two days poring over more than eighteen months of transactions with the bank. She had been right: money was unaccounted for. Many thousands of dollars.

I called in the board's vice chair, Maurie Landsman, who was also an attorney. Melody walked us through the forensics, line by line. Landsman and I shared the same sense of disbelief. DiMenna had been an inspirational leader in countless dimensions, contributing to the dreams and skills of hundreds of young people. Neither of us had seen any evidence of a capacity to be deceitful. His exuberance, his ability to connect with genuine warmth and caring, his artistic brilliance . . . none of this seemed consistent with a thief.

Landsman and I considered whether we should confront DiMenna and simply work it through quietly. Perhaps in another case, that would have been the best course. But there were a couple of complicating factors.

First, the company was built on trust with parents and their children. Refusing to be honest about a major breach of that trust was unthinkable.

Second, the city had recently been rocked by a scandal at the community's other children's theater. In an explosive set of revelations, John Clarke Donohue, the founding and sole artistic director of the Minneapolis Children's Theater, had been prosecuted for alleged sexual misconduct with students. To compound the shockwaves from that story with a second example of misconduct in local youth theater—although it didn't involve any allegations of sexual abuse—was a painful prospect. And yet, to paper over it would have been worse, eroding any sense of responsible stewardship and trust.

I suggested to Landsman that I call a close friend, Tom Johnson, the Hennepin County Attorney. Tom was the epitome of integrity and a world-class attorney. He also was a compassionate guy. We agreed that we needed his advice.

Johnson listened carefully to my explanation. "This is, unfortunately, clear-cut, Rip. You have to hand the matter over to our office. Trying to rectify a criminal act by working something out is an invitation to disaster. Failure to act may also be an illegal act itself insofar as the theater's revenues are dedicated to uses to which they are not being put." He got one of his lead prosecutors on the line, who was also unequivocal. Landsman and I should step back; Johnson and his team would review Melody's documentation and take appropriate steps.

His exuberance, his ability to connect with genuine warmth and caring, his artistic brilliance . . . none of this seemed consistent with a thief.

It didn't take them long to ascertain that DiMenna had indeed embezzled from the theater. Although not at the level of corporate fraud, it was substantial and merited prosecution. DiMenna was charged.

Before the prosecution hit the press, Landsman and I arranged a meeting with all the current students and their parents. We braced ourselves for an outpouring of outrage at our decision—given the loyalties of the students, many of whom had been with the theater for five or six years, we felt sure they would be incredulous that we couldn't have worked out something short of a criminal prosecution.

Every student and parent came. I laid out everything we knew, and explained why we'd chosen to act as we had. There was an extended silence; shock, disbelief. Then, one of the students who had worked with DiMenna for a long time raised her hand. I tensed, knowing what was about to come.

"Thank you," she said, with tears streaking down her face. "We can't imagine someone—especially Steve, who we all love—violating our trust this way." A second student stood up and said the same. And a third, and a fourth. It was cathartic. The parents were clearly waiting for their children to set the tone. They then spoke up one after another, all expressing shock, but support.

I asked whether the students and parents wanted the theater to continue or to close. They were unanimous: there were other adult artists deeply involved in Fuller, all of whom shared DiMenna's artistic vision. One of them could certainly carry on.

So, we did. Another brilliant young director took over and guided the theater through the rest of the year. And into the next. But within a couple of years, the energies diminished, and the Fuller Young People's Theater closed its doors.

The media story was more subdued than I feared it would be. DiMenna tried to make the case that he was simply extracting what he was entitled to, that we'd never paid him a wage commensurate with the value he offered the organization. That he was not paid enough was indisputable. That it was profoundly wrong to seek to rectify that through embezzlement—rather than through negotiations with the board—was equally clear. DiMenna pleaded guilty, received probation, and paid restitution. He moved out of state and reinvented himself, although again in theater.

To this day, I have difficulty holding simultaneously the two Steve DiMennas. It isn't so much that he would take money for his own use; rather, it was the disconnect between the person who built a pathway based on putting other people first, particularly youth in their formative years, and the person who put himself first.

That isn't compartmentalization, with one set of behaviors in one situation and another in others. It is diametrical behaviors in the same situation.

Artistic Janus.

Working years later in the mayor's office, I would come to see that this was not so unusual and inexplicable as I thought when reflecting about DiMenna. It was the adaptive behavior of people who believe that playing straight won't achieve what they want, who delude themselves into thinking that they will escape detection, who conclude that their actions are justified by a different moral compass.

It's more than expediency, more than Machiavellianism: it's the absence of integrity. And without integrity, leadership is a sham. The young people at our meeting grasped that immediately, even as Landsman and I were unsure what the reaction would be.

> **I would come to see that this was not so unusual and inexplicable as I thought.... It was the adaptive behavior of people who believe that playing straight won't achieve what they want.**

During my negotiations with DiMenna's attorney before the plea deal, he argued that I should have noticed and addressed DiMenna's behavior early on. I had the nagging feeling he may have been right. It's entirely possible that the charisma, the self-assurance, the loftiness of the theater's purpose clouded my clarity of view.

Indeed, I was caught unprepared again at least twice over the next several years by people whose big personalities and abundant self-confidence created a veneer of inspirational energy, reliability, and honesty. Once by a long-serving employee in the mayor's office who resented the authorities I carried, and worked actively under the table to undermine me with the rest of the staff. And later by a philanthropic employee who created a back channel to my board of directors to argue that I'd failed to adequately resource that employee's role.

That I failed to detect warning signs in these instances made me rethink the line of sight a leader needs in order to build genuine trust. In all three cases, I had remained at too high an altitude—board chair, deputy mayor, foundation president—to detect the nuances of staff behaviors that would have enabled informed analysis of character, motive, and method.

That begs the question of what early detection mechanisms should be in place when a colleague's behavior is tinged with a tendency to manipulate or undermine institutional norms. In a perfect world, those traits would reveal themselves during an initial interview, but that rarely happens. Unfortunately, those traits become manifest through crisis, as was the case with DiMenna.

Perhaps nonprofit environments, characterized by endemically low wages and scarce resources, require a hypervigilance beyond what the private or public sectors require. But I don't think so.

Or perhaps more likely, when an organization is oriented strongly toward a mission of public service, a leader needs to continually and intentionally fortify structures and norms of trust that are rooted in an ethic of being in service to others. The exceptions—the cases in which colleagues pursue paths rooted in self-interest—might then be more readily illuminated and more susceptible of resolution.

In either event, Feldman's demeanor when he first approached me probably should have served as more of a warning flare to me than it did. What could possibly be objectionable about running a children's theater? Turns out, quite a lot.

Working back channels to quell gun violence

The George Floyd murder in Minneapolis in the summer of 2020 was a haunting echo of the police-community tensions that same city was feeling in the early 1990s.

In that earlier time, media accounts were filled with sordid, chilling stories of the violent, chaotic world of the Sereno 13s, Vatos Locos, Rolling 30s Bloods, Gangster Disciples, and Vice Lords. Long a fraught relationship, the chasm between residents and the police department was filled with racial animus and distrust. Activists and rank and file community residents alike protested systemic police misconduct. Conservative politicians decried the breakdown of law and order. The acquittal of Los Angeles police officers in Rodney King's beating made the situation even more combustible.

Mayor Don Fraser's tenure since his 1978 election had been dedicated to redefining the mayor's role in supporting children and families. He had established a Youth Coordinating Board to coordinate youth services across the city departments, as well as among the independently governed park, library, and school systems. He had partnered with United Way to create the Success by Six early childhood development initiative. He had formed Way to Grow, a nurse-home visitor program to promote maternal and infant health. He had convinced the corporate community to underwrite new neighborhood early learning centers that brought under a single roof Head Start, parenting supports, childcare, and health screening.

The toxic brew of the drug wars and gang violence threatened to push these efforts to the margins of community life. The mayor had to pivot with greater intensity to public safety.

In a series of efforts that eerily foreshadowed today's police reform energies, Fraser zeroed in on community-based approaches to public safety. He worked with Police Chief John Laux to establish the Safety for Everyone (SAFE) program, in which police officers were paired with civilian organizers who could call on their relationships in the community to prevent routine calls from escalating into dangerously volatile situations.

Responding to neighborhood demands (through a program called the Neighborhood Revitalization Program, described in Chapter 12), Fraser and Laux created a handful of pilot police substations that would get officers out of their squad cars and walking the streets. And Fraser convinced the Park Board to house youth outreach workers in the city's park buildings, where they could organize after-school programs, athletic leagues, and social events.

And yet, the gunshots and deaths and fear persisted. Members of the Black community set out to create a new playbook.

In the summer of 1992, a group of self-identified gang members joined with community activists—led by community activist Spike Moss, the Rev. Jerry McAfee, and Vice Lords gang leader Sharif Willis—to form United for Peace. Moss and McAfee had long been known as media-savvy racial justice advocates with deep credibility in the low-income neighborhoods of Minneapolis, particularly in North Minneapolis. Willis was new to the mix. All three were unequivocal: the Black-on-Black youth violence was a cancer that would ultimately destroy the community.

In a major break with expectations, Chief Laux authorized his deputy chief, Dave Dobrotka, to see whether the department could find common ground with United for Peace. As Fraser's deputy, I was tasked with assisting Dobrotka in any way he needed.

It was a roll of the dice. The rank and file of the police department didn't trust United for Peace one iota, believing that Dobrotka and I were being played. Moss and McAfee were, in their eyes, media-hound snakes in the grass who would only hurt the department's gang-busting efforts. And Willis had served time for murdering a man over a gambling dispute and carried convictions for armed robbery. Mother Teresa he was not.

Dobrotka spent enormous time—and personal political capital—seeking to build bridges with United for Peace. But the deep seated distrust of anyone with a uniform and a gun was powerful not only among the United for Peace members, but in the broader communities of color as well. After many weeks, Dobrotka had little to show for his efforts.

They wanted to open a back channel with a third party, completely under the radar, to explore ways to reach into both the gang community and the police department to take down the heat and start chipping away at the walls between the two.

In the midst of all of this, I received a call from Jim Nelson, the founder and director of The City Inc., the Northside community's hub of social services and job training for hard-to-employ adults. Nelson had offered to house United for Peace's operations. Indeed, he had both put Moss and McAfee on contract and hired Willis in an attempt to convey to gang members that The City Inc. could be a safe, protected zone for conversations about possible alternatives to gang life.

Nelson told me on the phone that United for Peace was skeptical that Dobrotka's good intentions would work. They instead wanted to open a back channel with a third party, completely under the radar, to explore ways to reach into both the gang community and the police department to take down the heat and start chipping away at the walls between the two.

Nobody in the police department fit that bill. The mayor's staff person dedicated to public safety was seen as too cozy with the department. The mayor himself would call too much attention. Civil rights leaders would be seen as having too much of a prebaked agenda.

My name had been suggested as someone who might thread the needle—by whom, I wasn't told. Nelson predicted that my community-focused work over the last three years would give me some credibility, but that it would go only so far. I'd have to overcome suspicion that a white public official was a Trojan horse.

I was skeptical. “I’m not sure there’s any viable end game; I can’t make meaningful commitments, Jim. The police department will never agree to an agenda developed outside their culture. And United for Peace would likely see anything I might come up with as inadequate from the jump.”

Nelson was quiet. “Maybe,” he said. “But we’re out of alternatives. Kids are dying because nobody cares enough to find some path out of the swamp. And it’s a swamp on both sides. Fraser’s trying in his own way, but early childhood programs and youth workers aren’t going to cut it. We’ve got to go to the heart of police behaviors.”

We talked about what that might look like. The litany sounds all too familiar today: reforming use-of-force protocol and tactics, implementing checks on racial profiling in traffic stops, recruiting more Black cops, and others.

We agreed that although I couldn’t unilaterally deliver those kinds of policies, there could be value to my listening, bearing witness, and surfacing ideas within the city’s power structure. That was when Nelson threw the curve. “I want you to meet with Willis: just the two of you, way off the grid. United for Peace agrees.” No fanfare, no entourages, no press.

Willis’s formal title was Minister of Justice of the Almighty Nation of Conservative Vice Lords. He had a reputation for being mature, conciliatory, and soft-spoken—but also steely, commanding, and feared.

I hesitated. This was a risky piece of business, to say the least. I made clear that both the mayor and the police chief would have to sign off. Nelson agreed and said that was something Willis understood. It could be a complete dead end. Or it might be a first step toward something meaningful.

Fraser and Laux consented. Laux wanted to take all sorts of precautions, but we rejected that. Instead, after a week of clandestine communications straight out of a bad spy movie, I walked into a small coffee shop off Plymouth Avenue North to see a tall, thin man in a black coat, black jeans, and black sunglasses seated in one of the booths well-shielded from the street. He looked up the minute I walked through the door, stood up, and offered me his hand. He held my grip for a few seconds, as if to convey that it wasn’t perfunctory. Big smile: “Mr. Rapson, Sharif. I appreciate your meeting me.”

Willis’s formal title was Minister of Justice of the Almighty Nation of Conservative Vice Lords. He had a reputation for being a mature, conciliatory, and soft-spoken—but also steely, commanding, and feared—presence in the city’s gang culture. He spoke deliberately, precisely, unemotionally, all the while apologizing for regularly checking the outside for anything unusual. He told me what he knew about me, what gave him pause, what led him to believe I could help.

He made clear that this was dangerous for him. The gangs of Minneapolis were in a fierce struggle for turf, for power, for street credibility. Even talking with me could lead to retribution from within his own organization. But he felt that things had gotten out of control: that young Black men were gunning one another down for no good reason, and that personal grievance and revenge had torn apart the neighborhood he’d grown up in.

Willis wanted to find some way to keep young gang members from making the mistakes he had made and to give them a sense that someone cared. He wanted to help them believe they would have alternatives to taking a bullet before they turned 16.

Just as Nelson had predicted, Willis believed that what we had done in the Fraser office seemed a genuine move in the right direction. But—and it was a big but—these young people needed a very different kind of intervention from a midnight basketball league, or counseling sessions with outreach workers, or job training programs that would land them in minimum-wage jobs.

He wasn't yet sure what that would be, but it would need to be developed with them, for them. Perhaps job apprenticeships with firms owned by people of color . . . or new forms of community service that paid well . . . or, he said as his voice trailed off, perhaps something neither you nor I can imagine.

"We've got to work both sides of the street, Rip. There's no other way to break the code—the gang code or the cop code."

And that's only the first part, he continued. All that is moot if police keep harassing young Black men because they're hanging out on a corner, throwing them up against the car because of a broken headlight, using brutal physical suppression methods.

"We've got to work both sides of the street, Rip," he said. "There's no other way to break the code—the gang code or the cop code."

He was right, of course. And I told him that Fraser knew it and would be committed to moving on parallel tracks. I also I told him that I knew that the mayor would be open to breaking the mold, but I reiterated that Fraser wasn't the whole equation. And I wasn't an entirely free agent: I was wary of making commitments I might not be able to deliver on.

Moreover, with each act of new violence, we would get cynical, vitriolic pushback from council members. Persistent skepticism about the sincerity of United for Peace could make it difficult to defend the wisdom of high-visibility risks. With convicted felons leading the effort, we would inevitably struggle to gain the hearts and minds of patrol officers.

I told Willis that we would swallow all of that and try. The outlines of a framework seemed to be there. After more than three hours, we left agreeing that we would keep talking.

But that would not happen.

On September 25, 1992, Minneapolis transit police on a Northside bus route forcibly removed a passenger who didn't have fare money. The passenger was Black, and blind. A large crowd materialized quickly to protest police abuse, and, in a subsequent melee, one of the transit officers was punched.

Later that day, Chief of Police John Laux was in a previously scheduled meeting at a Northside community center when a crowd burst in demanding justice for the ejected bus rider. Laux knew nothing about it, but agreed to look into it immediately. As he approached his squad car, he found the windshield smashed.

A few hours later still, at 1:45 a.m., Minneapolis Police Officer Jerry Hoff had taken a break for coffee at a Pizza Shack on the city's Southside. Hoff was looking forward to his retirement from the force in three months. He was sitting with his back to the door when two men suddenly burst in and shot him. Officer Hoff was able to radio for help, but died at the hospital within the hour. It was the work of the Vice Lords, carrying an unmistakable message of revenge for the bus incident.

All efforts at coffeehouse diplomacy evaporated in that moment. A manhunt ensued for one Shannon Bowles, who had pulled the trigger, as well as three accomplices. He was nowhere to be found.

About three weeks in, with community tensions rising by the day, I received a call from Willis. "I've been in touch with Shannon," he explained. "He doesn't want to go down in a gun battle with the cops. But he also doesn't trust the cops to take him in alive. I've given him my word that if he surrenders to you, he won't be harmed. Your choice whether you want to do that."

A complex proposition. On one hand, Bowles and Willis both knew that I would immediately turn the suspect over to the police; nothing would change that outcome. But Bowles was looking for a guarantee that he would not be harmed during the course of the arrest. On the other hand, the arrangement might be interpreted as debasing theater, with me being manipulated by a cop killer; people could well question why in the world Bowles would put himself in my hands, however briefly.

But in the end, it was no choice whatsoever. Willis trusted me enough to reveal that he had spoken with Bowles. I trusted him enough to believe that his engagement was limited to the message-carrying function. Rejecting his proposal would only invite the horrors of a continuing search or a horrific shootout down the line.

Willis and I set a time for the rendezvous. I insisted that it be at the back steps of City hall. He agreed.

He was true to his word. A nondescript Chevy pulled up to the back entrance to City hall at the appointed hour. Willis emerged, with his hand on Bowles' arm. As Willis removed his hand, I placed mine where his had been and walked Shannon Bowles up the steps. At the top, Chief Laux took him into custody.

I've since wondered whether—but for the brutal treatment of the bus rider—we might have bent history, even just a little.

Bowles, and his three accomplices, were subsequently tried, convicted, and sentenced to life in prison.

There were no more meetings with Willis. Incidents of gang violence worsened. It would take Minneapolis a decade to reduce the temperature on city streets.

The chain of events raises a host of questions about improbable alliances in the public space. United for Peace knew it had to start at the top of a waterfall of risk if it was going to break into new territory; so did city hall.

The kind of trust that materialized between Willis and me grew out of a sense that neither side had the right levers to change the trajectory of young people engaged in warfare over drug turf. Indeed, trust may be the wrong word. It seems improbable that a gang leader could so summarily "trust" a white representative of the political power apparatus based solely on the counsel of colleagues and his reading of a three-hour meeting.

And yet, it felt to me that some connection was created that went beyond transactional: that the kind of risk-taking implicated in the situation couldn't rest solely in logic. There had to be a ground wire to something more intangible: intuition, emotional judgment, good faith.

My engagement with Willis came to a crashing, inconclusive end. But, for a moment, it suggested the possible. Neither he nor I alone could have delivered on the promise of illuminating alternative pathways for disenfranchised young people. Neither he nor I alone could have ushered the kind of meaningful reform capable of altering the ossified norms and dynamics of police culture. Three decades later, both sides of the challenge remain woefully incomplete.

And yet, I've since wondered whether—but for the brutal treatment of the bus rider—we might have bent history, even just a little. Not in the way George Floyd has, to be sure. But in more incremental ways, by showing that bridges can be constructed between the perceived radicalism of community activism and the assumed entrenchment of municipal government. The right parties working the right terms at the right moment to get something started.

Situational trust.

Willis was later convicted on a drug and weapons charge when he held a dozen people at gunpoint at a gas station, claiming that they had stolen from him. He was sentenced to 25 years in federal prison.

When he was released from prison in 2017, Willis immediately turned to combatting gun violence in Minneapolis, organizing a conference among ministers, gang members, community organizers, that also featured Stevie Wonder and Civil Rights leader Benjamin Chavis. It was a return to his dream of reconciliation and hope—to his trust that things could be better.

Welcoming arts and culture into City Hall

I hadn't been in the mayor's office for even a year when I was thwacked by a blunt force instrument named Walt Dziedzic.

Chair of the City of Minneapolis' powerful Ways and Means Committee, Dziedzic was an old school, blue collar pol full of bluster and rugged charm who was elected to the council from the heavily Eastern European First Ward some thirteen years earlier and would go on to serve another ten. A large, powerfully built man, he had lettered in football, baseball, and hockey in high school; served in the Army during the Korean War; played three years of professional baseball with the Brooklyn Dodgers before attending college; and joined the Minneapolis Police Department, where he rose to become a burglary detective. Not someone to mess with.

But that's exactly what I did, albeit unintentionally.

I had received a call from Cynthia Mayeda, the president of the Dayton Hudson Foundation, the corporate philanthropy arm of the Dayton-Hudson retailers (which would later be dissolved in favor of the Target Corporation). She asked if I would meet her for coffee to explore an idea she'd been considering about how the city might ramp up its support for the arts. She said she had admired my legal work on behalf of arts organizations and thought I might be interested in carrying forward that interest in city hall.

I had never met Mayeda, but knew her by reputation. The Dayton Hudson Foundation had been forged from the deep civic values of Ken Dayton, the last of five Dayton brothers to run the company after their father, George Draper Dayton, founded the Dayton Dry Goods Company in 1902. Ken Dayton had run the company like the brilliant businessman he was, but his orientation of the corporate foundation stood in stark departure from its peers. He eschewed the impulses of cause marketing—using corporate philanthropy as an arm of the mothership's marketing department—in favor of positioning the corporation's philanthropy as fully independent, focused solely on creating "a better environment in which to work and live."

In Mayeda, Dayton had selected a leader who believed strongly in the power of arts, culture, and design to foster and reinforce that kind of environment. During her twelve years as the head of the foundation, she had come to be revered within the arts community as a champion of all forms of creative expression—perhaps second only to Ken Dayton himself, and his wife Judy.

When we sat down for coffee, Mayeda explained that the foundation's fiscal year was coming to a close with some $90,000 still unspoken for. She asked whether the mayor's office might be interested in receiving a grant to explore ways of elevating the arts in the eyes of public decision-makers. If so, she would leave it to the mayor and me just how to approach the question. Although Mayeda couldn't guarantee a grant, she smiled and said that since the idea had come from her, she was pretty sure a request would be well-received. But I would have to move quickly: she'd need my response within two weeks.

I didn't stop to think about the complexities of working customary city hall grant application processes. I simply said yes.

After talking to dozens of people who had long advocated for moving the arts inward from the periphery of municipal priorities, I crafted a proposal suggesting we open the question to the larger community by launching a yearlong set of discussions, to be managed by two longtime cultural professionals, called CultureTalks. The conversations would engage all quarters of the community and touch on everything from promoting arts education to recognizing arts as a community development tool; from creating a dedicated arts office in city hall to providing arts funding from the city's budget. The resulting themes and recommendations would be submitted to the mayor's office.

Within twenty-four hours, Mayeda called me to say that the grant had been approved.

A slight problem, though: as a member of city government, I hadn't taken the process through the obligatory channels. And those channels flowed right through the Ways and Means Committee—which meant Walt Dziedzic.

Dziedzic wasted no time in letting me know how he felt about what I had done. He exploded into my office two days after I received notification from Mayeda and said: "You know you can't do that!" he roared. "Do what?" I asked, somewhat innocently. "Go freelancing for money without working through the Grants and Special Projects Office." I tried to explain why I had acted so precipitously, and why it would be a shame to turn our back on the opportunity.

Dziedzic wasn't impressed. "Well, we'll then need you to come before the committee to make your case. Next Monday. By the way," he added before stomping out, "you should know that the committee has enough on its plate with budget cuts in every direction without having to worry about a cutesy arts project that the [affluent] Seventh Ward may like, but the people of my ward don't have time for."

If residents of the tony parts of the city wanted to pay for art galleries and opera performances, they could do it on their own dime.

I dutifully appeared at the next Ways and Means meeting. Dziedzic gaveled the meeting to order, saying the first order of business would be to hear directly about this arts project that had caught the council by surprise. In fairness, he let me give about four minutes of explanation, but he then unloaded. Lots of frustration about my not respecting the process—and even more vitriol about why I would think that a foundation grant of this size should go to the arts. People worked too hard to see their taxes squandered. If residents of the tony parts of the city wanted to pay for art galleries and opera performances, they could do it on their own dime.

Fortunately, I'd been able to previously explain myself to several of the committee members, who were a bit more forgiving than the chair. They came to my defense, noting that a project of this kind would be possible only if underwritten by a foundation. They seemed sympathetic to not looking a gift horse in the mouth. Dziedzic grudgingly acknowledged the points, but made clear that he wanted no part of it; it was a waste of money and would come to nothing. He let the measure go through.

Not an ideal way to launch a project that would have the imprimatur of the mayor's office. I realized I had some repair work to do.

I let Dziedzic cool off for a week, then paid him a visit. I asked if he would be willing to attend the very first CultureTalks event: a discussion at St. Constantine Ukrainian Catholic Church, square in the middle of his Northeast Minneapolis ward. "There you go again, Rip. You didn't even let me know," Dziedzic bellowed. "That's why I'm here," I replied. "We set it up right after Monday's hearing so that you could be the first council member to see what we're up to."

He came to believe even more strongly in the intangible, invisible role the arts play in creating social cohesion.

"Waste of time," Dziedzic grumbled. But he agreed to show up the next Thursday evening. It involved his constituents, after all.

We met in the sacristy that evening. About a dozen community members were sitting in folding chairs. The council member showed up about twenty minutes late, obviously annoyed at the command performance. We introduced ourselves around the circle: the parish priest. The choir director. The creator of Ukrainian Easter Eggs distributed at holidays, and her daughter. The seamstress who tended the vestments. The stained-glass artisan, the tile artisan. The owner of the flower shop down the street that supplied altar bouquets. The organist.

And others. Some young, some old. Some in the first generation of artisanship, some in the second, and one in the third. All constituents of Dziedzic, and all known to him.

Dziedzic was a deeply religious man, and his ward was home to more churches per square mile than any other part of the city—Baptist, Lutheran, evangelical, Methodist, and particularly, Catholic. As each participant described his or her relationship to the church and the role played by the art form they represented in church life, Dziedzic's body language softened. He looked over at me and nodded. Two speakers later, he smiled. Before long, he was asking questions about how they learned their craft, whether they were professionals or volunteers, whether they worked in other churches as well.

The discussion went on until 9:30, when the Ukrainian Easter egg maker said it was an hour past her bedtime. As we left the church, Dziedzic put his huge hand on my shoulder and turned me around. "Well done, my friend. I wasn't expecting that," he said. "Count me in. You need anything to help this project along, you let me know."

And he was true to his word. He became the council's biggest booster of CultureTalks. He showed up unannounced at meetings even outside his territory. He subsequently created an open tour of hundreds of arts studios in Northeast Minneapolis called Art-a-Whirl, which became the largest event of its kind in the Midwest. At year's end, he championed the recommendation emerging from CultureTalks that the city create an Office of Arts and Cultural Affairs.

Walt Dziedzic was certainly moved by the tangible artistic expression: the music, the painting, the objects. But my sense is that he came to believe even more strongly in the intangible, invisible role the arts play in creating a sense of social cohesion.

We witnessed through the Covid crisis the infinite ways those qualities can help fortify civil society's ability to cope, to adapt, and to imagine the future. To paraphrase the great British cultural writer, John Tusa:

[The arts] can detect order within disorder: think of the powerful poetry so many created or shared to help make sense of the insensible. They can substitute the unexpected and fresh for the conventional and insular: think of the virtual musical and theatrical performances on YouTube. They can offer a vision of connection as an antidote to isolation: think of the singers on the balconies of Italy or in the windows of Manhattan. They can offer beauty in the face of the repellent: think of the countless examples of self-expression popping up in windows, on sidewalks, and along the streets in places like Detroit, or Memphis, or New Orleans.

Dark Matter.

Astronomers have a pretty good handle on how much total matter is in the universe, calculated through absurdly intricate analyses of how light behaves. But when all tangible light sources are gathered up and calculated, the sum accounts for only about 15 percent of total matter. The only explanation for the remainder is dark matter: the "stuff" that can't be observed directly.

But the *effects* of that stuff on visible space-places, like solar systems or galaxies or nebulae, are indeed observable. Astrophysicists have demonstrated with increasing clarity, for example, that dark matter's gravity "controls" how galaxies rotate and how they are bound together.

The idea that something is there, and has properties and effects—even though we can't really measure or "account" for it—is a wonderful gateway into Walt Dziedzic's universe: the invisible civic dark matter that holds us together as community.

Diverting trash to where it belongs

The algorithms so religiously observed by the engineers at Hennepin County weren't as infallible as they were cracked up to be.

The engineers' cost-savings calculations seemed straightforward. Collect garbage from the homes and businesses of South Minneapolis, drop them off at a transfer station in the Phillips neighborhood, and then consolidate loads for hauling to the downtown Hennepin Energy Recovery Center (the "Burner").

Responsible for trash disposal, Hennepin County had mapped out the most efficient location for the transfer: a vacant property at the east end of the Phillips neighborhood, which was easily reachable from all points south and was near the industrial north-south Hiawatha Avenue arterial. Although Phillips was one of Minneapolis' poorest and most racially diverse neighborhoods, the garbage wouldn't be disposed of onsite; just "stored" there until a mega-truck would carry it to the incinerator. The transfer station would accordingly require fewer direct hauls to the burner.

The residents of Phillips weren't pleased. The prospect of garbage trucks from throughout the city running through their streets at all hours to deposit waste right by where they lived and worked struck them as a safety risk and an environmental hazard, with the heightened noise and air pollution and potential for diesel oil and other effluents contaminating groundwater.

That kind of noxious presence didn't exactly signal neighborhood livability. The neighborhood was already a case study in health disparities created by a concentration of industrial sites; the Native American, Black, and Hispanic populations living there suffered (and continue to suffer) disproportionately high rates of asthma, lead poisoning, cardiovascular ailments, and cancer.

A coalition of neighborhood residents approached the mayor's office to ask us to give them a hearing. This was more than a bit sensitive: the county, not the city, controlled the disposition of Minneapolis' garbage. But the coalition argued that they had no other options. The county had concluded an environmental review and, finding no undue risk, was preparing to start construction.

Mayor Fraser was willing to give the matter consideration. He asked me to see what, if any, options we might have.

I started by talking with Peter McLaughlin, the county commissioner who represented the area. McLaughlin was sympathetic; he agreed that there was no need to rush to judgment about something his constituents saw as so detrimental. But he didn't feel he could undercut a decision his colleagues on the county board had already locked onto. He told me that he would be willing to place the project in temporary abeyance if the mayor's office created a process that would enable the community to voice their concerns more fully. He warned me not to expect a different outcome—the engineers had presented an open-and-shut case to the commissioners. He said he'd like to sit in on the process as an observer, not as a participant.

I worked with a dozen community representatives to map out a series of meetings that we fully expected would be heavy on community grievance and personal testimonials. We agreed we would meet regularly for two months, hoping to move beyond expressions of injustice to develop possible mitigating measures or, less likely, to design alternative solutions. The first meeting was set for two hours on a Thursday evening at the brand new Third Precinct police station, which had a large conference room. We gave the effort the elegant title of the Garbage Transfer Station Task Force.

That first meeting attracted scores of longtime residents and business owners deeply concerned about the health and stability of their neighborhood. Indeed, the very first speaker was a passionate, but unpredictable, community activist named Annie Young, who pointed out that the Phillips neighborhood had just completed a comprehensive plan as part of a citywide process I oversaw called the Minneapolis Neighborhood Revitalization Program (see Chapter 12). The Phillips NRP plan, she reminded me while looking at McLaughlin, was centered in constructs of neighborhood environmental sustainability. It would be hypocrisy to permit county government to undermine that intention.

But members of the group had clearly pre-caucused and come ready to move beyond grievance—in fact, to dissect and reassemble the particulars of what the county was proposing. After Young spoke to the community's frustration with the very idea of a garbage station in their midst, Susan Gust, who ran an architectural materials recycling business called The ReUse Center, reset the tone. "We all know full well that Phillips has been treated as a dumping ground for every environmentally harmful use possible," she said. "So, we don't need to make that case. We instead want to use this process to challenge the methodology of how this decision came to be made."

Surely the engineers had run the numbers; they couldn't have made such a fundamental miscalculation.

Gust looked across the table to a man with Coke bottle glasses, who added, "I'm trained as an accountant, not as a traffic engineer. But I know enough about quantitative methods to suspect that the county jumped over several assumptions. When you make different assumptions, their conclusions don't hold up."

A third community member then raised her hand, saying, "I've just completed my master's of urban planning thesis on the history of this neighborhood, and I'd like to suggest that city government should challenge the county's plans as a violation of the most basic principles of prudent long-term land use planning—something the city has the authority to do."

There were others. A former industrial engineer. An artist. A small business owner. Residents who didn't necessarily have technical training, but who instead reflected generations of people who knew, lived in, and worked in the neighborhood. It was clear that the Garbage Transfer Station Task Force would be a contentious piece of business.

The next meeting, we heard from the accountant who had called the county's assumptions into question. He had calculated how long it would take a dozen of the garbage trucks serving South Minneapolis to get from their usual last customer to the proposed transfer station—then contrasted that with how long it would take to go directly from that last customer to downtown. The aggregate numbers favored the downtown direct haul: the detour to the transfer station *added* time rather than reducing it.

That seemed like such a basic flaw in the county's data. Surely the engineers had run the numbers; they couldn't have made such a fundamental miscalculation, I said. That's the point, the accountant responded: one's data are only as good as the algorithms those data are run through.

It was clear that the Garbage Transfer Station Task Force would be a contentious piece of business.

I asked a series of questions about his own assumptions: How did he know the routes the trucks would take? Where their last pickup would be? He replied that he'd simply studied maps and relied on routes that would be reasonable. And that was the point: what we really needed was an analysis of the full universe of sensible assumptions, with real travel times calculated from them.

We agreed we would enlist citizen volunteers to do exactly that, and then we adjourned for the night. These volunteers—not computers—would map the comparative travel times from the farthest reaches of southside city households to the proposed transfer station and to the downtown burner. McLaughlin agreed to provide the county's data on the number of households each truck served and their current travel times to the burner.

We recognized that human data-gathering would take a while, so we extended our two month shelf life. And we agreed to intersperse, between data-parsing sessions, conversations about alternative uses for the vacant land.

As more data became available, the accountant's analysis got sharper, more comprehensive, and more definitive. By the end of the ten months, he had calculated and vetted with a neighborhood subgroup every single garbage truck route in the service area, creating an aggregated differential between haul to the transfer station and haul to the burner that was light years from what the county's numbers had suggested. It wasn't even a close call: his analysis was exhaustive and airtight.

Meanwhile, the wish list of alternative land uses began to be whittled down. The group deliberated ideas that were true to the spirit of environmental stewardship the Phillips NRP Plan had elevated, while remaining mindful of economic sustainability.

To his credit, McLaughlin let the process play out. He endorsed the task force's work and, as the commissioner representing Phillips, he persuaded his colleagues to pull back on the plan and give the task force an opportunity to develop a serious alternative.

The plan that emerged was as audacious as it was ironic.

In place of a waystation for household waste that would be incinerated, the group proposed a multipurpose environmental sustainability center. The first move would be to relocate and expand Susan Gust's existing architectural salvage and reuse center. The second would be to create a "green" office park dedicated to environmental innovation.

In community representatives' vision, the new center would serve as an incubator for businesses offering goods and services geared toward restoring the environment. It would also provide community space for classes and trainings about environmental sustainability.

All told, they estimated that the enterprise would create 40-50 jobs for Phillips neighborhood residents. The complex would be named the Green Institute.

It was a breathtakingly bold idea, even today. Thirty years ago, it was visionary.

That pie-in-the-sky concept became reality. Once completed, the Green Institute served the community for some fifteen years before closing its doors.

Social alchemy.

The Garbage Station Task Force process—by injecting community values, relentless grassroots gumshoe efforts, iconoclastic insight, and vision into a public decision-making apparatus inclined toward the tried and predictable—became a vehicle of creative community transformation.

It wasn't a process suitable for all disputes. But it suited this one. And along the way, it demonstrated the breadth of possibility inherent in blurring the lines between public and community decision-making.

11 CRIMINAL PRESERVATION

Treating architectural heritage as irreplaceable, not disposable

Knocking down a historic armory to make way for a new jail seemed eminently justifiable in the tough-on-crime zeitgeist of the early 1990s.

Hennepin County's jail was housed in the upper floors of city hall, across the street from the county courthouse. Inmates were taken from overcrowded, out-of-date cellblocks to a dedicated elevator that had only a single stop: the basement. They were then escorted in handcuffs along a long underground tunnel under Fifth Street and brought up to the courtrooms via another secure elevator.

County policymakers wanted an alternative solution—preferably a free-standing facility that could accommodate an ever-rising prisoner population. But the alternative had to be proximate to the courthouse. Given that facility's location smack dab in the core of the financial district, options were limited.

They had long had their eyes on the Minneapolis Armory three blocks away. The armory had been an important gathering space since its construction in 1935 through the Public Works Administration: first as the home of the Minnesota National Guard, then as a tank training facility during World War II.

After the war, it became the home, for more than a decade, of the Minneapolis Lakers before they moved to Los Angeles in 1960. Then, for the next twenty-five years, the armory served as a venue for political conventions, sporting events, trade shows, and concerts. But it had sat empty for more than a decade—windows shattered, interior moldering, roof threatening to collapse.

That state of dissolution served the county's purposes perfectly. The county purchased the building in 1989 for $4.7 million, and its planning department started laying the groundwork for its demolition.

During my three years in the mayor's office, Don Fraser had taken multiple steps to course-correct the neglect of historic preservation that had characterized the city's periods of urban renewal and downtown expansion. We had developed a "state of the urban environment" address to complement the mayor's annual state of the city and budget addresses, emphasizing our commitment to preserving what remained of the city's early 20th century architectural patrimony.

Fraser had agreed with my recommendation to veto a demolition permit for the Ivy

Tower, an iconic eight-story ziggurat-like structure built in 1930. That veto was upheld by the city council. He had singlehandedly blocked the efforts of a private developer to create an enclosed shopping mall by building a dome over the west end of the Nicollet Mall, designed in 1961 by Lawrence Halprin. And we had convinced new owners of the 800-room, 1908 Leamington Hotel that the structure should not be demolished for a new glass building, but instead renovated, guided by an advisory design-review process.

The destruction of the armory, however, wasn't being proposed by private developers, but by a sister unit of government—under the direction of seven county commissioners, each holding an election certificate. Challenging that decision would likely be seen as a political affront or worse, a publicity stunt.

To make matters worse, Fraser could only give the matter limited attention. He was running to lead the National League of Cities, a post he sought to convince the member mayors and the league's staff to develop a robust agenda focused on children and families: a stark departure from the league's traditional bread-and-butter concerns.

Challenging that decision would likely be seen as a political affront or, worse, a publicity stunt.

Fraser was sympathetic to my sense that we shouldn't sit by as a building of such importance was removed from the city's landscape. He just couldn't see a path forward, given the energies he would have to spend pushing his agenda onto the national stage.

Without perhaps thinking it through completely, I said I would be willing to develop a strategy.

Fraser paused before responding. "This is completely different from anything we've done," Fraser said. "How strongly do you feel about this? And is there really a solution?"

"On the first: very. On the second, I'm not sure," I replied. "But letting the county have a completely free hand in obliterating our most important work of architecture from the PWA period would be irresponsible—almost an act of municipal malfeasance.

Fraser smiled. "Well, that's a little strong. But I take your point. There's also the small matter of John Derus. He's not about to do this office any favors."

The John Derus in question was chair of the county board—and a longtime Fraser foe. Derus was as conservative as Fraser was progressive. He filled a room with his physicality and projection of bravado, not above putting his face right in yours until you blinked and backed away. Derus and Fraser had tangled for years over policing and social policy. There was no question that Derus had his eye on Fraser's job.

"I don't have the history with him that you do," I offered.

"No, but your boss does," Fraser replied. "And Derus will view you, appropriately, as my surrogate. Just be careful. Do your best and let the chips fall where they may. We may not be able to win this."

That was sobering, to say the least. So before reaching out to county officials, I had multiple conversations with members of the historic preservation community. They were adamant that the fight was worth the candle. The armory was unique, even among other armories built throughout the United States during the WPA era.

Listed on the National Register of Historic Places, it was the state's most significant example of the Moderne Public Works Administration style, with elaborate ornamentation throughout. It contained two floor-to-ceiling Federal Art Project murals painted in the

Social Realist style by Else Jemne and Lucia Wiley. It could seat 8,500 people on its main floor. The upper floors contained office spaces, and its basement was a garage sufficient to accommodate tank maneuvers—or to park more than 200 automobiles.

Reinforced by those conversations, I sat down with the county planning director. She was blunt, and annoyed: the county had purchased the site for $4.7 million, the plans were too far along, and there were no alternatives. If I wanted to make an issue of it, I'd have to convince the county board to give me the time of day. She wasn't going to.

Conversations with the board made clear they weren't interested, either.

If we were going to slow the process down, we needed some other way to raise the stakes. There seemed little basis for a lawsuit. A community engagement process like that we used for the Garbage Transfer Station would be seen as contrived and irrelevant in the context of a downtown development project. And it wasn't clear that threatening permitting or other regulatory obstacles would have leverage against the county government under these circumstances.

That left only one option: elevating public attention and trying to generate a bit of heat. But the public safety versus preservation angle made it a long shot. A very long shot.

I underestimated the architectural and heritage preservation communities, though. Buoyed by the Fraser administration's previous successes in pursuing preservation of significant historic structures, they mobilized—quickly, forcefully, and effectively. Preservationists orchestrated a flood of commentaries and letters to the editor in the *Star Tribune* and neighborhood newspapers. They elicited letters from constituents to their county commissioners asking them to consider alternatives. And they organized several public forums at libraries throughout the county.

That left only one option: elevating public attention and trying to generate a bit of heat. But the public safety versus preservation angle made it a long shot. A very long shot.

It was at one of those forums that the calculus unexpectedly changed.

After I'd made a presentation to a large public meeting about the peril the armory faced, an elegant young couple approached me: a small woman with dancing eyes and a tall man with unruly graying brown hair swept back from his forehead *a la* Michael Douglas. The man spoke first: "Rip, we've wanted to meet you. I'm Bill Morrish. This is my wife, Catherine Brown, and we just moved to Minneapolis to establish the Design Center for the American Urban Landscape at the University of Minnesota's School of Architecture. We specialize in taking on tough architectural and land planning challenges." Brown added, "You've certainly got one here. We've got some ideas about how you might solve it."

They spoke confidently, without arrogance. Their tone was even, but intense. Their affiliation with the school that my father had led for thirty years made their introduction all the more weighty. I asked if they could visit city hall for a deeper conversation.

Morrish and Brown were trained as architects. But what they really were was a problem-smashing machine. In their subsequent decade-long tenure at the Design Center, they would launch a six-year project to help aging suburbs manage new social and economic challenges and create design charettes aimed at revitalizing commercial corridors in North and South Minneapolis.

They would also help the Department of Housing and Urban Development convert a site in North Minneapolis—in which Depression-era public housing was sinking due to a high water table—into a mixed-income, mixed-use project. Morrish and Brown convinced HUD that the solution lay not in rebuilding on top of the water table, but instead in bringing to the surface an ancient creek flowing beneath the property and making it the centerpiece of a new development, which became known as Heritage Park.

That was all in the future. But Morrish and Brown had already begun thinking about both tracks of the armory conundrum: its possible reuses and potential alternative jail locations.

The reuse question was, in the abstract, the easier of the two challenges, and where they began in earnest. It could be an event center, but that would require a private sector buyer. It could be an adjunct to the newly constructed Minneapolis Convention Center, but that was over a mile away. Morrish and Brown landed instead on a public use with a friendly partner.

The armory was tailor-made for recreational uses; its vast, readily adaptable floorplate could accommodate basketball courts, volleyball courts, badminton courts, soccer pitches, or pretty much anything else that involved athletic competitions—or some combination of these. It had second-level seating on both sides of the floor: perfect for spectators. It could park 200 cars or more in the basement. The "head house" office space could be built out to accomodate a couple dozen offices.

Morrish and Brown suggested that we approach David Fisher, the superintendent of the Minneapolis Park and Recreation Board, an independently elected and governed body. Not just to use the building, but to make it the park board's headquarters.

Fisher was a respected executive who held a continuously expanding, and expansive, vision for the Minneapolis park system. With a public park within a ten-minute walk of every city resident—and an unparalleled natural abundance of a dozen lakes, the Mississippi River, three major creeks, and the 769-acre Theodore Wirth Park—the Minneapolis park system was regarded as one of the premier park systems in the country. Fisher had inherited a great deal, but was committed to reimagined programming, further physical expansion, and broader reach into city neighborhoods.

He was not about to declare—overtly anyway—war on the county. He looked at me with a slight grin and said, "That's your job."

Making as bold, potentially controversial a move as taking over the Armory didn't give Fisher a moment of pause. Indeed, he was enthusiastic. It would take the park board's offices out of a cramped, nondescript building. It would integrate recreational programming with administrative functions. It would provide opportunities to host large gatherings. *But*. . . .

He made clear that he was not about to declare—overtly anyway—war on the county. He looked at me with a slight grin and said, "That's your job."

That was enough for us, and Morrish and Brown went to work. My father developed concept drawings, an engineering firm prepared construction estimates for stabilizing and retrofitting the building, Fisher projected operating costs and revenues, and the preservation community started spreading the word that there might be an alternative use that made sense.

It was still a race against time. Fortunately, we had caught the attention of Nina Archibald, president of the Minnesota Historical Society, who was strongly sympathetic to the effort. She agreed to have the Historical Society file a lawsuit seeking a temporary injunction against the facility's demolition.

The county wasn't about to allow grandiose visions of the armory's future to supplant its perceived need to break ground for a detention facility—soon. But the plan had generated considerable public attention, amplified considerably by the lawsuit. The county could no longer ignore it. Within days of the lawsuit's filing, I got a call from John Derus telling me to appear before the full board and justify making life difficult for its members.

It quickly became clear, as his analyses grew more refined, that the Morrish-Brown option was a thunderbolt of opportunity.

I immediately called Fraser, who was out of town on National League of Cities business. "That's entirely their prerogative, Rip, and to be expected," he said. "The only question is whether it will be a hearing or an inquisition. You've raised issues Derus and his planning staff don't want to deal with, so you'll have to make the case that considering an alternative isn't an arbitrary, incendiary act, but instead something of real merit. Can you get Fisher to go with you?" I told him no; that went beyond Fisher's commitment. Silence. "Well, good luck."

So, armed with those good wishes and all of our planning documents, I appeared the next week at the regularly scheduled meeting of the Hennepin County Board of Commissioners.

The chair, Derus, was brutal, domineering, and dismissive from the get-go. Although I was representing the mayor's office, I was not an elected official, so he let me know for well over an hour not only that I was meddling where I had no authority; I was also impeding efforts by the people's elected representatives to keep the county safe. Commissioners Mark Andrew and Peter McLaughlin tried to soften the onslaught, but they agreed with Derus that the project had to move forward without further delay.

The takeaway from the "hearing" was crystal clear: the issue was dead.

Morrish and Brown, who had observed the proceedings, walked with me back across the street to city hall. I realized that the smackdown we'd collectively received was not the kind of soft landing that any reasonable people trying to be helpful to their new community might want. I suggested that we might let the matter breathe; for the moment, the armory was protected by the Historical Society suit. "I don't think we're done quite yet. I have an idea, but need a bit of time to work it out," Morrish offered vaguely. After all they'd done, I couldn't say no. But I certainly wasn't hopeful.

Less than two weeks later, Morrish and Brown invited me to dinner. A wrap-up wake, I assumed. But we hadn't even gotten as far as the dinner table when Morrish, clearly very excited, announced that there was a solution hiding in plain sight. Somehow, these newcomers to town had heard that a large commercial printing company, Winslow Printing, located on the block kitty-corner from the county courthouse, was looking to expand on a larger site and might be open to being purchased.

I was incredulous: first, that they would have uncovered intentions that weren't generally known. Second, that the complexities could be sorted out quickly enough to argue its viability as a solution. Morrish could read my reaction.

It wasn't as much of a stretch as it appeared, he explained. The building was not architecturally distinguished or historically significant, so it wouldn't violate anyone's preservation principles. It had an underground space covering an entire city block, so it could be connected directly to the courthouse with a tunnel—obviating the need for the county to bus inmates some four blocks back to the armory site after court appearances. And its basement was an open plan, so it could be reconfigured without extensive demolition.

Morrish and Brown had previously brought on a nationally known jail design expert to assess the county's needs and scope possibilities. We now enlisted his support to test the Winslow Printing option. He methodically matched the site against the physical configurations and operational needs of state-of-the-art facilities elsewhere. He prepared a construction budget and matched that against the considerable costs of tearing down a structure built to accommodate tank battle simulations.

The consultant carried enormous credibility. And partly because his bill was being paid with the Design Center's budget and not through taxes, the county was willing to give him considerable leash. It became clear, as his analyses grew more refined, that the Morrish-Brown option was a thunderbolt of opportunity.

And when the Minnesota Supreme Court ruled in the Minnesota Historical Society's favor in 1993, finding that the Minneapolis Armory was indeed protected by state historic preservation law and could not be torn down, the deal was sealed. The county negotiated the purchase of the Winslow block and invested in stabilizing the armory's deteriorating roof, replacing its windows, and tidying up its interior. Five years later, it sold the building to a private company.

The 500,000-square-foot Hennepin County Public Safety Facility, housing 270 inmate cells, was completed seven years later. The former jail on the top floors of city hall was converted to an adult detention center. All told, the courthouse, the jail, and the detention center created a "campus" on three adjacent blocks.

It is a fraught business to introduce unconventional ideas from the outside and late in the game.

Various maneuverings and delays meant that the armory did *not* end up becoming the park board headquarters. Instead, it served a variety of functions over the next twenty years, before its central location between the new U.S. Bank football stadium and Wells Fargo headquarters made it a hot property. It was converted in 2018 to a high-tech, high-capacity event space and concert venue.

There were plenty of naysayers during the twenty-year search for an alternative use. But Minneapolis learned a valuable lesson about the value of a preservation ethic. If the animating impulse is to make an immediate, irreversible move that is expedient for political or commercial reasons, the community may be deprived of the objective distance required to assess which places have enduring value . . . which places reflect the accretion of civic experiences, symbols, and values that contribute to community identity . . . which places, if creatively reimagined, could contribute to a diversity of form within our physical environment . . . which places merit patience until energies can emerge that help a community look forward, renew, and delight in the transformation of the old into the new.

In addition to those lessons, however, was another: a lesson in the complexities of working with public agencies inclined to hold, with a death grip, decisions they have made. It is a fraught business to introduce unconventional ideas from the outside and late in the game. Public agencies are loathe to spend taxpayer money outside the box of fixed positions and predictable outcomes. I was able to critique that predisposition and suggest a creative, alternative problem-solving process, but it took mobilizing outside resources through Morrish and Brown to lever innovation into the county's closed box.

It's not as if we could substitute independent external judgment for the judgment of those with election certificates. We instead had to forge a parallel path that gained credibility incrementally as the various puzzle pieces began to fall into place. Then, and only then, could it be brought back into the established bureaucratic and political structure and framed as a realistic alternative to the conventional solution. That path carries extremely high stakes—the county board's hearing/inquisition was a perfect case in point. But when the stakes of inaction are commensurately high, working through external resources, perspectives, and processes may not actually be so risky after all.

Changing the center of gravity in neighborhood planning and investment

It didn't take long after my 1989 arrival in the mayor's office to douse any expectations I might have had that the job would be all glitz, glamour, and glory.

Indeed, the cold water started flowing immediately.

One of the first meetings to which I was summoned was in the offices of Jim Heltzer, the director of the Minneapolis Community Development Agency (MCDA)—the city's quasi-independent housing and development agency—to talk about "the 20-year plan." Sounded like something straight out of Mao's *Little Red Book.*

Representatives of all the city's departments were there. So were representatives of the city's park board, library board, and school board—each governed by independently elected members. Staff from the MCDA were there in force, removing any doubts about who would be in charge.

We were there to determine how to fund neighborhood revitalization efforts. Mayor Fraser had commissioned a citizen's task force two years earlier to assess the development needs of the city's neighborhoods. That group had suggested that just as the city had created a year-by-year schedule by which every city street would be repaved over twenty years, it should also have a twenty-year plan to systematically improve each of the city's 81 neighborhoods. Accordingly, the commission called for dramatic increases in spending on housing and other forms of community-based development outside of downtown.

We needed to identify where those additional financial resources would come from, Heltzer explained. His staff, along with City Council Member Tony Scallon, had been exploring the feasibility of capturing and repurposing "excess" tax revenues generated by downtown development projects. Scallon had floated the financing scheme with his colleagues on the council, and they were supportive. It was now up to the leaders of the city's agencies and departments, Heltzer said, to determine whether it could be implemented.

The financing mechanism was at once complex and simple. The city had created tax increment finance districts in the 1980s to provide public incentives for new office and retail construction; bonds were issued to pay for immediate costs, with the expectation that the projected increases in tax revenue in properties adjacent to the new development in future years would enable repayment of those bonds. Nearly a decade later, the projects within those districts were generating more income than was required to support the bonds. Capturing the excess tax increment and using it to support a new bond would spin off some $400 million that could be applied—$20 million a year for twenty years—to neighborhood needs.

The new pool of money would signal to the neighborhoods that the city was as concerned with their development as it was with downtown business growth. And it would give life to Fraser's neighborhood commission's recommendations.

Creating a fund—as brilliant a move as that was—was only the first step, Heltzer noted. The city had to develop a mechanism for its distribution. I assumed I'd been invited to learn just how Heltzer and his agency proposed to do that.

That was partly correct. Midway through the meeting, Heltzer stated the only way the effort could work was with the full and enthusiastic participation of all city departments and independent agencies, together with Hennepin County—all of those entities had a claim to those "incremental" city tax revenues. Every dollar that went into a twenty-year-plan funding pool would be a dollar less available to them. That, he said with a grimace, posed a problem.

I looked across the room at Harvey Feldman, deputy to Minneapolis Park Board Superintendent David Fisher, suspecting that it was the park board that was the cause of Heltzer's grimace. Fisher and Heltzer were frequently at loggerheads: whereas the MCDA saw the city's open space as an inexcusable neglect of a development opportunity, the park board saw it as an invitation to continual stewardship of the city's natural inheritance. With each side prevailing about half the time, the battle was ongoing—and fierce. The park board wouldn't want to sacrifice any of its funds to the cause of economic development.

Sure enough, Feldman was the first to react. "We strongly support moving these kinds of monies into the neighborhoods. But it's not going to work if the MCDA is in charge," he said, looking directly at Heltzer. "Putting the city's economic development agency in charge is placing the fox at the entrance to the hen house. It will only serve to siphon resources that should be shared equitably by all the departments and agencies of the city."

Heltzer clenched his jaw, and chose not to argue. His long tenure at the agency had made him one of the city's most powerful actors. He was wily, savvy, and consummately political. The impetus for launching the program had come from his most powerful ally, Councilmember Scallon, who chaired the city council's Committee on Community Development. Heltzer couldn't let the initiative fall apart.

And to his credit, Heltzer also recognized that Feldman was right. For the other entities of the city to go along, his agency would have to relinquish control—or at least *appear* to do so while finding ways to ensure that it continued pulling all the most important levers. Heltzer also knew that his second preferred option, turning the process over to the city council, wouldn't work. That would inevitably devolve into a chaotic, thirteen-way political food fight for control and credit.

That left him with his least favorite, but only viable, alternative. Dropping all the niceties, he turned to me and said, "Unless Mayor Fraser's office agrees to step in and take responsibility for the design and implementation of this program, the MCDA will not participate." That certainly cleared the air.

Everyone in the room understood the implications: the MCDA's withdrawal would kill the initiative before it even got started. You simply couldn't run a revitalization program without the city's housing and economic development body. Heltzer's ultimatum had its intended effect; nobody in the room could see another way forward. And again, the reasoning was correct. Only the one public official elected citywide—the mayor—would have the standing, perceived neutrality, and political leverage to foster the collaboration necessary among the full range of players.

I told the group I thought that Mayor Fraser would be amenable, but would of course need to be walked through the argument before making such a momentous decision. Heltzer leaned forward and said with a hint of threat in his voice, "I hope you'll help him find his way to seeing that it's in the best interest of everyone." Message received. I simply nodded and told the group that we'd let them know soon.

As Fraser and I talked through the idea, it became clear just how complex the undertaking would be. It would be a defining act of his administration, something that would shape the city for a generation. Just sprinkling the money among the thirteen city council wards would be too blunt an approach: different needs in different neighborhoods would require different strategies with different price tags, all in a different cadence. And the funds would have to be allocated within the constraints of citywide policies; we couldn't have neighborhood-specific road design standards, garbage pickup practices, or emergency response regulations that were potentially inconsistent with one another, or with city ordinances or regulations.

Different needs in different neighborhoods would require different strategies with different price tags, all in a different cadence.

Fraser sat back, closed his eyes, and said nothing for a painfully long time. "OK," he said at last. "We need to do this. But we need to do it *right*. It needs to be designed apolitically, with care. It needs to be implemented efficiently, impartially, and fairly. I want you to take charge of that. From beginning to end, it needs to be perceived by all the city's neighborhoods as balanced. No favoritism for one ward or neighborhood over any other. It's a tall order—but it's the only way I'll agree to it."

We agreed we needed to create a policy board that included not only the mayor, but the president of the city council, the heads of each of the independent boards and the county, together with representatives from the Urban Coalition, the Central Labor Union, the United Way, three neighborhood representatives, and a Minneapolis-based representative each from the Minnesota Senate and the House of Representatives. The board would set policy, manage whomever was chosen to run the program, and reconcile conflicts that would inevitably arise among the various interests.

We also agreed this policy board would be supported by a technical group—an implementation committee—comprising the city coordinator, the heads of the city departments (police, fire, law, regulatory services, transportation, MCDA, engineering, planning, and others), the superintendent of parks, the superintendent of schools, the director of the libraries, and three neighborhood representatives to be selected in a new citywide election process. The committee would oversee the program's "plumbing," designing a community involvement process for each of the city's 81 neighborhoods, developing a proposed formula for distributing the $20 million annual pool, and creating a way to blend neighborhood funding requests with the budgeting processes of each of the public agencies.

And we realized we needed a full-time executive director at the helm.

With the high stakes, numerous moving parts, and the gnarly politics, executing the plan would be enormously complex. But Fraser was a consummate technician who paid meticulous attention to detail. In his spare time, he would descend to his basement to build, repair, and tinker with televisions, short-wave radios, toasters, and a strange hodge-podge of other electronic devices. He knew that good planning meant little without skilled execution.

Fraser removed his glasses and looked at me for a while. "OK, I think Heltzer is just waiting for us to stumble so the agency can step in and shape a process more to its liking. So I'm going to need you to figure out how to thread all these needles.

"Use me as you need to; I can chair the governing board," he continued. "But we need to make clear that you have the authority to create the architecture and processes to guide this plan. Why don't you first draft a memo that describes the architecture we've talked about. Make whatever changes you think are necessary, but be detailed and thorough. Let's shoot for having a blueprint a week from now."

With the high stakes, numerous moving parts, and the gnarly politics, executing the plan would be enormously complex.

Fraser and I met frequently over the ensuing days to fine-tune the machinery I was designing. We then shared a working paper with the department heads, made some well-advised adjustments, and then walked it around to each of the city council's thirteen members.

We dubbed it the Minneapolis Neighborhood Revitalization Plan—or NRP for short. The policy board would be chaired by Fraser, and the implementation committee by me; when Fraser wasn't available for meetings, I would chair the policy board as well.

At the inaugural implementation committee meeting, we settled on a handful of first principles. Expenditure of NRP funds would be shaped by neighborhood "action plans," not by dictates emanating from city hall. Neighborhoods would also have the latitude to propose changes in the design and implementation of city programs, including how departments and agencies could work together to advance neighborhood goals. The implementation committee would reconcile the ideas contained in the neighborhood plans with municipal priorities, and figure out how the "new" monies could be blended with city and agency budgets.

The next task was to settle on an executive director. After interviewing a dozen of the most talented neighborhood organizers in the city, the implementation committee recommended an unlikely candidate: Earl Craig.

The choice was as brilliant as it was unexpected. Craig had run the Minneapolis Urban Coalition for many years after unsuccessfully running against Hubert Humphrey for the U.S. Senate in 1970. While head of the Urban Coalition, he had hired two promising young analysts: Steve Cramer, who would become the city council majority leader, and Peter McLaughlin, the Hennepin County Commissioner who'd played critical roles in the garbage transfer station and the armory issues. Craig knew his way around politics.

A powerful advocate for civil rights—he was both Black and gay—Craig was sought frequently on issues of community engagement. During his interview, he would memorably note, "the one infinite asset we have as a community is residents well organized where they live." That perfectly summed up the program he would lead for two years.

Craig was also a case study in balance: fearless but not impetuous, brilliant but not arrogant, acerbic yet possessed of a velveteen touch in dealing with people. He was creative and possessed a firm grasp of the urgency of moving quickly. And even though he was methodical, Craig had a predilection to, as he liked to say, create "constructive disruption." He would turn out to be the perfect person to shepherd the endeavor.

Although Craig would formally report to the policy board, it was agreed that I would be his primary contact. He felt strongly that my role would be strengthened if I could chair—at least in the initial few years of the program—both the implementation committee and the policy committee. That would, Craig believed, send a clear message that the mayor's office held primary authority for building connections: both vertically between elected policymakers and staff executing the program, and horizontally among the multiple agencies who needed to develop the musculature of cooperation.

When it was time to select a neighborhood in the "stressed" category, Craig leaned over and whispered, "Please, God, don't let it be Phillips."

It took us six months to design the process. Each of the city's neighborhoods would be given money to organize their plan. The city's departments and agencies would serve as resources to the neighborhoods, at the discretion of the residents. Final drafts of the neighborhood plans would come to the implementation committee for review and comment. There would be a heavy presumption that the plans would ultimately be incorporated into city programs, budgets, and policies, but would first go through a reconciliation process to ensure they didn't contravene legal or regulatory requirements.

Because we knew some neighborhoods were better positioned to turn their plans around quickly and that we could pick up the pace as more neighborhoods completed their work, we categorized the neighborhoods three ways: those that were relatively prosperous; those that were at risk of decline ("tipping neighborhoods"); and those that were highly stressed. We would use a lottery to select one neighborhood of each type during each round.

The first round was launched with considerable fanfare. We had a huge Powerball-type event in the Minneapolis Public Library auditorium, complete with a big plastic drum spinning ping-pong balls emblazoned with the neighborhood names. Craig and I sat in the front row. Pilot neighborhoods in the prosperous and tipping zone categories were picked without incident; Craig was confident that both were on their way to developing sound, implementable plans. But when it was time to select a neighborhood in the "stressed" category, he leaned over and whispered, "Please, God, don't let it be Phillips."

He was referring to perhaps the most challenging neighborhood in the city: highly diverse, profoundly underresourced, and frequently rent by dizzyingly complex and rancorous community politics. Craig knew that the Phillips planning process would be protracted, almost certainly contentious, and likely to produce a plan that would unapologetically challenge city spending patterns.

The lottery balls bounced around for what felt like three hours before the winning ball popped up. It was, of course, Phillips. It's probably a good thing that I didn't take a picture of Craig at that moment, slunk down in his chair with his hands covering his face, shaking his head, only to emerge finally with a forced grin and shoulder shrug.

But Craig was both pragmatic and creative. He knew the program was better off being tested right out of the gate. Although it was easy to view Phillips as an impossible case, that struck Craig as the wrong lens. He understood that the Phillips plan would demonstrate whether we could serve exactly the kind of neighborhood for which the program was conceived—while garnering the support of the more risk-averse policymakers in city hall.

In fact, Phillips proved to be one of the most formative experiences of the early NRP years. The neighborhood developed a complex, high-functioning organizational structure. It pressure-tested city public works, housing, and regulatory services polices. It called for new investments, including the emerging ideas for the Green Institute discussed in Chapter 10.

Perhaps more than anything, the Phillips plan crystallized the necessary role city hall would have to play in mediating between grassroots resident reform impulses and public sector inclinations to safeguard existing programs and investments. The plan—indeed, the planning process itself—generated a gray zone that required compromise, modulation, and relinquishment of control on both sides.

Mezzo mediation.

Phillips wasn't the only neighborhood to activate this phenomenon; because it was an intentional design element of the NRP, other neighborhoods in the queue also stepped into the tension zone.

The "tipping" neighborhood selected in the second round of the lotto drawing was Whittier, just west of Phillips. Shortly after Whittier's ball popped out, Craig and I were approached by members of the Whittier Alliance, which was led by one of the city's most talented community organizers, Kris Nelson. (Indeed, Nelson had been one of three finalists for Craig's job.) The alliance had a track record as a sophisticated neighborhood organizing and planning organization, giving the neighborhood a running start on formulating a full-blown NRP plan.

I was momentarily proud of myself for being so tactically clever. The moment was fleeting.

Nelson, accompanied by Lisa Kugler—a housing expert who was his no-nonsense second-in-command—wanted to convey that the Whittier neighborhood would form a plan on its own terms. Working with city agencies would only corrupt and water down the process, they explained. And they would refuse to negotiate away from the components of the plan: what they handed to us, they expected to be funded.

Craig spoke first: "Well, you know, Kris, it would really be good if we could model out a different kind of behavior here. If you could have the city departments and the county working with you to develop this, you'd have buy-in by the time you got to the end."

Nelson wasn't convinced. "I'm pretty sure that's not going to work for us," he said. "We've been at loggerheads with public agencies for years, and they just won't bend." He and Kugler then walked us through—agency by agency, department by department, initiative by initiative—where Whitter planned to push for change.

"Maybe there's a third way," I ventured. "If you insist on prevailing without compromise on every detail, you'll push the agencies into a corner—and there's only so much Earl and I will be able to do to get you across the finish line. And even if we advocated for every single component of the plan, you'd run straight into your council member, who is almost guaranteed to dig in her heels. Why don't we go back over your priority list and explore whether there might be room for engaging well-intentioned staff at these agencies? I'm not trying to force premature compromise. I just think that setting a tone of possible collaboration will avoid a train wreck."

Nelson and Kugler exchanged looks. "I don't see how we do that without undermining the clearly articulated priorities of the neighborhood," Nelson said. I persisted. "Let's give it a chance," I replied. "If we can avoid starting out with rigidity on both sides, the process will have a fair chance to play out to Whittier's benefit."

Nelson's face reddened. "That's not good enough. We've been 'playing it out' for years, with precious little to show for it." He and Kugler got up to leave.

"Wait," Craig urged. "This isn't just about the money that is hard-wired into city and agency budgets. It can involve new dollars as well." I quickly added, "It might be possible, for example, to use those dollars to push the MCDA and school district to blend their existing funds for a combined housing and neighborhood school project. Or you could use the new funds to sweeten the MCDA's pot, to encourage them to contribute commercial corridor improvement funding that could help the police department justify creating a police substation."

Nelson tilted his head in attention: a community school and police station were both priorities for Whittier. I was momentarily proud of myself for being so tactically clever.

The moment was fleeting. Nelson shook his head. Kugler broke the silence. She stiffened in her chair and answered: "No, thank you. We simply wanted you to know what we intend to do. We didn't come here for your permission." Craig and I had no choice but to shrug and smile.

"Well, I guess we've got our marching orders," I managed to get out. "Let's hope we can work things out."

The "marching orders" phrase became an NRP shorthand. Not for intractability, because ultimately the neighborhood did have to negotiate and compromise. But instead for the understanding that the presumption had shifted: decision-making would lead with neighborhood priorities, and it would fall to the NRP process to find out how to meet their spirit.

If balancing neighborhood priorities and city ones was the first challenge, managing the money was the second.

Neighborhoods were spending months and months to engage citizens, prioritize community needs, situate them within a spectrum of responses from public agencies, and negotiate with local government representatives over additional funding and the extent of reimagined policy needed to animate the identified priorities. As a result, by the end of the program's first year, we had very few plans to fund. The first year's bond proceeds ($20 million) were sitting in a bank account waiting to be deployed, which drove the elected officials crazy.

It was the mayor's office that would incorporate actionable neighborhood plans in the city's budget; but so far, there were none. And it would be the mayor's office taking the heat from the council members. So, like any person caught in the middle, I tried to redirect the heat. I suggested to Craig that we find ways to move dollars into neighborhoods whose emerging plans contained elements that were clearly aligned with city priorities.

Craig disliked that idea. Intensely. "Look, it's about the entirety of the plan, Rip," he said, more than once. "If I don't have a neighborhood plan, I'm not going to spend the money. And I'm *not* going to pour all the money into the first one or two or three plans that waltz in the door—no matter how good they are. We have 81 neighborhoods to attend to."

He was just getting warmed up. "I'm not going to cherry-pick pieces of a plan that's intended to be a complete, integrated package. And I am *certainly* not going to have the council members, park board members, or anyone else tell me how we should earmark the money. That's the antithesis of what we're trying to accomplish."

I understood and appreciated where he was coming from. I also knew that letting funds sit unused in the bank would test the public officials' patience and erode support for the process. "Let's keep the decisions in the hands of the neighborhoods," I suggested, "but carve out a portion of the yearly allocation for early access. We can ask the neighborhoods to identify parts of their plans that are 'shovel-ready' and could be funded at relatively modest levels."

"I'm *not* going to pour all the money into the first one or two or three plans that waltz in the door—no matter how good they are. We have 81 neighborhoods to attend to."

Craig listened carefully. "So, it wouldn't preclude funding other parts of a neighborhood's plan?" he asked. "No," I answered. Craig continued: "And it wouldn't deplete monies that need to be set aside for later neighborhoods?" "No," I replied again. A smile began to form, slowly. He then nodded. "OK. That works."

We called it the First Step program. It effectively served as a political pressure-release valve, permitting ribbons to be cut and laudatory press releases to be issued by our political representatives without compromising the fundamental integrity of the neighborhood planning process.

As completed plans began rolling in, the two initial challenges—priority-bridging and money management—became one. The question of how to mesh aspirations and policy became a question of how to budget: even if city agencies signed off on neighborhood priorities, we still had to pay for them. Because the NRP funds would be one-time allocations to a neighborhood, the challenge became how to recalibrate agency programs and budgets so the work envisioned in the plan could be sustained over time. The expansive and intricately thought-through Whittier Plan—championed by the contrarians Nelson and Kugler—became the test case.

Every delegate to the implementation committee came to hear Nelson's presentation of the plan. It called for a new neighborhood school; a sub-precinct police station and foot patrols; subsidies for a mixed-income commercial and housing project; traffic calming along residential roads; and much more. The pricetag was enormous. But it was the challenge to established city policies that generated most of the debate.

Robert Ferrara, the superintendent of Minneapolis Public Schools, began by stating that neighborhood schools were a violation of school district policy, so that was off the table. Minneapolis Police Chief John Laux explained that the department didn't have the money or personnel for substations or beat officers. City Engineer Mike Monahan doubted that the speed bumps would meet the city's traffic-flow requirements. Minneapolis Community Development Agency Director Jay Jensen—Jim Heltzer's successor—said the housing project was not on the agency's list of priorities.

Not quite what we had hoped for. As Craig kept his powder dry, I told the group we owed the neighborhood the respect of exploring how we might meet the spirit, if not always the letter, of the plan. Nelson took umbrage: “We’ve been through that, Rip. Everything we’ve offered can be done; each idea has been due-diligenced to death. Each is important to our community’s health. Smiling and telling us it was a good try is not going to cut it.”

About three hours into the increasingly tense—and unproductive—meeting, Craig and I called a recess. I was a bit deflated. As we stood in the hallway, Craig picked up my mood. “We had to let it play out this way, Rip,” Craig said. “We knew that what Whittier would propose would be seen as unrealistic by the departments. We knew that the departments wouldn’t come to a different view on their own.”

Nelson took umbrage: “We’ve been through that, Rip. Everything we’ve offered can be done; each idea has been due-diligenced to death. Each is important to our community’s health. Smiling and telling us it was a good try is not going to cut it.”

Then he added with a smile, “Time for the mayor’s office to weigh in.”

That was curious. I wasn’t quite sure what the mayor’s office weighing in would look like, but I knew Craig was right: this was the inflection point. We needed to dig into the mayoral moral, financial, and political toolbox.

Back in the room, I asked the group to revisit each of the department requests one by one. We started with what was ostensibly the hardest case: a neighborhood school request in a school district that didn’t allow for neighborhood schools.

I suggested to the superintendent that the district take a forward-leaning position by forming a task force to explore, on an expedited timeline, the legal and practical feasibility of a neighborhood school in Whittier (and perhaps elsewhere). Fraser would express strong support, providing some political cover. And the action would signal the willingness of the district to treat the NRP process—and the residents of Whittier—seriously.

Ferrara embraced the idea. Within weeks, he appointed a talented young administrator named Carol Johnson (who would later go onto to serve as the superintendent of the Minneapolis, Memphis, and Boston school districts) to lead the task force. After many months of study, their recommendation was to create a neighborhood school in Whittier, and to incorporate neighborhood schools into the district’s overall system of school choice.

We next turned to the second hardest nut: the police department. The department had dug in not because the Whittier request was so terribly unreasonable, but because the department simply didn’t trust outsiders to tell them how to protect public safety. “A substation with beat cops would be a net contribution to public safety,” I argued to Chief Laux.

“Not if it means we have to transfer money from other functions,” he replied. “We’ve weighed our priorities carefully, and this didn’t make the cut.”

“Well, let’s not force you to make that decision,” I said. “Let’s instead have the mayor make the decision for you by including funding for a precinct substation in his budget. We’ll also make clear that Whittier is entitled to designate part of its NRP allocation to public safety. You can choose whether to use those additional NRP monies for the substation or for another piece of your budget.” Seeing that it was possible to test an untried and risky idea within the political cover of the mayor’s budget, Laux agreed.

Laux eventually became an ardent proponent of the NRP process. To nobody’s surprise, public safety became a priority in every neighborhood plan. Not everyone tapped the

Whittier recipe of a substation and beat patrols, but the department reached a willingness to adapt existing approaches—and explore new ones—to find common ground with neighborhood groups.

Third up was the traffic department. Having watched the flexibility of the schools and police, Mike Monahan was in an accommodating frame of mind. The Kenwood neighborhood—among the city's most affluent—had begun to form a relatively modest suite of NRP requests, including installation of speed bumps as part of the First Step program. Monahan had no problem with extending the experiment to the busiest Whittier streets. He and Nelson agreed to explore other methods of traffic calming as well.

Other departments quickly fell in line. The final agency in the queue was the MCDA.

I had no concrete strategy for confronting the gorilla in the room: the one singled out by Whittier for a large affordable housing project and the one which, if Fraser was right, was biding its time until things began to unravel. I dreaded the exchange to come.

I couldn't have misjudged the situation more. Obstruction might have been Heltzer's dance of choice, but it was not Jay Jensen's.

Without any prompting, Jensen said the MCDA would consider combining NRP money and the agency's existing housing funds to pursue the housing project. He added that the agency would be willing to work with the neighborhood to adapt a housing maintenance revolving loan fund like the one that had previously been developed in the McKinley neighborhood: a model that creatively reimagined the MCDA's underused housing fix-up program. This was exactly the kind of retooling Craig and I had hoped would characterize the NRP process.

Whittier was pleased. Craig was pleased. But, despite acknowledging the need for compromise, the departments were less pleased. They were drawing down new dollars, but they were also being asked to reallocate their existing budgets and contemplate new models of service delivery not of their invention.

Whittier was pleased. Craig was pleased. But, despite acknowledging the need for compromise, the departments were less pleased.

We had begun—and it truly was only the beginning—developing a novel budgeting, prioritizing, and public-service-redesign apparatus that would be forged in the mezzo space between bottom-up aspirations and top-down prerogatives.

Over time, neighborhoods not only nested their priorities into city department budgets, but also conveyed a different set of priorities for the quality of neighborhood life. When Council Member Scallon conceived of the NRP refinancing, he assumed it would be put into bricks and mortar projects—housing, mostly. But the neighborhoods had other ideas: park upgrades, water quality assessments, tree plantings, bike lanes, traffic calming, new lighting standards, community gardens, mural projects, and other ideas Scallon thought were just hooey. He was frustrated beyond expression. But over time, even he saw the value in diversifying the agendas emerging from resident engagement.

Beginning with Whittier, and accelerating with the diversity of successive neighborhood plans, skeptics across the city came around to a more balanced view of the NRP's potential. A final example.

The Bottineau neighborhood, which sits on the east bank of the Mississippi River in Northeast Minneapolis, prioritized the river in its plan: attention to water quality, shoreline beautification, pedestrian access. But rather than going it alone, their plan proposed using the NRP to gather thirteen Minneapolis river-adjacent neighborhoods to imagine and plan collectively. The Mississippi River Neighborhood Coalition was born.

The coalition would endure beyond the NRP planning process. Its work would result in enhanced resident access to the river through parks and trails. It would produce ambitious, sophisticated inquiry into what it might take to convert highly industrialized areas along the river to other, less noxious uses—a process that has crystallized in the last decade, some thirty years later. It would birth collaborative beautification and cleanup initiatives for the riverbanks.

With each NRP Plan, it became increasingly clear that neighborhoods sought a holistic and integrated vision for their community.

The coalition drew heavily on the resources of the MCDA, the park board, the planning department, and other units of the city, all of which were instrumental to the progress the coalition achieved. But the agencies couldn't have undertaken this kind of effort without the passionate commitment of hundreds of neighborhood residents over many years.

With each NRP Plan, it became increasingly clear that neighborhoods sought a holistic and integrated vision for their community. Housing was important, but it had to be considered in relationship to safe streets, access to public parks and open space, and neighborhood schools. Safety was critical, but it had to be integrated into well-lighted streets and vibrant block clubs.

Slowly, steadily, the agencies caught the wave, and the impulse of participatory budgeting, cross-agency cooperation, and public service redesign stuck. It survived new mayors, new council members, new neighborhood residents. By the time the program sunset twenty years later, its imprint was indelible—both on the neighborhoods themselves and on the municipal agencies that serve them.

Leadership came from all quarters: residents willing and able to adapt big thoughts to practical investments; public officials learning to mediate between citywide priorities and neighborhood-based objectives; a program director with inviolable integrity steering the ship; a mayor's office using its leverage to pull all the strings together.

Indeed, Minneapolis introduced a novel, challenging, and profoundly prescient municipal management concept: distributive leadership. Communities equipped with the tools to drive technically challenging approaches to improving quality of life and basic city services. Public officials designing novel financial instruments dedicated to community revitalization. Municipal agencies permitting resident aspiration and knowledge to reshape the policies and practices driving service delivery.

So utterly novel some thirty years ago. And today, evident in the practices of countless American cities.

Running for mayor

Sharon Sayles Belton was adamant: she had no desire to be mayor of Minneapolis.

As president of the Minneapolis City Council, Sayles Belton was a logical candidate to succeed the mayor of sixteen years, Don Fraser, in the city's 1993 election. As deputy mayor, so was I. Sayles Belton and I had worked as close allies, so it was time to clear the air. We had the opportunity when sitting next to each other on a trans-Atlantic flight in mid-1992 to establish a sister city relationship between Minneapolis and Tours, France.

With Mayor Fraser unable to make the trip, Sayles Belton and I were designated to represent Minneapolis in Tours, the largest city of the Centre-Val de Loire of western France and the gateway to the Loire's chateau region. Tours was to become Minneapolis's third sister city—joining Ibaraki, Japan and Novosibirsk, Russia—with the aim of fostering cultural, artistic, academic, and economic exchanges.

When the trip rolled around, I was strongly considering running for my boss's seat when he retired in 1993. But Sayles Belton was a friend, a close legislative ally, and a formidable political force. In a council often at odds with Fraser, Sayles Belton had been a consistent and ardent supporter of his agenda, sharing the mayor's deep commitment to improving the welfare of children and families. She had served as a parole officer for sexual assault offenders and a neighborhood activist before being elected to represent the city's Eighth Ward, its most diverse, on the council. She served for seven years before her colleagues elected her council president in 1990: the first Black person to hold that position.

Sitting next to her on the long flight from Minneapolis to Paris, I told Sayles Belton about my thinking. But I turned to her and said, "I would like to run. But it doesn't seem right to do that if you're thinking about running. I'm prepared to hold off on my decision if you're considering it." She shook her head.

"I've thought about it and come to the conclusion that that's not where I want to head. I'm more of a legislator than an executive," she explained. "I enjoy the process of working both sides of a question and forming policies from that. My real hope is to run for Congress when Marty Sabo steps down . . . you should go ahead and declare. There will be quite a few other candidates, and you'd be the best of the group. I'd advise you to get in the race early." It was vintage Sayles Belton. Direct, thoughtful, respectful. I made the decision to jump into the race when I returned.

She was right about the crowded field. Others soon announced their candidacies: Steve Cramer, the 11th Ward city council member, who was the body's majority leader; John Derus, chair of the Hennepin County Board of Commissioners; Richard Jefferson, Minnesota's first Black state representative; and John Wodele, a former mayor of Wabasha, a small Mississippi River town southeast of Minneapolis.

In the months after the trip to France, I assembled a campaign committee, hired a campaign staff, secured early endorsements, and made a public announcement of my candidacy. We named seven cochairs of geographic, racial, sexual orientation, and gender diversity, including a rising young attorney named Amy Klobuchar. It was early, so neither Fraser nor Sayles Belton endorsed any candidate. That changed a few months later.

Sayles Belton had an annual winter tradition of vacationing in a Mexican beach town with several of her closest women friends. All were political activists and highly accomplished professionally. On their 1993 trip, Sayles Belton's friends agreed that it was past time for a woman to lead the city; so far, the field comprised five men. Sayles Belton at first demurred, suggesting that her co-vacationer Kathy O'Brien, the Second Ward council member and powerful chair of the city's Ways and Means Committee, should run.

In a daylong meeting, we deliberated whether I should withdraw to leave as much room as possible for Sayles Belton—with whom I felt not only ideologically aligned, but personally connected.

O'Brien wasn't sure she could win—but she knew Sayles Belton could. She pressed Sayles Belton forcefully: not only was it time for a woman mayor, it was also time for a Black mayor. The group agreed with O'Brien. They convinced Sayles Belton to run.

Her decision, announced after she arrived home, was—to say the least—a surprise to me (and to many others). And it was tectonic. It prompted several of my campaign workers to tell me they felt bound to sign on with her campaign. It put Fraser in a complicated dynamic, with his closest legislative ally and his deputy in the field together. It threatened to split off supporters of Representative Jefferson, who sought to be the city's first mayor of color. And it immediately transformed the field's dynamics: now it was Sayles Belton and everybody else.

In a daylong meeting of my campaign staff and advisers, we deliberated whether I should withdraw to leave as much room as possible for Sayles Belton—with whom I felt not only ideologically aligned, but personally connected. But by then, we were six months into my campaign and encouraged by the progress we'd made.

We'd developed a campaign theme that distinguished us from the others, drawing on my work in fashioning the Neighborhood Revitalization Program: "Make Rip Rapson Your Neighborhood Mayor." Sounds a bit stilted in retrospect, but it grounded the campaign fully in the grassroots planning and engagement I'd spent three years supporting.

With the help of almost two dozen workgroups, we were finishing what would become a seventy-five-page, graphically rich campaign book, the first in the city's political history, outlining the campaign's policies in housing, transportation, economic development, environment, the arts, and children and families. We had formed "Out for Rip," a separate working group focusing on LGBTQ issues and led by two prominent gay activists. And we were aggressively expanding our volunteer base.

A few veteran politicos in the group warned that if we stayed in the race, we would split the progressive vote, giving the conservative candidates—Steve Cramer and John Derus—the opening they would need to win. But the majority held a different view: I should stay in, but avoid campaigning negatively about any of the candidates. I could run entirely on my background and the issues our campaign had elevated.

Beyond the ethically attractive quality of the proposition, it seemed tactically compelling. It might well mobilize constituencies not necessarily attracted to more traditional "downtown" candidates. It would convey a continuity of purpose from the Fraser administration, which had placed integrity and effectiveness above the political fray. And, knowing the likely conservative positions of Cramer and Derus in particular, it would give the city's voters real choices.

Our test would be the Democratic party's endorsing convention in June. A longstanding tradition in Minnesota politics, party endorsements were conferred when one candidate received sixty percent of the more than 1,000 delegates elected to a citywide convention through in-person caucuses in each of the city's thirteen wards. That endorsement would propel the candidate into a September primary, in which the two top vote-getters would advance to the November general election. Receiving the convention's endorsement wasn't required for entering the primary, but given the party's strength in Minneapolis' progressive political climate, it carried considerable weight.

Sayles Belton, Jefferson, and I pledged to honor the endorsement, which meant that whoever lost at the convention would drop out and not participate in the September primary. It was not at all clear whether Derus, Wodele, or Cramer would do the same, or simply enter the primary without an endorsement.

Over the next many months, we adhered faithfully to our game plan of sticking to the issues. Mostly. Sayles Belton and I were able to remain civil and talk about the policies we believed defined our campaigns. But, behind the public curtain, our wires crossed when we made our appeals for endorsements to interest groups. Two in particular.

The first was the DFL party's Feminist Caucus.

On one hand, this endorsement was presumed signed, sealed, and delivered for Sayles Belton the minute she announced her candidacy. She had been a single mom, a hardscrabble parole officer in a man's world, and a political pioneer. On the other hand, our campaign had mobilized large numbers of women who were deeply involved in neighborhood politics, the environmental movement, and the arts.

One stunning afternoon, the caucus decided to endorse both of us. Sayles Belton's team was livid. The possibility of the first woman mayor? A woman who was eminently qualified? From that point forward, the Sayles Belton campaign staff started taking off the gloves.

The second endorsement echoed, in some ways, the first: the party's Gay-Lesbian Caucus.

Here, the question wasn't exactly who was "entitled" to the endorsement, but who had been most effective in raising and embracing issues of concern to the LGBT community (as it was then termed). Painfully, the two sides divided along gender, with the Out for Rip committee being mostly men and Sayles Belton's campaign drawing heavily on women.

My campaign was co-led by Jerry Fladmark. Fladmark was an exuberant optimist who'd helped organize several campaigns on behalf of the Twin Cities gay community. He was deeply respected in the community for his fierce advocacy of domestic partners benefits, gay marriage, heightened attention to teen homelessness and mental health, AIDS education and prevention, and many other issues.

Equity for the gay community was a key focus for our campaign—from the get-go. At one of our earliest campaign meetings, John Killacky, head of performing arts for the Walker Arts Center and an outspoken gay rights advocate, turned to me and said, "If you want me to be involved, you have to be all-in in advocating for LGBT issues. We won't accept tokenism. You have to believe enough in LGBT rights to put our community front and center—in your speeches, in your campaign materials, in your leadership structure." Within an hour of that statement, we had formed Out for Rip.

The Sayles Belton campaign went from livid to nuclear.

Killacky had every intention of holding my feet to the fire. Putting his well-honed impresario skills to work, he organized multiple events that none of the other campaigns would go near. He arranged a performance at the city's leading gay bar, the Gay 90's, by Miss Richfield 1981, a drag queen who retold the Medea legend through Cher songs. She did a completely over-the-top performance piece at the Bryant Lake Bowl, dressed in strings of sausages. And she helped advocate successfully for the cover photo of the campaign book's chapter on families to feature a gay family.

So by the time I walked into the LGBT caucus, we had made clear that the issues the caucus members cared about were front and center in our campaign. We received their endorsement.

The Sayles Belton campaign went from livid to nuclear. They weren't about to let this go unchallenged. They urged their candidate to go negative, which she largely resisted—but many of her campaign operatives did not. They began whisper campaigns about my "true" sexual orientation, even going so far as to suggest that my marriage to Gail (who was pregnant with our first child) was nothing more than stagecraft. They started publicly questioning what I had done that would cause Fraser to withhold his endorsement of me. They seized on a scandal involving one of my cochairs, a longtime friend, to insinuate I had knowingly overlooked signs of misbehavior.

So much for a campaign on a higher plane. Although neither Sayles Belton nor I went negative, animosity between the two campaigns burned hot. Probably because that development was so unexpected, I found myself almost oblivious to the other four candidates.

It became clear that the endorsing convention would be the crucible. It wouldn't just break up the candidate logjam; it would also likely leave only Sayles Belton or me still standing. In more than a half century of conventions, the delegates had made an endorsement every single time. Everyone expected the same to occur here. Pundits projected that Sayles Belton would run ahead right out of the gate, picking up delegates after each round of voting, steadily eliminating candidates failing to meet required minimum vote thresholds, and finally pulling away when the field was narrowed to two.

Derus—with a very conservative base and a long history of winning his county board seat in the northern part of the city by huge margins—decided he would skip the convention and simply engage in the primary. Wodele made the same decision, fearing he would be dropped early in convention voting.

That left Cramer, who became something of a stand-in for Derus among the conservative factions on the North Side, and Jefferson, who was widely regarded as a man of deep integrity and unquestioned historical importance, but who had run a decidedly lackluster campaign.

The convention began at 9 a.m., but after all the speeches by officeholders, candidates, and other dignitaries, it was mid-afternoon. We then moved to the balloting, which moved at an excruciatingly slow pace. Jefferson was eliminated after the second ballot, and Cramer after the fourth. By evening, it was down to Sayles Belton and me, each of us with roughly half the ballots. Neither of us had been able to reach the 60 percent of the 1,000+ delegates required for endorsement.

We learned that we were very likely to stay right where we were. In meticulously orchestrated political shenanigans after Cramer was dropped from the voting, his delegates and those who preferred Derus had decided they would split their votes strategically to prevent either Sayles Belton or me from gaining momentum: if I pulled ahead, votes would shift to Sayles Belton, and vice versa. It was a tactic designed to deadlock the convention, orchestrated and executed with precision by a master organizer named Brian Rice, whose father was a legendary legislator and power broker in Northeast Minneapolis.

On the fifth ballot, Sayles Belton was ahead by just a few votes. It was 1 a.m. People had been dribbling out, exhausted by more than sixteen hours of speeches, arm-twisting, vote-counting, procedural votes on motions to adjourn without an endorsement, and countless other energy-draining maneuvers.

But very few of our people had fled. In fact, they were energized. We had battled the clear favorite to a standoff. And we had a secret weapon in the form of our dynamic floor organizer—a journalist, environmental activist, and longtime friend: R.T. Rybak. Rybak was like the Energizer Bunny after eighteen energy drinks. He started the political equivalent of conga lines snaking their way through the hall, picking up delegates as he went . . . indefatigably worked our ward coordinators to keep their spirits up . . . made speeches from the stage on behalf of the campaign. The Sayles Belton campaign had no equivalent.

None of us could know it at the time, but this was the same R.T. Rybak who, eight years later, would begin a twelve-year tenure as mayor of the city.

None of us could know it at the time, but this was the same R.T. Rybak who, eight years later, would begin a twelve-year tenure as mayor.

Minutes before the sixth ballot was scheduled to begin, the Sayles Belton campaign sent a message asking if my finance chair, Sam Kaplan, and I would step into the hallway for a conversation with Sayles Belton and her campaign manager, Sixth Ward Council Member Jim Niland.

Niland was regarded as a political wizard who had cut his teeth on labor organizing and had his own political base in the central part of the city. One mistook his youthful, almost cherubic appearance at one's peril—he had masterminded every move the Sayles Belton campaign had made over the last months.

Kaplan, a respected corporate attorney, had come into political prominence three years earlier when he became the first major civic figure to endorse and champion an unknown Carleton College professor and farmer-rights advocate in his quixotic run for the United States Senate. That professor, Paul Wellstone, would unseat the well-financed incumbent, Rudy Boschwitz, and go on to become the Senate's leading populist and progressive voice until his horrific death in a 2002 plane crash. Kaplan would remain one of the senator's closest confidantes and advisers.

When we met Sayles Belton and Niland outside the hall, Sayles Belton looked exhausted, almost in a state of shock. Niland spoke immediately, complimenting us on such an unlikely show of strength. "I don't suppose you want to throw your support to us," he said, only partly in jest. Kaplan and I chose to hold our fire; clearly Niland had something up his sleeve.

Indeed he did. With his usual disarming smile, Niland moved right to the point. "The Cramer and Derus people are manipulating the vote of their caucuses so that neither of us can get to sixty percent—they're just instructing them to divide up the vote. We have to leave here with an endorsement. But it'll be past 2 in the morning by the time the next votes are counted, and people just won't stay beyond that. We'll lose the opportunity to endorse. Let's agree that whoever is ahead after this sixth ballot will receive the endorsement."

Kaplan and I looked at each other in disbelief, then shook our heads in unison. "You know that we can't change the rules unilaterally, Jim," I said. Sam said, "How would it look for us to tell more than a thousand people—who have committed eighteen hours today, and all the countless hours of attending caucuses and working for candidates—that four people have taken it upon themselves to decide how a nominee is selected?"

Niland simply nodded his head, while Sayles Belton remained quiet. "But you know if this breaks down," he said, "we'll go into the primary with six candidates and neither of us may come out. People will understand that we will have had no choice."

"But we do have a choice, Jim," I replied. "And we're making it. Let's let this play out."

So, we went in and conducted the sixth ballot. The irony of the result was stark: I won the sixth ballot by one vote. Had we accepted the Sayles Belton-Niland compromise, I would have "won" the endorsement. But it would have come at too high a price—it would not have been an endorsement worth having.

Niland had been right about another thing, though. After that sixth ballot, people were spent. A motion was made from the floor to close the convention with no endorsement. There was always a first time. The motion passed, and we all headed home at 2:30 a.m. All six candidates were headed for the September primary.

The Sayles Belton campaign went dark for many days. They never dreamed that they would be denied the endorsement, particularly by someone who had never run for public office.

Two days later, Mayor Fraser asked me to lunch. His normal reserve seemed extreme; I had no doubt that the results of the convention were on his mind. I assumed that he wanted to talk about how the dynamic between Sayles Belton and our office would play out in the coming months—something I'd thought a great deal about as well.

I began the lunch with a few suggestions about how the mayor's office and the city council might work together. It wasn't just a matter of working cooperatively and respectfully with Sayles Belton, but with Cramer as well. I told Fraser I didn't want to be an impediment to the work that needed to be done, and that I thought we could compartmentalize the issues in front of us and continue to do the citizens' work.

"That's what we need to talk about," Fraser replied, reaching into his suitcoat pocket and pulling out a two-page, handwritten letter. He handed it to me with a grimace. It was addressed to him from Council Member Kathy O'Brien, who'd been so instrumental in Sayles Belton's decision to run and was among her most able and passionate supporters. O'Brien had also been an ardent supporter and ally of Mayor Fraser, and he had enormous respect for her.

The letter recited all the ways that Fraser had championed civil rights over his career. O'Brien noted the 1972 Fraser-McGovern Commission that had rewritten the rules for how the Democratic Party selected its national delegates, ensuring that there would be greater influence of women, people of color, and young people. She discussed his focus on disadvantaged and marginalized children and families while in the mayor's office. She recalled his fierce civil rights activism of the 1960s.

O'Brien then came to the point: Sharon Sayles Belton represented all he had fought for—and stood for—during his forty-year public service career. She needed his support, and had earned it. Indeed, unless Fraser was willing to endorse her immediately, Sayles Belton would have to drop out of the race. She would make her decision in the next two days.

Fraser looked at his plate, not saying a word. He didn't need to. He'd been put in an impossible position. I considered suggesting that he could endorse us both, but then thought better of it. O'Brien's letter made clear that the consequence of a dual endorsement—just as powerfully as no endorsement at all—would be a Sayles Belton withdrawal. It wasn't difficult to read his mind: as much as he might be impelled by my having served him with deep loyalty and distinction in two different roles, endorsing me would prevent the citizens of the city from the opportunity to elect their first female, and Black, mayor.

The reality crystallized that Fraser's endorsement of Sayles Belton would deal a death blow to my campaign.

There wasn't much for me to say. I certainly wasn't going to argue my case; this wasn't about that. It was his decision, not mine. I asked what he intended to do. He said he wasn't yet sure.

We walked back to the office in silence. With every step, the reality crystallized that Fraser's endorsement of Sayles Belton would deal a death blow to my campaign. It would only be natural for voters to wonder how the mayor's two-time aide didn't enjoy his boss's support. I considered, for one tenth of a nanosecond, making public the O'Brien letter if he chose to endorse Sayles Belton. But I knew that would be wrong, deeply wrong. The voters of Minneapolis should not know the letter had been written or the ultimatum made.

Two days later, I opened the *Star Tribune* to see a simple two-paragraph letter to the editor from Fraser. The mayor began by briefly describing his respect for both Sayles Belton and me. He said either of us would be a strong mayor. But, he concluded, he had only one vote to cast, and it would be for Sayles Belton.

Our campaign team assembled that evening to assess the damage. Two of Fraser's closest friends were apoplectic. They saw in his decision a political knife in my back, and urged that we characterize the move as a betrayal of loyalty and common sense. But that clearly wasn't the answer.

Others noted that even if we didn't react directly to Fraser's letter, we needed to shift our tactics.

First, and most immediately, I needed to leave my position as deputy mayor and spend the next three months working as hard as possible to make the case for my campaign—Fraser's position notwithstanding.

Second, we had to accept that one of our strongest bases of support, senior citizens, would likely follow Fraser's lead. Fraser enjoyed enormous popularity among seniors—well above 70 percent—and they turned out heavily in primary elections. Until now, we had every reason to believe (and our polling affirmed) that they would transfer much of that support to me, as a suitable successor. No longer.

Third, we needed to continue distinguishing our campaign as clearly as possible. Our issues-rich campaign book had already helped define the campaign as one of ideas. So had producing the first campaign video the city had seen. Investing heavily in visually arresting and sometimes offbeat campaign materials had conveyed a sense of freshness. Holding events in unorthodox locations had attracted a mix of artists, architects, community organizers, and other constituencies that often eschewed engagement in local politics.

At the office the next day, I suggested to Fraser that that my resignation would be the best route to avoid my role becoming a distraction over the next three months as he, I, and others sought to clarify how it would possible to separate my campaign activities from my responsibilities for advancing the mayor's interests. We spent the entire day walking through how to prioritize and reassign matters I was working on. We then exchanged thanks, and I left city hall for the last time.

The next months were a blur. But the tide had gone out. Senior citizens were now polling for Sayles Belton at an 80-20 split. It became clearer by the day that undecided progressives were breaking for Sayles Belton, and uncommitted conservatives for John Derus. The other candidates were becoming afterthoughts.

That's exactly how September's primary election went: Sayles Belton won first by a wide margin, and Derus came in second, both advancing to the general election. Two months later, Sayles Belton swamped Derus, with nearly 60 percent of the vote. She was sworn in on January 4, 1994. Sayles Belton would go on to serve two four-year terms.

I've been asked more times than I can count why Fraser and I remained cordial, even working together closely, years later, on a series of early childhood development initiatives. Many of Fraser's closest political allies never forgave him, and they were perplexed by why I had. I think there were four reasons.

First, Don Fraser was an honorable man—a once-in-a-generation public figure who took a risk on me, not just by bringing me onto his congressional staff and, in the Boundary Waters dispute, giving me responsibility for one of the gnarliest issues of his career. But also by choosing me from a large and distinguished slate as his deputy in city hall. In each case, we had worked as closely as two people in public service can work, with my enjoying his complete confidence to act on behalf of him personally and on behalf of the office he held. I felt, and will always feel, a profound gratitude for that confidence. He earned my loyalty.

Second, the political exigencies of 1993 made it virtually impossible for him to have behaved differently. As O'Brien so bluntly and skillfully underscored in her letter, Fraser causing Sayles Belton to drop out of the race would have irrevocably tarnished his reputation as a warrior for civil rights and racial justice. And it would have left him in profound personal doubt about whether he'd impeded the kind of racial progress to which he was so deeply committed.

Third, his wife, Arvonne, was Fraser's most trusted counselor. Arvonne had run his congressional office in D.C., had been the coordinator of the Office of Women in Development within the United States Agency for International Development, and was a globally recognized advocate for women's rights. If anyone would have the last word on whom he should land his endorsement, it would be Arvonne. She, Fraser, and I had spent countless hours in the Fraser's living room talking about ideas, job challenges, and policy disagreements. I believe she respected me, and I certainly respected her. But if a choice had to be made about whether Fraser's successor would be me or a well-qualified woman, she would argue there was really no choice.

And fourth, Fraser's decision may have been the kind of historical milestone the city needed in 1993. Electing a woman and a person of color was momentous. Our community could look to a mayor with a powerful biography of having overcome countless structural obstacles to her success. They could see in her the promise of a political leadership progression that for generations had calcified as the exclusive domain of white men. They could witness and assess how a mayor whose race, gender, and lived experience set her decision-making apart. Sayles Belton had not initially seen herself in the mold of leading the city, but now the citizens of Minneapolis could judge whether she did, in fact, have an executive temperament suitable to the office.

Best not to fight against a political riptide.

It's hard not to fast-forward thirty years and see in Minneapolis a community that continues to struggle at the razor's edge of race relations, crystallized in the murder of George Floyd. Sayles Belton wasn't only a pioneer; she also represented a newly conceived politics that might approach that struggle in a different way.

So, "forgiving" Don Fraser wasn't really the question. Few decisions of any import in positions of leadership default to absolutes, and certainly Fraser's didn't.

Best not to fight against a political riptide.

Looking back, the more vexing question is whether this kind of campaign—run with clear-cut issue definition, rejecting the trivialization or denigration of political opponents—would be possible today. My first reaction is no, for all the reasons current political contests degenerate as they do.

But, and perhaps this is answering a slightly different question, my second reaction is that this is exactly the kind of campaign I *would* run today. Indeed, eight years after the Sayles Belton election, my friend R.T. Rybak ran exactly that kind of campaign—and won.

Today, when my campaign manager, Jerry Fladmark, reflects on this question, he reaches a different conclusion. He believes a civil, positive, strictly issues-based campaign is worth little if one loses. That's certainly the prevailing ethic today. Preserving a candidate's viability is paramount, protected at all costs.

I come at it differently. It comes down to why you're running for public office. It's certainly true that you can't bring your leadership values into a role that you haven't won. But putting important issues on the table, sketching clear paths to addressing them, and mobilizing constituencies that share your convictions is another way to gauge the importance of running for public office.

I believe even a "losing" campaign can have lasting impact. My campaign inspired an effort to keep a particular suite of issues in the civic arena—and it also helped spark the candidacies of several others who championed those issues. Rybak frequently said that the issue strategies we articulated in my printed "tome" became a blueprint for his agenda in his early years as mayor. Indeed, parts of that blueprint were widely apparent by the time Mayor Rybak retired in 2013.

So, my advice to current political hopefuls is probably really bad career advice. But, over the long term, it may be relatively good civic advice.

14 Generative Friction

Forming a loyal opposition

Although losing political campaigns typically go quietly into the night, that was not to be the case after mine.

Days after the general election, I wrote a commentary for the Minneapolis *Star Tribune* suggesting six lessons I believed we could extract from the city council and mayoral elections. The incoming leadership at city hall provided not simply an opportunity to pursue new ways to strengthen municipal services, but also a moment to confront issues of concentrated poverty and urban disinvestment by fortifying neighborhood-based problem-solving capacity.

My piece wasn't intended as criticism of our new mayor; I wanted instead to underscore important ideas that could easily be lost as the aspirational energies and articulations of the campaign season gave way to the nuts-and-bolts realities of governing.

Within two weeks, I received a call from John Kostouros, one of the city's finest community journalists and a lead writer of my campaign book. "I've been thinking a lot about your op-ed piece. I'm wondering if you'd be willing to meet with a couple dozen of your campaign volunteers to see whether there might be ways to continue to give oxygen to the ideas you raised," Kostouros said.

I explained that I wasn't keen about doing another autopsy of the campaign. Kostouros laughed. "Oh no," he said. "That's not the point. We've had enough of that. No, we want to see if you would be willing to help start an effort that would keep your ideas about neighborhood revitalization alive."

I paused and took a deep breath; reengaging policy discussions so soon after an unsuccessful run wasn't at the top of my priority list. Kostouros could hear my reluctance, and turned the screws a bit tighter: "It's a bit of torch-passing. I think you'll appreciate who will show up," he continued, listing some familiar names. John hit a nerve: these were people who had poured their time and passion into a campaign grounded in community issues, and it seemed only fair and reasonable to have a conversation with them.

About two dozen people gathered in my living room on December 11. A campaign volunteer named Joe Barisonzi had circulated a three-page document entitled "The Rapson Project" to frame the conversation. It opened with the following paragraph:

> Since the 1993 mayoral primary, many people have been throwing around ideas on what form the Rapson mayoral campaign should, or could, now take. The setback of

> the primary derailed the basic goal of the campaign: to elect Rip Rapson mayor. But it did not necessarily defeat the other goals. Social, economic, and environmental issues; political issues for the [party]; and the personal values of integrity, communication, and collaboration.... The purpose of this document is to... suggest a plan which will have the opportunity to meet those undefeated goals.

The meeting lasted for hours. Clearly, this was not an effort to remount a campaign against Mayor Sayles Belton, but rather a way to sustain the energies the campaign had elevated around better supporting the livability and economic vitality of urban neighborhoods.

Myron Orfield, a state legislator who had developed Minnesota's sweeping metropolitan property-tax-base-sharing laws, advocated creating an entity to make the case that the fate of urban neighborhoods was inextricably tied to broader metropolitan policy. Orfield noted that the Community Connections Project I'd signed on to lead at the University of Minnesota's Design Center (see Chapter 15) was explicitly aimed at helping older first-ring Twin Cities suburban communities grapple with many of the same issues facing the region's urban core: aging infrastructure, diversifying demographics, insufficient affordable housing, poor public transportation connections, and countless other forces. He argued that city hall, regardless of how effective Mayor Sayles Belton might be, was prevented by structure and politics from taking a broader view of metropolitan connectivity.

Betsy Sohn, a community organizer from the Phillips neighborhood, took a different tack. "The Neighborhood Revitalization Program is focused on the priorities of individual neighborhoods," she said. "While you were in the mayor's office and Earl Craig was in charge [he had died unexpectedly two years before], you developed a direct pipeline from neighborhood plans into city budgeting and policymaking. That may evaporate in the new administration. We need some way to look across all the neighborhoods to try to add things up—a neighborhood agenda from the outside-in."

City hall, regardless of how effective Mayor Sayles Belton might be, was prevented by structure and politics from taking a broader view of metropolitan connectivity.

There was widespread agreement that Sohn's approach was the best place to start, connecting over time into the issues Orfield hoped to address. We also agreed that a new group was necessary to hold, organize, and advance the work. Our group could identify the best ideas emerging from the NRP planning process and find ways to increase the wind behind them.

Gretchen Nichols, a community organizer who would later join the Community Connections Project team, had recently written me a note sounding the same theme: "At a Fannie Mae housing discrimination colloquium last weekend, it became painfully clear that while millions of dollars are invested in research, few resources are actually allocated to community efforts to address these problems." She urged that the group focus on "how to develop the capacities of community-based organizations to find their own solutions or alternatives."

Kostouros jumped on that. "My hope is that we can create a think tank that stretches people's ideas about what's possible, as a matter of both policy and practice. We could convene roundtables, invite neighborhoods to participate in workshops, and write up the results in a newsletter or in community newspapers," he said. "And if we could raise some money, we might also commission research and new analysis that could work independently from the city and county, but ultimately be helpful to them.

"Look, there's no reason to rope off the electeds," Kostouros continued. "We should welcome them into the conversations and incorporate the work they're doing. But there will always be ideas and approaches beyond what they can embrace. Things they see as too provocative, or politically sensitive, or unfeasible. But wouldn't it be great if we had a center that could raise and advocate for those ideas? It's the only way they'll get raised. Our challenge will be to get city hall to take the organization's efforts and role seriously."

But despite the groans and the less-than-stellar grades, city staff were taking the suggestions emerging from neighborhoods seriously.

Paul Ostrow, a young attorney who would later be elected to replace Councilmember Walter Dziedzic, the powerful boss of the city's First Ward, nodded. "That will be the challenge: getting policymakers to take the platform seriously. But it's doable. First, we need to pull together a group of thoughtful, diverse people willing to commit time to this. Second, we need to combine resident perspective with external thinking. And third," he said looking at me, "we need you. You laid the groundwork. You have credibility. And you can call on the resources of the Design Center to get us started."

Bill Morrish, director of the Design Center, had been quiet up to this point. Now he smiled and spoke. "It's a good fit. Our work with aging suburbs was always grounded in the Minneapolis experience. That's why we asked Rip to join us. Let's give it a try."

Quite a lot of progress for an initial meeting. But we all understood that constructing and animating the skunkworks would take time. Darcy Seaver, a brilliant planner, writer, and researcher whom we'd lured to the Community Connections Project, offered to create a work plan. The group agreed to meet monthly under the moniker of the Minneapolis Center for Neighborhoods.

Seaver delivered impressively. She drafted a statement of mission and objectives culled from the inaugural meeting. She proposed that we prepare articles of incorporation and create a 501(c)(3) to enable the group to attract the modest support needed to convene public forums, underwrite periodic publications, and eventually, hire an executive director. She suggested creating a membership structure of interested stakeholders, anchored by issue teams to develop ideas, attract people with expertise to contribute, organize community workshops, and develop analyses and recommendations.

Over the next year and a half, we convened or cosponsored dozens of neighborhood roundtables. We started with a discussion of a half-dozen neighborhood commercial corridor planning initiatives. We gathered more than a dozen neighborhoods to explore a new community safety and policing model they were developing. We conducted a working session among four neighborhoods undertaking cultural plans and projects. We organized a public forum about reusing the million-square-foot abandoned Sears building on Lake Street for a multicultural food and retail hub.

We organized a series of multi-neighborhood workshops about how to encourage citywide social service organizations to partner with neighborhoods with weak human development infrastructure. We tested neighborhood affordable housing plans against obstacles in the city's planning and regulatory documents. We partnered with the Mississippi River Neighborhood Coalition to accelerate their environmental stewardship efforts.

These discussions, and many others, fulfilled Kostouros's hope that the center would raise and advance issues that elected officials couldn't tackle, politically or otherwise. The discussions were, in and of themselves, useful in bringing together residents who were working on similar challenges. As word spread of the opportunity for neighborhoods to network with and learn from one another, attendance rose and interest grew.

We coupled neighborhood case presentations with external perspectives: academics, practitioners, representatives of other communities.

We wrote and incorporated summaries of each roundtable into a quarterly newsletter, *Neighborhood Connections*, which also included commentaries from those outside our orbit, including public officials. That pre-internet publication grew to some 2,000 subscribers.

The center also launched, in partnership with the Metropolitan Interfaith Council on Affordable Housing, a monthly Neighborhood Leadership Breakfast series focused on longtime "elders" in community organizing and development.

The sweep and depth of the conversations was making the Neighborhood Revitalization Plan director, Bob Miller, nervous. He and his staff had their hands full just helping create individual neighborhood plans, so they couldn't give full attention to the frequent cross-neighborhood workshops we were conducting. We accordingly began more intentionally coordinating our efforts with his work, piggybacking on meetings he already had scheduled and cosponsoring events.

That, in turn, suggested the possibility of holding an annual State of the Neighborhoods summit to pull together the multiple threads of neighborhood work into a comprehensive picture of what was going well and what wasn't—particularly in relationship to city policies, practices, and budgets. Miller didn't have the inclination—or the capacity—to lead that kind of event. So working with him, the center took it on.

We'd provided a vehicle to cultivate long-view perspectives that transcend the vicissitudes of election cycles.

The first State of the Neighborhoods Address took place on January 4, 1995, at the Mixed Blood Theatre with about 100 people attending. It highlighted examples of neighborhood innovation and collaboration, and identified ways city policies were enhancing or impeding the work. We were delighted to see in the audience both the director of the Planning Department, Paul Farmer, and the director of the Minneapolis Community Development Agency, Rebecca Yanisch. They'd been paying attention to the center's roundtables, regularly sending department representatives to attend.

The second State of the Neighborhoods summit was a little edgier, incorporating a Design Center analysis of how well city agencies had adapted to the priorities identified in nineteen neighborhood plans. The presentation focused on a "report card" for each of the city agencies and independent boards, with various segments delivered by different neighborhood representatives. The marks were not great—overall, averaging out to a C. That got the agencies' attention. Indeed, a clearly agitated Yanisch strode up to the podium seconds after I delivered the address, asking, "What were you thinking, Rip? C-? I've never gotten a C in my life, and don't intend to stand still for one now."

It was perhaps an understatement of the city's frustration. The *Star Tribune* wrote the next day: "The estrangement between some political leaders and the center was perhaps best illustrated by the collective groan that went up [yesterday] from a caucus of city council members when they were reminded of the pending speech."

But despite the groans and the less-than-stellar grades, city staff were taking the suggestions emerging from neighborhoods seriously. Hennepin County selected a neighborhood in which to pilot a more flexible, results-oriented human development service delivery system. The Inspections Department initiated a training program for neighborhood residents to expand enforcement of city housing codes. The Planning Department and the Community Development Agency created a package of business assistance tools to help a half-dozen neighborhood commercial corridors overcome zoning, regulatory, and funding challenges. All tied back to the center's work.

Indeed, in 1997 the summit became an all-day conference that combined a State of the Neighborhoods report, a keynote address from the president of the McKnight Foundation, "pupa" awards for the most promising small-scale neighborhood improvement projects, and workshops on housing rehabilitation, transportation calming, commercial node development, and more. Eventually the center expanded its horizons to include St. Paul neighborhoods as well.

The center showed that developing, championing, and trying innovative ideas outside the fence-line of public sector strategies wasn't an act of sabotage, but a gesture of constructive civic engagement. We'd demonstrated the potency of enabling eighty-one neighborhoods to learn from one another and to create networks of collaboration around shared interest. We'd provided a vehicle to cultivate long-view perspectives that transcend the vicissitudes of election cycles.

It anticipated a later era of distributed, participatory democracy, in which a city's full civic infrastructure informs public priority-setting, budgeting, and implementation. And it enabled the harnessing of a collective voice that, while not substituting for electoral decision-making, could create the kind of generative friction that enhances it.

Finding clarity by illustrating problems

It wasn't so much the stories that intrigued her than it was the illustrations.

My mother was a self-trained librarian. For twenty years, Mary Rapson donated her time to the University of Minnesota Libraries' Kerlan Collection, one of the world's most expansive archives of children's literature. With more than 100,000 children's books—many inscribed by the author and/or illustrator—as well as original manuscripts, galleys, and color proofs from nearly 2,000 authors and illustrators, the Kerlan was created in the 1940s by Dr. Irvin Kerlan, a longtime chief of medical research at the Food and Drug Administration and an avid collector of rare books.

Mom was a cataloguer. But in the dark ages before computers, that meant proceeding book by book, entering in block script on a little index card—actually twice, since they required duplicates—the author, title, date, and place of publication, together with a wealth of other information about the work. All organized according to the mysterious Dewey Decimal Classification system, which called for an erudite choice among ten different classes, each divided into ten divisions, each of those broken into ten sections. One card went in the back of the book, one into the index file. Times 100,000.

My mother also devoted time to the library's Sherlock Holmes collection. She catalogued every one of the 115 books by Sir Arthur Conan Doyle, or about him or about his fictional creation.

My visits felt like coming out the other side of the wardrobe in *The Lion, the Witch, and the Wardrobe*. We'd take the stairs up to the third floor, open a huge wooden door, and enter a room with books everywhere: those already Dewey Decimalized stacked neatly on the shelves; those in the queue piled on file cabinets; and those just arrived splayed across the floor and wedged under the desks. A young person's paper forest, with imaginary places and people and things hidden behind the spines of books reaching in every direction and up to the ceiling like roots and branches.

Each trip would begin with my mother asking what I wanted to see that day. Dr. Seuss? She would grab one of her meticulously handwritten cards, find the right shelf, and hand me the book (provided it wasn't an irreplaceable first edition, a particularly fragile manuscript, or filled with original illustrations). Did I want to see how Beatrix Potter created *Peter Rabbit?* That might mean looking at the shiny metallic production plates, located in one of the scores of flat files along the wall. We'd go through the same careful, loving process over and over until the library closed.

The magic of children's books made its way into our home, with lovely—if less rare—early editions of *The Hardy Boys, Winnie the Pooh,* and other lesser-known works. I'm pretty sure that my mother chose our small collection based on captivating illustrations. The Norse fairytales of *East of the Sun, West of the Moon* were terrifying to a child, but Kay Nielsen's meticulously detailed and sumptuously colored illustrations imbued them with a magic that made them less traumatic. And it was the visual images from the pages, even more than the stories themselves, that stayed with me.

Any child would have been well advised to steer clear of a hero whose life ended in fiery martyrdom. But M. Boutet de Monvel's glorious oil paintings chronicling the fate of Joan of Arc were like a magnet; in fact, I mentally blocked the story's ending until I was much older.

> **The magic of children's books made its way into our home. . . . It was the visual images from the pages, even more than the stories themselves, that stayed with me.**

No such luck with *Pinocchio*—not Disney's Jiminy Cricket version, which I probably could have ingested without undue discomfort, but the 1883 version by Carlo Collodi, which I couldn't. Here, the illustrations by Tony Sarg only augmented the story's terror: terrifying circus masters, evil foxes, man-swallowing whales, boys being turned into donkeys.

One might think that all these pictures exploding off the pages would inevitably lead me to want to draw myself. In a way it did, I suppose: my mother's challenge was to convince a young boy that the books at home weren't coloring books. I shudder to this day when looking through these wondrous books and seeing my random crayon entries. Horrible.

But that was as close as I would get to trying to draw until decades later. I had absolutely no natural ability. None. Perhaps that it was just a matter of being intimidated: it was inconceivable that I could produce anything remotely close to such transcendentally beautiful images.

Or perhaps it was because of the awe I felt watching my father completing sketch after sketch on bumwad in his basement office, endlessly—and seemingly effortlessly—exploring different solutions to a particular architectural challenge.

Or, most charitably, maybe it was the dawning realization that my one, exceedingly limited artistic outlet, the trumpet, constituted the entirety of my creative capacities.

Whatever the reason, I didn't draw. At least not in any meaningful sense of the term (I still have hanging in my kitchen a kindergarten "drawing" of a turkey, which almost certainly convinced all concerned parties that crayons and I shouldn't be in the same room).

That changed after I joined the University of Minnesota's Design Center for the American Urban Landscape in 1993. The Design Center was led by the couple who'd helped shepherd the armory project, Bill Morrish and Catherine Brown (see Chapter 11). They asked me to join them to run a project I had proposed to them after leaving the mayor's office. Called the Community Connections Project, it created a team of architects and landscape architects, a geographer, a community organizer, a planner, an economist, and others to explore how aging first-ring suburbs could address challenges traditionally associated with inner-city communities.

We worked with a half-dozen suburban communities to identify potential solutions to gnarly civic challenges: blending a new transit center into an existing downtown; creating a multicity consortium of cities unified by their proximity to an interstate freeway; helping remove the stigma from social service agencies in suburbs not accustomed to them. These were the kind of problem-sets my time in city hall had prepared me to attack. Morrish, meanwhile, brought an entirely different dimension to the problem-smashing toolbox: drawing. Or more accurately, the ability to distill highly complex situations into ingeniously original and lively sketches.

After meeting with a community, the Design Center team would gather around a large conference table and watch Morrish talk and draw. With each insight, he would—like my father—try out a different visual metaphor to describe it. Houses swirling like tornados and landing in a street grid altered to accommodate a light rail station. Clouds representing different issues of shared concern hovering over a tilted, fanciful geography of cities clustered along the I-35W freeway. People gathered around meeting tables connected by arrow-like vectors to depictions of ever-larger forums for community conversation. The repertoire was endless.

The drawings would then become the jumping off point for our next meeting with community representatives. Morrish would prepare a sequence of drawings contextualizing the problem by identifying its essential components. He would then move on to reorder, combine, connect, or discard them in ways that permitted the problem to breathe.

The power of the method was its dynamism. It wasn't like looking at a static section-drawing of a building plan, but instead like walking through a series of doors into rooms where all the furniture had been rearranged, or discarded, or combined with entirely new elements altogether. It was visual systems thinking.

Morrish struggled when trying to translate these ideas into written form, but his drawings were virtuosic—brilliant in both their holistic thinking and their graceful expression on paper.

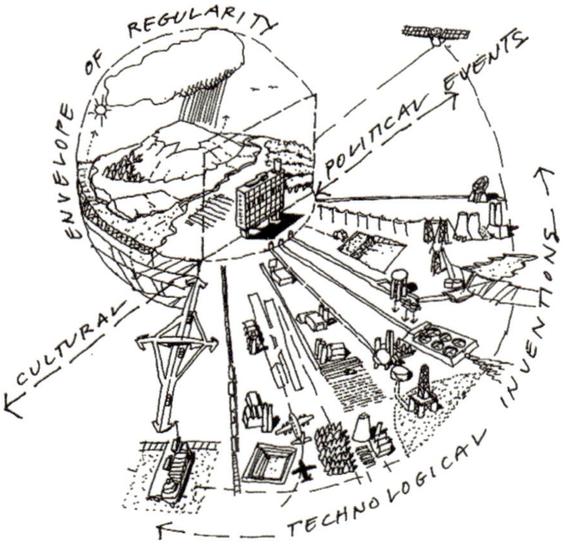

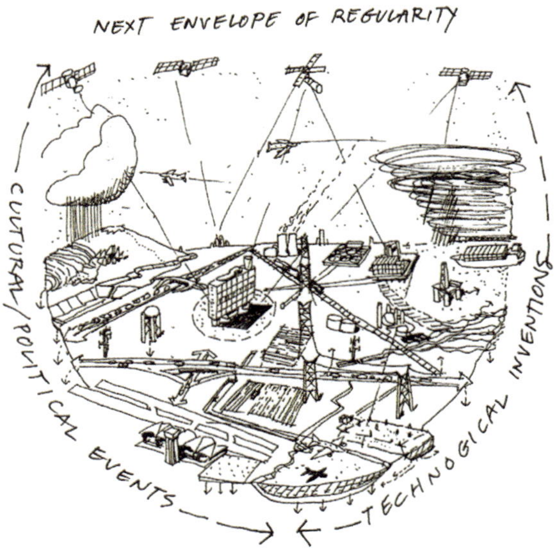

Morrish's drawings were virtuosic—brilliant in both their holistic thinking and their graceful expression on paper.

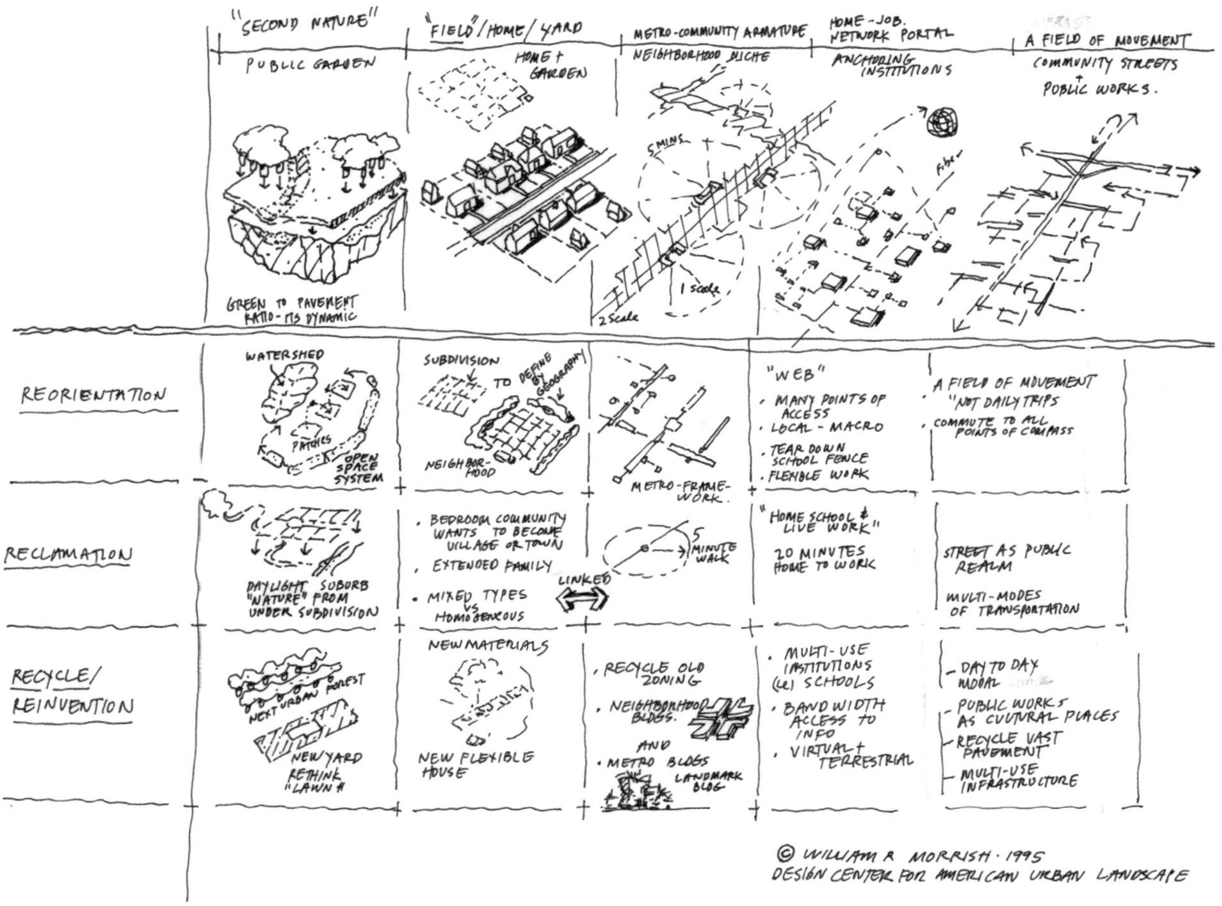

One had the feeling of sitting in an airplane, looking out the window, and seeing not just the physical elements of the landscape, but also the unseen tendrils connecting them. Genius.

Before arriving at the Design Center, I'd regularly taken notes during meetings by using a traditional outline format, sometimes embellished with a few arrows or boxes to suggest how pieces of the conversation were linked. Morrish's techniques were from a different planet. I gradually began to incorporate some of his symbols and images into my note-taking, discarding lined paper for 11x17 sheets that freed me to rearrange elements of an argument or set of ideas.

Morrish was amused at first, recognizing an absence of talent when he saw it. It would have been easy for him to be dismissive and conclude that remediation just wasn't in the cards. But he took just the opposite tack, realizing that I was serious about trying to learn a new skill. He started making suggestions.

He was infinitely patient. When we would schedule conferences, for example, I would map out the planning timeline with icons representing different activities: simplistic little tables of people for breakout sessions, stacks of paper to suggest briefing materials, books to represent reports, megaphones to depict speeches, and the like. Morrish would then critique it. Each successive drawing got a little less primitive, a little more effective.

Midway through my tenure, I received a call from Ralph Smith, vice president of the Annie E. Casey Foundation in Baltimore. Smith explained that Casey was embarking on its next generation of grantmaking in support of children and families. He had invited the nation's leading academics and practitioners focused on family health and stability to discuss what pathway might best advance the field. He had admired Mayor Fraser's work in centering children and families within municipal government. Knowing that I had played a role, he asked if I would be willing to attend his gathering and inject a public sector perspective.

When I arrived at the conference room in Casey's Baltimore offices, it was filled with the hum of energetic conversation among people who clearly knew one another. They were there both because Smith had a reputation as a brilliant thinker, and because he and Casey's president, Doug Nelson, had firmly established Casey as the nation's premier philanthropic player in addressing the needs of children and families.

> **It would have been easy for him to be dismissive, but he took just the opposite tack, realizing that I was serious about trying to learn a new skill. He started making suggestions.**

It became plain, however, as the meeting progressed, that for all his brilliance, Smith wasn't very good at herding strong-minded people toward consensus. I decided I might be most helpful by trying to capture the key threads of the conversation rather than by forcing my way through its increasingly dense intellectual haze.

That turned out to be a wise choice. Hours into the meeting, I despaired that the conversation was just going around and around. Arguments were being repeated ad infinitum, each with the highly particularized gloss of someone with a very specific expertise. Smith was deeply deferential: an admirable trait, but one that sacrificed the opportunity to synthesize and shape what was being said. The discussion seemed stalled, with the same ideas being raised from different angles.

I determined to exercise my Morrish muscles, outlining on my 11x17 sheet of paper five or six themes—each with a handful of sub-themes—accompanied by icons suggesting how the themes might be connected. I was sitting next to Smith, who, about four hours in, looked curiously at my paper. "What's that?" he asked quietly during one particularly long-winded exegesis.

"I really am paying attention," I replied defensively, afraid he thought I was just doodling to pass the time. "I'm struggling a bit to follow the thread of such a complex discussion, so I thought I might try to make sense of it by mapping it out." Smith smiled wryly and announced to the group that we would take a break. He asked me to walk him through the drawing's structure. Nodding as I spoke, he then asked if he could copy it. Of course, I said, thinking that it might simply help him steer the remainder of the meeting. He left the room with the drawing in hand.

Smith returned about fifteen minutes later and handed a copy of the drawing to each of the participants. "Let's work from this for the rest of our time together," he suggested. That wasn't what I had expected, and I could see several people around the table bristle. Morrish had helped me make my pictures more interesting, but they were still pretty rudimentary. I couldn't help but suspect that people with these kinds of credentials and experiences were offended by having their sophisticated ideas reduced to such simple—indeed, overly simplistic—form.

But it was Smith's meeting, and this was the way he wanted to organize it. The resistance gradually dissipated, and the meeting began to take shape along the broad contours of my diagram. We emerged with a set of conclusions and recommendations that Smith assured me were what he had hoped to extract. That might have been the result regardless, but Smith was effusive in his thanks.

I didn't think much more about it; I was simply glad I had been able to help. But a few weeks later, Smith called again, this time with Nelson, Casey's president. They asked if I'd be willing to do more of this visualization work with them as they developed new strategies. I explained that I had a day job and needed to check with Morrish. He was bemused, but agreed—delighted to think the center might contribute to Casey's efforts.

Over the next couple of years, I met periodically with Nelson, Smith, and their project manager Miriam Shark to "translate" their thinking into visualized form. The concept drawings I created could not have been more different from the tomes of carefully crafted briefs they'd written to guide their process, but the Casey team concluded that it was useful to have both: with the pictorial syntheses conveying the overarching constructs, and the narratives filling in nuanced underlying meaning. Increasingly, one medium fed the other, and vice versa.

I was startled when Nelson called me to say that he'd used one suite of a half-dozen drawings as the conversation starter during the Casey board of directors meeting dedicated to approving the foundation's new Strong Families, Strong Communities strategy. Sensing my horror, Nelson quickly told me that the drawings had introduced an element of lightness to a pretty high-stakes meeting. Many years later, when Nelson retired, I had that batch of drawings laminated so that he could use them as placemats on his sailboat.

"I've never seen anything like this—except for a guy at Harvard who charges $2,000, and his visuals aren't as good as yours."

The use of my drawings to advance the Casey board conversation was likely my most significant contribution to the foundation. But perhaps the most unexpected use of them was an earlier request from Shark and Nelson that I create several schematics for an information platform that would describe for potential grantees the foundation's emerging strategies—a "website" before that was common parlance.

I had sent along a dozen drawings depicting what the home page architecture might look like, and what you might see if you made a series of decisions about an information pathway: what would open up with one "click," or with a follow on click to go deeper, or even with a third to go deeper still. I was a considerable distance outside my zone of competence in any technical sense, but Shark conveyed that it seemed to do the trick. She asked if I could come to Baltimore to meet in person.

I met Shark, and a handful of others I didn't know, in their main conference room. Each had my stack of drawings. Introductions were first name only, no description of role. One participant asked right out of the gate if I did web design for a living. I couldn't help but sense an attack coming. "No, I don't," I replied, turning crimson. "I would never claim that these are anything other than basic working tools to help Casey get conceptually grounded before they launch full-bore into what I know will be a profoundly complex project."

Another participant sitting next to him didn't seem convinced. He followed up by asking what my methodology was: did I use computer analytics, engineering formulas, or something else? I thought he was kidding—or really annoyed at having his time wasted by someone with no business in what should be a web professional's realm.

I explained that I'd tried to visualize the waterfall of decisions a user would be inclined to make to get the information she needed. And I'd tried tried to do that in a way that Shark and her Casey colleagues could readily follow without becoming entangled in the complexities of coding—that could come later, once the fundamental architecture was in place.

The two men looked at each other, shook their heads, and guffawed in unison. Uh-oh, here it comes, I thought. I still didn't know to whom I was talking.

But then they smiled. "We're from Microsoft, and this *is* what we do for a living. I've never seen anything like this—except for a guy at Harvard who charges $2,000 an hour, and his visuals aren't as good as yours. In our shop, we do our first-cut designs by putting yellow sticky notes on a wall, and then adding more and more stickies to track the path of different decisions. You've done that on 11x17 sheets of paper. It's a lot simpler, and more digestible."

"In our shop?" That would be the world's largest computer software firm. I reassured them that I certainly wasn't in this business. The second guy chuckled and said, "You should be. You can come work for us any time." The rest of the meeting went on as planned. I chose to stay at the Design Center.

Two years later, I was invited to interview for consideration as third president of the McKnight Foundation, a family foundation based in Minneapolis. The outgoing president, Michael O'Keefe, was a nuclear physicist who'd helped build out sophisticated programs in international crop research, neuroscience, human services, the Mississippi River, the arts, housing, and rural development. The job description indicated that the family hoped to maintain these focal areas, but also to reimagine how the foundation invested in children and families as well as regional economic development.

I prepared for my final interview by doing a three-panel drawing that sought to capture the complexities of maintaining the bedrock of the foundation's strategy while adapting to their emerging interests. I attached it to a large foamcore board. Arriving early, I was met by the head of the search committee, Cynthia Boynton, who was the daughter of Virginia Binger, McKnight's founder.

"What in the world is that?" Boynton asked. After I explained, she asked me to walk her through it quickly. She said she was a visual artist and appreciated that kind of visual thinking. "But I don't think it would be wise to share it with the other board members during the interview. Not all my family members are visual thinkers, and you might lose them with something like this. I'd leave it out here." After the interview, though, she took me aside and asked if she could keep the drawing to think more about. "I'll return it, promise."

It's hard to know whether the drawing had much to do with their decision to hire me. But Boynton later told me, without tipping her hand on the question, that the board had discussed it at length after the interviews were complete.

After I arrived at McKnight and we began to build out new programs, it struck me that variations on what I'd prepared for the job interview could be useful to that process. I started with our relatively small staff, who wanted to see ways of weaving together the programs they knew with the potential new initiatives. I took a page from Morrish's book: after staff discussions supported by background briefing papers, I'd pull together conceptual roadmaps—we could move this way, or that, or somewhere else altogether. It became easier to see where our choices lay and how we might share them with the board.

Once we had narrowed our options, I drew inspiration from another person I'd watched using visuals to such powerful effect: Bud Heinselman, whose mylar overlays of the

Boundary Waters Canoe Area had been a fertile conversation starter in countless meetings with members of Congress twenty years earlier (see Chapter 3).

My version of "Bud's maps" had, as its base, a depiction of the foundation's existing grantmaking focused on nonprofit organizations. The first overlay began to create a pyramid-like visual, with the second layer depicting baskets of work tied to fields of discipline, both existing and potential. The third set of overlays related to working in place: McKnight's existing rural Minnesota development initiative, along with a proposed field of Twin Cities regional development.

We dubbed this new framework "tiers and baskets." The term stuck as a shorthand for how we proposed to tie our various bodies of work into a coherent whole. Little did I know that it would again be called into play six years later in an entirely different setting.

Right-brain thinking isn't right for everyone, as Cynthia Boynton warned me before my McKnight interview. But there is a power in visual conceptual drawings that extends beyond simply complementing speech and writing. I've been fascinated, for example, at the proliferation in recent years of visual note-takers at convenings. It suggests that, at least in some circumstances, visualizations can be a superior form of communication.

Pictures imprint on memory in a way that recalling words on a page, or uttered from a podium, can't. They can invite people into conversation while conveying that the analysis isn't ironclad. They can be suggestive, like a Rorschach test but with more definition. They can be playful or whimsical, letting people dwell on idiosyncratic or intriguing images before engaging the deeper substance. They can challenge a predisposition to let the left brain's logical, categorical thinking take full control. They can contribute to problem-solving by depicting the simultaneity of issues, the multidimensional qualities of a problem or solution, the sinews between different players acting in separate spheres, the cascading of consequences over time.

16 Concretizing Culture

Designing streets as community spaces, not commuter pass-throughs

One might think that my standoffs with Hennepin County over the garbage transfer station or the Minneapolis Armory would have/should have ended once I left the mayor's office.

No such luck.

That familiar antagonism reemerged as I began my tenure at the McKnight Foundation six years later. The same cast of characters remained on the county board, with Peter McLaughlin again front and center.

In early 2004, the county began a community planning process for reconstructing a two-mile stretch of Lake Street, the city's main east-west artery. Running through the city's most ethnically and racially diverse neighborhoods, Lake Street was a county road governed by state highway standards and not subject to planning, design, or construction oversight by the city.

The proposed Lake Street Reconstruction Project would widen the street, carve out more turn lanes, eliminate street parking, narrow the sidewalks, and otherwise facilitate the movement of cars through the area with the fewest impediments and highest feasible speeds. All adding up to what had long been seen by county engineers and officials as an upgrade to the region's transportation infrastructure.

But that stretch had become the hub of fledgling Somali, Ethiopian, and Latino entrepreneurship—brimming with markets, restaurants, and community gathering spaces, virtually all operating on the razor's edge of viability.

The collision of these two worlds—traffic efficiencies and ethnic business viability—was, in retrospect, inevitable. For county decision-makers, Lake Street was not a destination, but a funnel through which cars needed to move swiftly to get somewhere else. And for the county engineers, a "planning process" was more an exercise in informing residents of what would happen than an act of engagement: they would present the technically viable options, solicit comments from residents and business owners, and attempt to reconcile the options and comments in ways that fit within accepted engineering doctrines and that didn't disrupt the predetermined scenario.

That was exactly how the process was unfolding. The county had formed a public advisory committee and had allocated $4 million for business stabilization during construction and for streetscape improvements. It was all by the book—specifically, the Green

Book containing the standard street design and practices prescribed by the American Association of State Highway and Transportation Officials, and religiously observed by traffic engineers.

As happened in the garbage transfer station saga, I received a meeting request from a group of residents and business owners who were concerned that the county's efforts would undermine a neighborhood plan published several years earlier. That plan called for the Lake Street business district to be tied to a proposed "Midtown Greenway Corridor," a rail-to-trails bike and pedestrian corridor parallel to Lake Street, one block north. It had been adopted with the full support of citizens, county officials, and city staff.

What we needed was an engineer sufficiently heretical to challenge Green Book dogma.

The neighborhood representatives argued that the reconstruction project's single-minded focus on traffic management would sacrifice the community plan's emphasis on small businesses development, pedestrian-friendly environments, and bike use. The distinctive identity of the emerging ethnic entrepreneurial district would be enhanced not by moving more traffic at higher speeds, but instead by narrowing the street to facilitate bus and bicycle travel, widening the sidewalks to promote outdoor dining, preserving on-street parking to encourage ready access to shops, and redesigning intersections so sections of the avenue could be closed off for community festivals and celebrations.

The phone call was not a surprise; McKnight had been watching the county's plans with concern. Working closely with a national consortium of foundations and lending institutions called Living Cities, we had created a multimillion-dollar pooled investment fund to support the ethnic businesses along the avenue.

After talking with the community representatives, I met with County Commissioner McLaughlin and the county's external engineering consultants. They were courteous, but explained that the Public Advisory Committee's comments had already been taken into account. Given the Green Book's requirements, further changes simply weren't possible.

One consultant pulled up a simulation on his laptop demonstrating current traffic "flows" along the street: lots of red dots moving herky-jerky both east and west. This was grossly suboptimal under "universally accepted" engineering standards, he said. He then punched in a second simulation, showing the effects of widening traffic lanes and adding separate turn lanes by narrowing the sidewalk and moving bicycle traffic off Lake Street to the greenway a block north. The red dots magically turned green. *Voilà*: the Green Book gods were satisfied.

I realized that there was little I—or any other layperson, including those on the Public Advisory Committee—could do to compete with the engineer's computer program. I thanked the group and said I would be back in touch.

What we needed was an expert engineer sufficiently heretical to challenge Green Book dogma. I called a friend who'd been a longtime student of, and writer about, livable cities while editor of the *Utne Reader* magazine, Jay Walljasper, to see if such a creature existed. Walljasper had a brilliant suggestion: he told me that an organization based in New York named Project for Public Spaces had exactly that kind of expertise and would be eager to help.

I called PPS founder Fred Kent to put the question to him. Sure enough, they had someone who might be helpful. Kent explained that they'd recently hired the former head of a major West Coast state department of transportation who was a pioneer in alternative approaches to urban mobility. He would be willing to fly to Minneapolis, hear the county out, and see if there was any room for maneuver.

McLaughlin and the engineering consultants agreed to meet a second time, this time with the PPS engineer and me. It began as a replay of the first meeting. The county's consultant pulled up the same simulation and played it again. Next, the PPS lead engineer asked what would happen if certain tweaks were made. Start with eliminating the turn lanes, he suggested. The consultant reluctantly typed in a different code, and some of the red dots started turning green. The PPS engineer then asked him to narrow the traffic lanes, remaining within state requirements. Again, a reluctant recoding. Now, almost all the dots had turned green.

The PPS wizard then asked the consultant to recalibrate the traffic flows, treating the street not as a continuous corridor, but instead as a connected series of community nodes able to absorb slowdowns at each intersection. The green dots turned even darker, indicating improved flow.

Next, the PPS engineer asked the county consultant to recode the program to accommodate bus bump-outs. Then, different water drainage systems, to serve as workarounds to Green Book street width mandates. Then, expanded street parking solutions. One by one, he suggested other modifications. By the time he was done, there was complete silence in the room.

The county consultant looked like he might explode. But McLaughlin intervened first. "Impressive," he offered. "But we can't make changes of this magnitude based on two hours in a conference room. What do you propose given how far along the process is?" I suggested that we relaunch what's known in the realm of public administrative decision-making as a "late stage review." The county would convene PPS, city officials who had helped develop the Midtown Greenway Plan, and members of the Public Advisory Committee to take another look at options. McLaughlin agreed.

We see the tendency of public officials to define problems narrowly. And to leap to, and lock into, technocratic solutions too quickly. That can put the officials, and their solutions, at odds with the people who have to live with those solutions day to day and year after year.

The process played out over another six months. Virtually every adjustment the PPS engineer had suggested in the McKnight conference room held up to deeper scrutiny as the reassembled group of actors more fully explored options. It was evident that McLaughlin had implored his team to be open to ideas that could be seen as strengthening the neighborhood plan; these were his constituents, after all.

In the end, the product was a street designed not to a single standard along its full length, but instead with varying configurations, with reduced width of driving lanes and a resulting increase in sidewalk width throughout. It included expanded on-street parking in some areas, and sidewalk bump-outs to facilitate bus stops in many others. It incorporated innovative curb drainage systems, and had dedicated turn-lanes in only a few sections. That is exactly how it was rebuilt.

The street today still suffers from motorists anxious to whiz through. But happily, it became far more conducive to short-trip stops to local businesses. To open-air gathering and dining. To bike travel. To tree plantings. In a word: to vibrant community life. Ultimately, the redesign process was faithful to the principle of elevating the identity, function, and integrity of a place.

As in the cases of the garbage transfer station and the armory, equipping community residents with tools to counterbalance the ostensibly unyielding nature of "expert" public sector perspective was transformational.

In all three, the solution lay less in blocking the will of the public sector than in widening the aperture of possible solutions. Garbage needed to be transferred; there was simply another solution that allowed it to be done more efficiently. Prisoners needed to be housed; but there was a way to accomplish that without violating the city's architectural heritage. Cars needed to be moved; yet we could achieve that while enhancing—instead of undermining—the economic and social vitality of an emerging cultural corridor.

In all three cases, the ability to slow down processes that had been moving inexorably forward on fast tracks afforded the time needed for a new dynamic enabling objective, third-party analysis, reasoned exchange and negotiation, and good faith synthesis to take hold.

And in all three, we see the tendency of public officials to define problems narrowly. And to leap to, and lock into, technocratic solutions too quickly. That can put the officials, and their solutions, at odds with the people who have to live with those solutions day to day and year after year.

It's difficult to break that tendency in any one case—and even more difficult to break it over time. In some of the coming chapters, we'll see attempts to do this more systematically by creating sustainable structures and processes that cultivate ongoing, integrative thinking. Mechanisms that set problem-solving tables across disciplines and sectors. Channels that feed community experience, wisdom, and perspective directly into early-stage policy deliberations. Platforms that broadly distribute leadership responsibilities for designing, implementing, and stewarding solutions to seemingly intractable challenges.

Shape Shifting

Translating business self-interest into a shared civic agenda

Nobody could remember a statement from a university president creating this kind of firestorm. But then again, Mark Yudof wasn't your run-of-the-mill university president.

In 2001, Yudof approached the rostrum to address the Minnesota legislature, along with other leaders, policy wonks, and public sector influencers, at the opening of the state's biennial legislative session. Trained as a constitutional law professor, Yudof had served as president of the University of Minnesota since 1997, after two decades in the University of Texas higher education system as a faculty member, law school dean, and provost. He had the reputation of being reliably candid and wickedly smart.

His piercing frankness probably shouldn't have been a surprise, yet his talk that day sent shockwaves through the room. In plain language, he told the 1,200 people assembled that the Twin Cities had become complacent and lazy. The region's impulses of innovation—exemplified by such forward-looking acts as the formation of the Metropolitan Council, one of only a handful of regional planning authorities in the United States; the creation of the Citizen's League, a pioneering regional research entity; and the corporate norm of donating 5 percent of pretax profits to charity—had atrophied. In a nutshell, Yudof asserted, the region was slipping into mediocrity, with no strategy for keeping the edge needed to compete in the 21st century.

The outrage and fury surprised even Yudof. Legislators were quick to point out that he was the head of the university, not the governor. In fact, they argued, presumably swallowing hard, it was professional-wrestler-turned-Governor Jesse Ventura who bore responsibility for pulling the state out of the economic downturn of the early 2000s, not an unelected law professor.

Yudof and I had gotten to know each other through a series of conversations leading to McKnight making a once-in-a-decade gift to the university. He called me immediately after his speech. Yudof realized that he couldn't ignite this kind of controversy without trying to do something about it, and had a plan to create a blue ribbon panel to formulate recommendations for a more competitive future. He asked if McKnight might support that effort.

I said we would. I suggested that he might take advantage of the freedom that came with *not* being governor to make sure the panel represented the best thinkers in the state, and wasn't just window-dressing or a vehicle for covering all possible political bases. Yudof agreed, naming two respected corporate leaders he'd lined up to lead the effort: Roger Hale of the Tennant Company, an industrial equipment manufacturer, and Larry Perlman of Control Data Corporation, a pioneer of supercomputer technology.

Unfortunately, appointing the remaining commission members did, in fact, become an exercise in check-the-political-boxes, undermining Yudof's early goal of promoting bold, long-term stretch thinking. Despite lengthy hearings and deliberations, the panel was something of a dud, ultimately producing only a handful of mushy, middle-of-the-road recommendations that tilted heavily in favor of the University of Minnesota. That fed skeptics' view that Yudof's broadside had simply been a self-serving attempt to generate increased legislative support for the state's higher education system.

His piercing frankness probably shouldn't have been a surprise, yet his talk that day sent shockwaves through the room.

Shortly after the panel's dissolution, Perlman came to see me. He was clearly frustrated: the problem hasn't gone away, he said. "We still need to mobilize the corporate and civic communities to create a path forward."

I didn't disagree. "And we're still prepared at McKnight to help support that," I replied. "But I think you're in a bit of a box, don't you?"

Perlman was a steely guy, and didn't flinch. "Yes, we are. But that's why I'm here. I think that you, as the president of the most prestigious and largest foundation in the state, are the one to get us out of that box," he said. "We need to start over from scratch. I think you're the right person to reset our approach."

It took me a bit to absorb that: the last thing I expected was that a corporate leading light would look to the head of a private philanthropy to mobilize civic impulses in the private sector. I expressed skepticism that I could deliver where he and Hale had not.

But Perlman persisted. "We were hobbled by the politics. You won't be. McKnight has feet in different worlds," Perlman said. "You'll be seen as credible by the business community. You work extensively with the public sector. You invest in nonprofits and academic institutions. You have no dog in the hunt. We need a neutral convener, and you're perfect."

Sensing my continuing apprehension, Perlman pressed on. "I'm prepared to weigh in whenever and however you believe it's useful, but you should design a process that makes sense to you." I suggested that it would be prudent to form a small planning group to explore how to construct the process: how we might identify the membership, how we might canvass possible issues, how it would be run, who would staff it, and the like. Perlman agreed.

My first call was to Jack Dorsey, a partner in the Minneapolis McKinsey office. When McKinsey first opened its Minneapolis office, Dorsey had approached me seeking a recommendation of a pro bono project that could have a strong impact on the city. I'd recommended that McKinsey help the new Minneapolis Public Schools superintendent, Carol Johnson, build an initiative championed by the Gates Foundation to create multiple small high schools within a single, traditional high school building. Dorsey told me McKinsey would be open to other opportunities if the schools project went well.

It had—hence my call. I asked Dorsey if he and some colleagues might be willing to help give shape to Perlman's idea. Understanding that the process would put McKinsey directly in touch with their new market's business executives, he readily accepted.

My next calls were to seven of the most thoughtful and imaginative people I knew: heads of a transit company, a publishing company, and a media company; a venture capitalist; a nonprofit executive; plus Perlman and Dorsey. I asked them to agree to two breakfast meetings to scope out a way forward.

That the participants started from a place of skepticism is an understatement. The group members weren't sure we could get busy executives to commit their time. Or that we could steer them away from the clearly defined priorities of existing business associations, like the Minnesota Business Partnership or Chamber of Commerce. Or that we'd forge consensus on anything beyond aspirational platitudes.

I snuck a glance at Perlman. He made a circular motion with his right hand, indicating that I should keep going.

"Let's roll back the tape and talk for a couple of minutes about what it would take to overcome all of that—about what's realistically needed for this to be successful," I suggested. That loosened the group up a bit. We quickly agreed that the purpose must be clear: the effort we sought to create needed to subordinate immediate and specific business interests to the broader goal of forging a regional business plan, one grounded in civic values and encompassing efforts that weren't being addressed in existing forums.

Someone suggested that could be accomplished only if we included institutions and leaders outside the corporate realm: the University of Minnesota, the Minnesota State College and University system, the mayors of Minneapolis and St. Paul, and likely others. Another urged that participants be limited to corporate chief executives. They needed to see their peers sitting across the table; permitting delegation to an organization's middle ranks would ensure its failure.

"We need to start over from scratch."

By breakfast meeting standards, this was progress; everyone agreed to a second meeting two weeks later. Between meetings, Dorsey and I discussed putting McKinsey more fully into play; given their entrée into corporate leadership suites, it made sense for them to be the front edge of our exploratory efforts. Dorsey pledged to confer with his McKinsey colleagues about strategies to engage chief executives preoccupied with running large, in some cases multinational, companies.

We began our second meeting with Dorsey's recommendation: McKinsey could use a senior team with connections and credibility to interview a hundred corporate CEOs over the next months to identify issues that most needed addressing. A couple of us agreed to take responsibility for socializing the idea with key public sector actors like Minneapolis Mayor R.T. Rybak, St. Paul Mayor Randy Kelly, and Governor Tim Pawlenty.

We soon realized that the architecture we were constructing was more complex, and would take longer to assemble, than we'd anticipated. More eggs and coffee seemed to be on the group's menu. Perlman said he would step away until it was time to persuade his CEO counterparts to participate, and everyone else signed on for an extended tour of duty.

We met every Friday morning for nearly a year.

The project became more compelling the more we mapped it out. As the McKinsey interviews began yielding recommendations, we were able to refine our objectives, our structure, our likely membership, and our strategies, envisioning smaller working groups to supplement the all-member meetings.

We also agreed to a name: The Itasca Project. It hearkened back to an endeavor launched by a handful of Twin Cities captains of industry decades earlier. In the early 1960s, a few business luminaries—Daytons, Pillsburys, Cowles, and others—would travel to the headwaters of the Mississippi River at Itasca State Park. They'd spend the weekend in a historic lodge, discussing ways to help the region thrive, and emerge with something resembling a collective agenda. Although the elitism of that approach seemed retrograde forty years later, the name felt apt.

By fall 2003, we'd wrapped up our last breakfast meeting. We were finally ready to launch.

I reengaged Perlman, and together we wrote a letter inviting 50 civic leaders to meet at the McKnight offices. It was an ambitious invite list, and a remarkable group turned out—including the CEOs of 3M, Best Buy, Medtronic, Wells Fargo, the Carlson Companies, HealthPartners, and Northwest Airlines. We also secured participation from Governor Pawlenty, Mayors Rybak and Kelly, the head of the Metropolitan Council, the new president of the University of Minnesota (Yudof left for the University of Texas in 2002), and the president of the state university system. Leaders of the two dominant business umbrella organizations, the Chamber of Commerce (focused on the state's small businesses) and the Minnesota Business Partnership (focused on the state's hundred largest businesses), were invited to sit as observers. A few businesses declined to accept—most disappointingly, Target, General Mills, and Pillsbury.

After Perlman and I opened with an overview of purpose, Dorsey began sharing a twenty-page PowerPoint of interview findings. With each slide, the displeasure from the Chamber, the Business Partnership, and the governor became more palpable. They had anticipated an affirmation of longstanding business concerns about corporate tax relief and regulatory relief. That wasn't what Dorsey was presenting. Instead, the interviews had identified four building blocks that corporate leaders believed necessary for regional growth and competitiveness:

1. Creation of a regional transit system
2. Improvement of the public education system, starting with early childhood development opportunities
3. Enhancement of patent transfer from higher education research and development to the private sector, and
4. Reduction in health disparities among Twin Cities residents

Governor Pawlenty was visibly flummoxed and annoyed. Rising to his feet the moment Dorsey finished, he noted that many people in the room sat on the governing board of the Minnesota Business Partnership, which was charged with advocating for issues of highest importance to the state's business community—and these weren't those.

After a minute of awkward silence, Marilyn Carlson Nelson, CEO of the Carlson Companies, leaned into the table and said in a calm, measured tone, "You're right, Governor, and that's why we've agreed to meet. What you see from the McKinsey analysis is that a critical mass of our corporate community sees the necessity of moving beyond tax and regulatory reform, as important as they are.

"We need systems that will help us move our employees and goods efficiently across the region," she continued. "Systems that will ensure we're training a skilled workforce, and that will capture the creativity and innovation coming out of higher education. And systems that will increase the likelihood that all our citizens can live full and healthy lives. We're here to chart a very different path forward."

Pawlenty was floored. He was looking at many of the same people who served on his political finance committee, and he found their divergence from well-trodden business priorities bewildering.

"But Marilyn, early childhood development? You can't be serious," Pawlenty rejoined. Nelson smiled and without missing a beat replied, "I couldn't be more serious, Governor. My employees need to know that their children have access to the kind of development opportunities that prepare them for kindergarten. Without adequate childcare, I lose good employees."

The group waited for Pawlenty's next move. Nelson's calm authority had unnerved him. Wisely, he chose to sit down, quietly slipping out minutes later.

Some group members questioned whether Itasca would be yet another staffed entity that would extract dues and devour the time of the members' own staff. Richard Anderson, CEO of Northwest Airlines (later merged into Delta), held up a grid of more than 15 umbrella business organizations along the X axis and their functions along the Y axis; every cell was filled with dots. "You've got to convince me that this is something different," he said.

Governor Pawlenty was floored. He was looking at many of the same people who served on his political finance committee, and he found their divergence from well-trodden business priorities bewildering.

Perlman replied that not only was the substantive agenda entirely different, but so too was the machinery to accomplish it. The Itasca project would be convened by McKnight and staffed pro bono by McKinsey; there was no intention to hire staff. Its efforts would be shaped by four working groups, each cochaired by CEOs but staffed and supported by subject-matter experts from the public, academic, and nonprofit sectors, along with corporate representatives. We would convene quarterly to track the work groups' progress toward formulating actionable recommendations. Each meeting would adhere to a tight ninety minutes with succinct supplementary materials distributed in advance. If the CEOs concluded that the meetings weren't worth their time, they could vote with their feet.

Head-nodding all around. We set the next meeting for three months later.

Everyone came back for that meeting—except the governor, who'd evidently seen enough (although he asked his chief of staff to sit in to keep an eye on things). The group signed off on cochairs for the four work groups and determined which McKinsey, McKnight, and nonprofit experts would staff each. We affirmed that Itasca would remain informal: no executive director, budget, or rigid governance structure. McKinsey would continue providing project management support, and McKnight would underwrite the carrying costs, including paying for the full-time secondment of a talented young McKinsey associate.

As the second meeting was about to adjourn, 3M's CEO Jim McNerney spoke up. "We still need one of us to run these meetings." Quiet. They all had day jobs. McNerney looked right at Jim Campbell, head of Wells Fargo's Upper Midwest operations, who promptly looked down at his shoes. "You'd be perfect, Campbell. You're about to retire. You're the only nice guy in the bunch. And we all steal most of our ideas from you already." Before Campbell could say no, the deed was done—by acclamation. Itasca had a chair.

The group had decided that regional transit would be its first, and highest, priority. The decision reflected growing frustration in the business and civic communities that the region had stalled repeatedly in trying to create a comprehensive public transportation system. The bus system was fragmented and only loosely coordinated among different municipalities. The region's sole light rail line ran along industrialized Hiawatha Avenue from downtown Minneapolis to the airport (and Mall of America), but not beyond. There was neither a viable plan nor a dedicated funding source to expand, connect, or enhance any of the pieces.

Itasca's efforts would change the arc of transit in the Minneapolis-St. Paul region over the next fifteen years.

The transportation workgroup was cochaired by Charlie Zelle, president of Jefferson Bus Lines, and Jay Cowles, immediate past chair of Cowles Media company. I suggested to Zelle and Cowles that we examine cities that had gotten transportation right. The blueprint of "intercity visits," started and refined into a precise methodology by the city of Seattle years earlier, had encouraged cities to explore new ways of working on issues by immersing civic leaders deeply in other communities' strategies. Zelle and Cowles agreed that should be the first order of business for their working group. McKnight accordingly would underwrite the costs of a trip to Seattle and Denver.

It was a revelation. Denver suggested how a regional taxing structure could underwrite the formation and ongoing expansion of a transit system. Seattle—just at the front end of a start-and-stop process of introducing comprehensive transit—showed the value of meticulous long-term planning and political patience. The Itasca group returned to Minneapolis less convinced of the applicability of the two cities' specific approaches than confident of transit's pivotal role in the health of a regional economy.

The question ricocheting through the debriefing session was how to embark on such an overwhelmingly complex undertaking. It wasn't simply a matter of identifying highest value routes, appropriate modalities, or even sustainable funding sources; it was also a question of what approach could avoid languishing in political purgatory, as multiple previous efforts had.

The politics were perhaps the most formidable obstacle. Governor Pawlenty had absolutely no appetite for a mass transit initiative: it would be all-consuming, and his priorities lay elsewhere. And it would be, he believed, prohibitively expensive. Which meant it would require raising taxes in one form or another—anathema to someone trying to build his national profile, and potential presidential aspirations, by underscoring his administration's no-new-taxes record.

But before worrying about the governor, we first had to convince our fellow Itasca members that we could develop a viable roadmap. I suggested we find someone with enough knowledge, skill, and credibility to distill the best elements of earlier plans, put them in the blender of current fiscal and political realities, and produce a working framework. The Itasca group would be the litmus test of whether that framework was compelling—and feasible. If they believed it was, we could begin building the public case and mobilizing key constituencies.

This was all a long shot. I could think of only one person capable of pulling it off: a unicorn with exceptional technical skills, deep political credibility, and unquestioned public stature.

His name was Curt Johnson.

Johnson had led the Citizens League, a public research and education group, for a decade. He had then been drafted by Governor Arnie Carlson to be his chief of staff for four years. Carlson subsequently appointed Johnson to chair the Metropolitan Council, the regional planning body for the Twin Cities. He'd recently retired from that post after a distinguished tenure.

All three experiences were critical. His Citizens League tenure had established him as a forward thinker who looked around corners in crafting public policy solutions. His stint with the governor had been a model of balance; Johnson was admired by key figures in the legislature and the executive branch as a fair and politically astute broker of conflicting perspectives. But even more, it was his service leading the Met Council that suggested to me that he was prepared to take on the challenge.

The Met Council was charged by the state with establishing regional growth policies and long-range planning for systems across the boundaries of its seven constituent counties: transportation, wastewater, aviation, housing, land use, regional parks, and others. That experience equipped Johnson to navigate the landmines of the countless transit plans that had been floated over the last twenty years.

Itasca's efforts would change the arc of transit in the Minneapolis-St. Paul region over the next fifteen years.

A humble and unassuming man, Johnson was deeply hesitant when I called to ask if he would take the assignment. "Nobody has been able to accomplish this, Rip—and there's a reason. Every transit line you propose is seen as a win for one community and a loss for another. Every municipal transit authority views a regional system as encroaching on its prerogatives," he said. "And even if you can solve the technical issues of routing and land purchase and heaven knows what else, the politics are impossible. Nobody in Burnsville wants to pay taxes for someone to ride a trolley car in Brooklyn Center. And Governor Pawlenty will be Dr. Death on anything that comes to his desk."

I waited until he finished. "So that's a yes?" I asked. Johnson laughed, albeit a bit nervously. "Not exactly. It's a maybe. We've never had a business coalition like this behind public transit, and that could make all the difference." Johnson asked for some time to think about it.

Three days later he called me back. "OK, I'm game. I'm going to need a month or two of radio silence while I comb through every plan that's ever been proposed, together with its political pathway to the graveyard," Johnson said. "My intention is to pull together a single master proposal: all the routes, all the technologies, all the price tags. My hope is that we can provide enough of a framework to support drafting legislation that could become law."

Johnson was true to his word. It was as intellectually virtuosic as it was technically precise and politically nuanced; he had distilled a dizzying set of possibilities into a single, comprehensive, up-to-the-moment plan.

That was part one of the assignment. Part two was to stress-test the plan with key constituencies before presenting it to Itasca. Johnson shared it with business groups, transportation trade groups, and anyone else who might add value—or throw up roadblocks—modifying or fine-tuning where appropriate.

It was a rollercoaster ride, as you'd expect with an effort that had become a hot-button issue on all sides of the question. But Johnson was preternaturally patient, politically agile, and intellectually commanding. His exhaustive "reconciliation" process entailed hundreds of adjustments—some scaling down, others scaling up, the ambition of the proposal. The magnitude of that ambition was reinforced by the plan's $20 billion price tag, even when stretched over multiple years. The cost alone was a guaranteed lightning rod, to say nothing of the plan's components.

Johnson had delivered beyond our expectations. Next up, part three of the challenge: securing the buy-in of the Itasca membership itself.

We set up an extended meeting of the full Itasca membership for a detailed briefing and the group's assessment of the plan. True to Johnson's prediction, Governor Pawlenty was livid about the very idea of Itasca endorsing the plan, conveying to the group that he would never sign legislation bearing any resemblance to it. He dispatched his chief of staff, Charlie Weaver, to the meeting to deliver that message.

Zelle and Cowles, who cochaired the transportation workgroup, opened. They reminded the group of the trip to Denver and Seattle and the stakes involved in this being Itasca's first major action item. Johnson then walked the group through the steps he'd taken to formulate the plan, including all the modifications he'd made following meetings with the various constituencies. He explained its structure, and detailed what the $20 billion would buy.

Before we could start the broader discussion, Weaver asked for a few minutes to articulate the governor's concerns about the proposal. The members listened but didn't take the bait, or at least not entirely. Someone suggested that we might be better served by selecting just a few routes to get small victories notched on Itasca's belt. Someone else noted that neither the Business Partnership nor the Chamber of Commerce—both of which included Itasca members—had seen fit to endorse the effort.

> **"I can't believe you're considering this. You're out of your zone—leave things like this to the legislature."**

Then Richard Schultze, CEO and founder of Best Buy, calmly but forcefully reset the tone. "I can't move my goods across the region without getting stuck in ridiculous congestion. Even locating our headquarters and distribution centers close to the airport doesn't help," Schulze said. "I'm losing employees because their commutes take forever. A world-class business can't survive in this environment—don't talk to me about baby steps." Heads nodded around the table.

Weaver couldn't help himself. He jumped up and stammered, "I can't believe you're seriously considering this. You're out of your zone—leave things like this to the legislature."

Big mistake.

Marilyn Carlson Nelson—as she had on the issue of childcare—diffused the tension. "Charlie, please remind the governor of our earlier conversation. The Twin Cities business community has joined arms with our mayors, our nonprofit community, and others to advance something that none of us in our individual capacities can: efficient regional public transportation. It is critical to every business in this room," Nelson said, "We need to move forward. If the governor can't get on board, so be it."

Ultimately this issue, as difficult as it was, was exactly the kind of challenge Itasca had been formed to tackle. Weaver was right: the elected officials of the state legislature would be the ultimate arbiters. But Itasca would put its weight behind the argument that this was sound, and necessary, public policy. The group voted to support the plan, along with a critical path for its adoption.

It was that critical path that represented Itasca's real coming-of-age. Part four.

Drawing on individual members' public relations capacities (Kathy Tunheim, for example, headed one of the state's most effective political communications firms), advocacy expertise, and internal lobbying teams, Itasca subsequently rolled out one of the most sophisticated and far-reaching public education and advocacy campaigns Minnesota had seen. It launched a multimedia campaign about the value of public transit. It called on advocacy groups to organize support within key legislative districts. And it provided unassailable case analytics for every component of the plan.

Perhaps most significantly, each CEO agreed to host a small dinner at his or her home with one or two legislators to talk through the plan. The effort focused on three dozen or so of the senators and house members whose support was crucial for passage. The prospect of an intimate evening with some of the nation's most respected business leaders ensured that the RSVP's came in at light speed. Not only did dinners permit the CEOs to hear out and respond to objections the lawmakers had; it also created a personal connection (that would be later reinforced by a handwritten follow-up note).

It was a disarmingly simple strategy, enabled by CEOs who were willing to put time, energy, and their personal reputations behind the effort. It was done quietly, without fanfare. A stealth strategy whose efficacy couldn't be gauged in real time. Our package of bills passed both houses of the legislature . . . and then Governor Pawlenty vetoed the package, as promised.

But in a political earthquake, the Republican House and Senate overrode the veto of a governor of their own party. I have absolutely no doubt that the stealth dinners made that possible. The package became law.

Core pieces of the plan have fallen in place steadily over the past two decades: the NorthStar Commuter Rail line, running from the far northern suburbs into Minneapolis; the Green Line light rail connection between the two downtowns; rapid transit bus lines crisscrossing the region; the Orange Line running due south from Minneapolis.

And Itasca continues its work today. It has moved on to other issues, welcomed new members, faced new organizational challenges. Its success conjures the *Star Trek* phenomenon of shape-shifting. The corporate community forged novel partnerships with the public, academic, philanthropic, and nonprofit sectors. The businesses, while never compromising their institutional interests, defined them more expansively than was customary. Itasca moved beyond the constraints of ossified trade organization priorities, with the group dynamic arcing above and beyond conservative political expectations.

And the shape-shifting wasn't limited to the business leaders. Nonprofits—initially skeptical of an elitist group of CEOs presuming to set regional civic priorities—worked hand in glove with Itasca to craft effective approaches to transit, childcare, and health priorities they too had been pursuing for years.

At first concerned about creating an impression that they'd relinquished public decision-making authority to unelected corporate leaders, mayors Rybak and Kelly took a back seat to—but threw their full weight behind—a process outside their scope of command and control.

And the McKnight Foundation, originally unsure whether philanthropy could contribute meaningfully to such an unprecedented effort, had realized Larry Perlman's aspiration. McKnight took the lead in designing the Itasca enterprise, set it in motion, and supported its early endeavors. And it then stepped away, as IRS guidance demanded, when a specific legislative proposal was born. For a foundation like ours, it was risky business. But it was the kind of risk, anchored in the pursuit of long-term public good, that private foundations are uniquely equipped to take.

Reinventing a storied philanthropic institution

I had no interest in transplanting my Minneapolis roots, even for a storied national institution like the Kresge Foundation.

Kresge was looking for a new president after John Marshall, the president of twenty years, announced his retirement in 2005. The search was led by Susan Boren, who was based in Minneapolis at executive search firm Spencer Stuart and whom I'd known and respected for many years.

Boren called to ask if I would sit down with her to talk about the opening at Kresge. Although I had left the McKnight Foundation a few months earlier, I expressed some reluctance, noting that I really wasn't familiar with Kresge's work. "Well, let me buy you coffee and tell you more about it," she replied.

Over coffee, I apologized for not knowing what a fellow foundation like Kresge did. She smiled and said, "That's not surprising. They are, in some respects, still a family foundation working quietly in a very narrow niche. But they are substantial—with $3 billion in assets—and have a reputation for excellence within that niche."

She explained that the Kresge Foundation was established in Detroit in 1924 by Sebastian S. Kresge, the founder in 1899 of the Kresge Five and Dime stores. That retail business had grown in scale and form over the next fifty years, becoming Kmart. By the mid-1960s, it was so large as to no longer be, in any meaningful sense, a family business. Sebastian's son and successor, Stanley, sold the corporation and began investing the proceeds into the foundation.

In the succeeding decades, the foundation invested in capital building campaigns for nonprofit organizations. Museum expansions, botanic gardens, new hospital wings, science centers at private colleges—virtually any expression of nonprofit bricks and mortar. Kresge believed that the undertaking of a capital campaign provided a window for a nonprofit organization to build an enduring donor base of individuals, ensuring its long-term financial sustainability.

Under John Marshall's leadership, Kresge perfected the concept of a "capital challenge grant." The foundation would commit to providing the last dollars necessary for completion of a building campaign. An organization would apply to Kresge once its major donations—those at a certain dollar level at the apex of a pyramid of giving—were in hand, with Kresge then issuing a "challenge" to the organization to raise the balance of the fundraising goal through individual donors. Once those donations were in hand, Kresge would release its funds, and the capital goal would be fully met.

This approach had helped thousands of capital projects cross the fundraising finish line. Indeed, the model was so effective that it became the gold standard for fundraising professionals. And it established Kresge as a sort of Good Housekeeping Seal of Approval for any nonprofit pursuing a capital campaign.

I was fascinated by Boren's description of Kresge's work—although not for the reasons Boren probably hoped.

I wondered how it was possible in my six years at McKnight to never have crossed paths with, or even heard of, Kresge. "For all practical purposes, McKnight and Kresge aren't in the same lines of business," Boren replied. "Both are privately endowed philanthropies working across the country, but that's where the similarities end. Kresge invests without engaging other foundations; their exclusive concern is fortifying the fundraising muscle of an institution. They're agnostic about what fields they fund into—with few exceptions, no particular part of the nonprofit universe is privileged. So whereas McKnight might seek to advance the larger environmental, or arts, or regional development field, Kresge works institution by institution. They do one thing, and they do it very well."

That struck me as a bit upside down. I couldn't imagine they'd be interested in someone whose philanthropic work was so completely different from theirs. But Boren said the Board's search committee wanted to explore how they might work differently. "Whether you talked with them as a candidate or as an adviser with deep experience in helping organizations reinvent themselves," Boren said, "you would be ideal."

I asked whether Kresge worked differently in their hometown of Detroit. "Yes and no," Boren offered. "My impression is that they largely adhere to their capital challenge grant approach, but are willing to make more flexible and larger grants in Detroit than elsewhere. They've made, for example, a $50 million grant—their largest ever—to reclaim the Detroit riverfront by creating a RiverWalk. They also provided early challenge grants to remodel the downtown library and build a new YMCA."

Boren had done her job well, piquing my interest. The last thing I was interested in doing was moving our family—my wife and two young children—from Minneapolis. But the chance to assist an important organization seeking to reimagine its possibilities felt hard to refuse. Boren could see the shift. "So, you'll meet with them? Not as an interviewee, but as an advisor?" I nodded.

> **The last thing I was interested in doing was moving our family—my wife and two young children—from Minneapolis.**

Two weeks later, I was sitting in the conference room of a metro Detroit hotel with the half-dozen members of the Kresge search committee. The cochairs introduced themselves: Elaine Rosen, the recently retired CEO of Unum Corporation (a Fortune 500 financial services company based in Maine); and Lee Bollinger, president of Columbia University and immediate past president of the University of Michigan. They were complemented by an equally distinguished group of committee members.

They began gently enough, with Rosen asking me to describe my work at McKnight. They zeroed in on how I had been able to work with the McKnight family board members to create new program areas in children and families grantmaking and regional growth.

They asked how, despite the different governance structures and programmatic orientations of the two organizations, McKnight's program expansion might be instructive to the Kresge board's interest in reaching a broader spectrum of nonprofit organizations.

Considering it presumptuous to suggest how to retool an organization with such a dignified and storied history, I asked whether I might take a different tack. "I would start with first principles," I suggested. "You might ask what qualities are unique to a privately endowed philanthropy like Kresge, and whether you're fully living into them."

"Invest in people who have been marginalized. That requires challenging practices and policies that block, rather than promote, opportunity."

That got the attention of Bollinger, who'd been pacing around the edge of the room. "Like what?" he asked.

"Let's start with four," I replied.

The first quality, I suggested, was the ability of private philanthropy to take a holistic, long-term view of its work.

That might begin with a more expansive view of an organization's needs. Kresge's laudable one-time investments in a specific building campaign might grow an organization's donor base and enhance its long-term fundraising capacities. But the potency of that approach largely evaporated at the conclusion of the transaction; it couldn't necessarily help an organization grow, adapt to external changes, or pursue new channels of work. And a more holistic approach might explore how a grant fits into a larger context: for example, whether a building project could create deeper connection to the surrounding community or advance the field of environmental sustainability.

The second quality was the extraordinary latitude that private philanthropy possesses to embrace risk.

I suggested that privately endowed philanthropy serves as society's social venture capital. Kresge's capital challenge grants were essentially risk-free to the foundation: if a nonprofit failed to attract enough individual donors to meet Kresge's challenge grant requirements, Kresge wouldn't make the grant.

If Kresge were willing to embrace higher levels of risk, however, it could begin freeing the foundation's methodology from some of its constraints. Placing a bet on an upstart organization without a heavily staffed, well-connected fundraising office and doing so early in the campaign's evolution, for example, could jump-start a campaign that might not otherwise be undertaken; a seeding function rather than a close-the-deal function. Much more akin to venture investing.

The third quality was the ability to use a wide spectrum of tools.

The Kresge challenge grant was an undeniably powerful tool. But there were others in the toolbox as well: commissioning research, communicating learnings across a discipline, fostering networks of organizations working in common purpose, making below-market-rate loans or even equity investments, and others. If all you have is a hammer, the saying goes, everything looks like a nail. The nonprofit landscape also includes screws, hinges, putty, and drywall; continue using your hammer, but also think about the screwdriver, the pliers, the trowel, and the tape measure.

The fourth quality, I suggested, was private philanthropy's freedom—indeed, its moral imperative—to improve the life circumstances and opportunities of economically, socially, and politically marginalized people, ideas, and causes.

Kresge was basically value neutral: its capital challenge grants made no distinction between an arboretum and a homeless shelter, a private college's athletic complex and the New Haven Brass Ensemble's renovated performance hall.

There's absolutely nothing wrong with supporting all those organizations, I quickly added. It certainly advances Sebastian Kresge's articulated mission for the foundation: "Making the world a better place." It's simply that private philanthropy has the freedom to take on society's gnarly, intractable issues. Issues that individual donors, corporate donors, and even governments find difficult to address. The great philanthropies of the twentieth century sought to do that: Carnegie with access to libraries, Rockefeller with food security, Robert Wood Johnson with public health.

Bollinger, whose room-pacing had unnervingly picked up speed, jumped on the last point. "Are you suggesting that philanthropy could actually make a difference in a place like Detroit?"

Up to this point, I'd been serving up general principles that might, or might not, be useful to a board intent on rethinking institutional direction. But Bollinger seemed to be changing the stakes. He wasn't interested in empty platitudes. I took a deep breath. "Actually, I am," I finally said. "The only way I could imagine a foundation with Kresge's history and heft working in a place so profoundly challenged by poverty, race, disinvestment, and reputational disadvantage would be to turbo-charge each of the four qualities I talked about."

Bollinger stopped pacing. "How?" He wasn't about to let me off the hook.

I quickly concluded that neither could I let them off the hook. "With all due respect, you're not going to do that with capital challenge grants," I ventured. "You have to make long-term commitments across a wide spectrum of issues, not just underwrite more building campaigns. You have to think long and hard about whether and how you're prepared to invest in the building blocks this community needs in order to revitalize its neighborhoods, bring commerce back downtown, prepare kids for school.

"You have to put your reputational equity on the line and take some substantial risks that are commensurate with the scale of the challenges. Your investment in the riverfront is an impressive start. How about placing some very significant bets on improved regional transit, small business development, or affordable housing?

"You have to pull every single possible instrument out of the philanthropic toolbox, even ones that you don't recognize," I continued. "Provide operating support to frontline community organizations that aren't building new buildings, but simply trying to keep their lights on. Offer working capital to nurture neighborhood businesses seeking to expand. Connect people from Detroit to other cities that have tested ideas that might be useful here.

The city had so much stacked against it. To many observers, it was the poster child for urban dysfunction.

"You have to sight unapologetically on systems that are blocking low-income people from participating fully in the economy. Invest in people who have been marginalized. That requires challenging practices and policies that block, rather than promote, opportunity." I stopped, pretty sure I had dramatically overstepped. But, I reminded myself, this wasn't an interview, so they could take my comments as they chose. It was hard to read the room.

David Page, a senior partner in one of the state's largest law firms, didn't seem convinced: "But that's not what we do."

"No, it's not," I replied. "But Mr. Bollinger's question suggested you might want to work differently, at least in your hometown. Forgive me if that's not the case. If it's not, your capital challenge grants will continue to confer enormous value in communities across the country. They just won't transform Detroit.

"If you *are* seeking to work differently, Detroit is exactly the place to start. You've already taken the huge step of investing $50 million in the riverfront. I imagine there's a long and compelling queue of opportunities beyond that—and many of them wouldn't require $50 million."

Page nodded. Bollinger sat down (although I wasn't entirely sure that was a good thing). Rosen smiled and said, "That's a good place to leave the conversation. Thank you for visiting with us." I thanked them in return for a challenging conversation, and wished them well in their search.

Pulling a page from the McKnight playbook, it struck me that the situation might benefit from a drawing (or two or three).

The next day, Boren called. "They loved it," she exclaimed. "They want you to come back and become part of the final pool of a half-dozen candidates." I was flabbergasted. How did I enter as an adviser and emerge as a short-list candidate, I asked? I reiterated my complete lack of desire to pull up roots, together with my reluctance to inherit a portfolio of, and predilection for, bricks and mortar grantmaking.

"But that's exactly what they took from your presentation. They wouldn't want to continue the conversation if they didn't find your thinking compelling. Please think about it, Rip," Boren continued. "Just imagine what a difference you could make in Detroit and in the foundation itself."

That made life complicated. Agonizingly so.

After many difficult conversations with my wife, Gail, she surprised me. "You have to play this out," she said. "I can't stand the thought of leaving our home. But Boren is right. This is a once-in-a-lifetime opportunity. At least talk to them again."

I did. Two more times. And then they asked me to accept the job.

I continued resisting. Although I had come to see that the Kresge trustees were deeply committed to substantive change, I wasn't sure they were prepared for what that might actually mean. The statement "that's not what we do" had stuck with me.

Moreover, the challenges Detroit faced were unlike those facing any city—certainly, unlike those in which I'd been immersed in Minneapolis. That reality cut both ways: if ever a community could benefit from a foundation of Kresge's stature and resources committing to deeper engagement, it was Detroit. But the city had so much stacked against it. To many observers, it was the poster child for urban dysfunction.

Add to the mix the heartburn of leaving a city I knew, loved, and felt loyal to—hauling with me a wife, daughter, and son who had known no other city—and the Kresge offer seemed a bridge too far. I told Gail that I had set a time to talk with Boren, to convey my deep regrets.

But I hadn't counted on Gail's adamance. "As disruptive and sad as it will be, we'll figure this out as a family," she said. "You have to take this step. You've contributed so much to Minneapolis. You should feel enormous pride in that. But this is a new chapter. It's time in your career to do even more in Detroit."

Leave it to those who love you to see things you yourself can't.

So comfort needed to yield to opportunity. I called Boren the next morning to say we'd come, family and all. I began in June 2006.

I'd told the board in our last conversations that my intention was to use the simple four-part framework we'd discussed to organize staff deliberations about the path Kresge might take. We all understood that we weren't sure where the process would lead us, but that we would learn as we went.

I assured the staff that our task wasn't to blow things up: the foundation's work was too well-developed, honorable, and effective for that to be wise or prudent. But we might think about the challenge in terms of "depreciating the asset"; slowly, thoughtfully asking what core aspects of the "old" model still held value and should be retained, while simultaneously exploring what aspects might be discarded in favor of innovation. We could take our time to be planful.

Some staff were apprehensive; the capital challenge methodology was so well defined, effective in its way, and deeply rooted. Most, however, were simply open—curious about how much change might be possible without breaking faith with grantees who'd come to depend on Kresge's grantmaking in its current form. And a handful took the opening to suggest varying degrees of disruption: how to make the application process less onerous and bureaucratic, how to open our doors to smaller organizations, how to supplement building support with other forms of support, and much more.

Pulling a page from the McKnight playbook, it struck me that the situation might benefit from a drawing (or two or three). For those staff and board members who were anxious, committing ideas to paper in visual form might convey that they were exploratory, not set in stone—suggesting a thought exercise rather than weighty decision-making. For those who were curious, sketches might convey an openness to flexibility and malleability. And for those who sought more radical departures from the past, drawings might facilitate "stretch" thinking.

But I hesitated to go down that path without ensuring I wasn't too far in front of the board. So we set a board retreat within the first months of my arrival to explore—with visuals—a framework we could build out over time.

Recognizing that cartoons were an unorthodox way to introduce a serious-minded board to a seriously intentioned process, I didn't send the visuals in advance; just a written memo summarizing my intentions.

I wanted to build an argument piece by piece. I started with a depiction (above) of what we had in place, the facilities challenge grant program. We came to call it the Blue Box. It was a deceptive depiction, reducing to a simple cube all the history, complexity, and impact of a program that had evolved over three decades. Imagine, I said, that the entirety of what we did could be contained within that Blue Box.

I asked the trustees to consider what it might mean to superimpose onto the box the four principles we'd discussed at the first interview.

I explained that in the five months between being offered the job and starting at Kresge, I had toured the country to ask other foundation leaders how they would answer that question. Could the box withstand the torque of these four values, or would that torque cause it to change into something else altogether? There had been universal agreement that you could indeed modify the box—focusing on capital campaigns that took more risks, or contributed to broader social objectives—but you couldn't accommodate all the principles from the outset. As the values were applied, the more compelling the case would become that an expanded, reimagined approach to grantmaking was needed. An evolution.

A first step in that evolution, I suggested to the trustees, might be to stick with providing capital support to nonprofits, but define "capital" in more expansive terms. Beyond facilities capital, a nonprofit might need planning capital, or operating capital, or growth capital, or loan capital. We could imagine "stretching" beyond the Blue Box to create a wide spectrum of capital support. (See below.)

The stretch suggested a way to respond to each of the four principles—but that act of stretching created a potential rabbit hole. The Blue Box was agnostic about the purposes for which Kresge capital would be used, provided it built fundraising capacity. But although only a select few nonprofits were building new facilities, most of the nation's 70,000 nonprofit organizations could identify capital needs of one type or another. We would have to develop an ability to prioritize.

The drawings introduced a thought challenge: how might we reimagine the ways in which Kresge's values could be applied to its longstanding "captital challenge" approach to grantmaking?

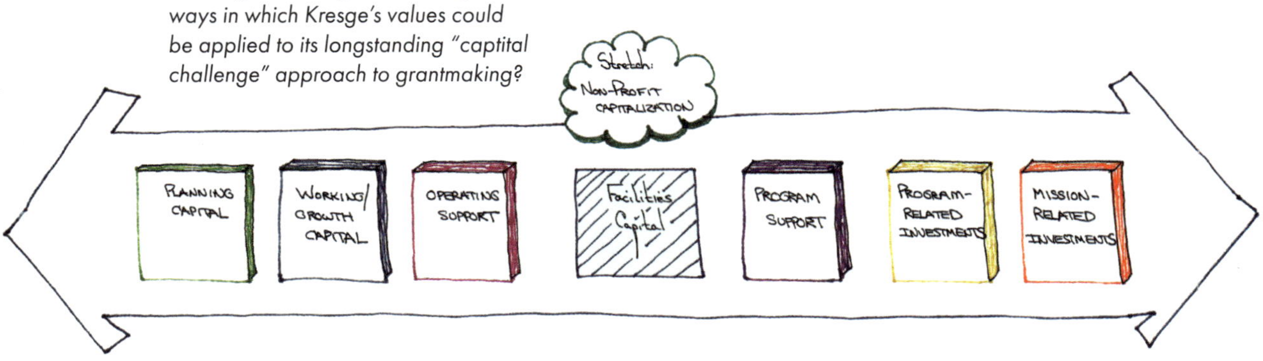

We could get part of the way there by applying the four principles to capital challenge grant applications, asking how the values might reshape our current program. For example, did a facilities capital request contribute to the revitalization of a low-income community (i.e., the holistic value)? Was it innovative (i.e., the risk value)? Did it help the organization expand its programming (i.e., the tools value)? Did it advance economic opportunity for people with low-incomes (i.e., the opportunity value)?

It would be neither wise nor justifiable—at least in the first stages of our redesign—to block a nonprofit from applying for a Kresge grant if it didn't meet all the values we articulated. We could instead weigh the variety of values advanced by one nonprofit against the variety of values advanced by another.

Could the box withstand the torque of these four values, or would that torque cause it to change into something else altogether?

And it wouldn't be easy to develop a consistent calculus in making those judgments, given the widely divergent missions and approaches each organization would present. A community health clinic in San Antonio might weigh heavily on the scale of community impact, for example. An art museum in Boston might be compelling for its innovation in hiring curators of color. A college campus in San Diego might be breaking new ground in environmental sustainability.

Still, though difficult, it seemed a logical first step.

We agreed that that first step couldn't be uncoupled from the dynamics of the field in which the nonprofit was working. The sources, forms, and channels of capital were very different for organizations in the healthcare, arts, education, human services, community development, and environmental fields. The values "funnel" would be inextricably connected, therefore, to a field funnel. (See below.)

I reiterated that this would have to be an incremental process—again, applied initially only to our Blue Box. We could breathe life into the capital stretch concept by asking how the values analysis, coupled with the field analysis, suggested whether and in what form a capital investment in a nonprofit should be made. It would enable us to develop much greater granularity in letting people know what we might, and might not, support.

That led, in turn, to a second "tier" of analysis. It wasn't simply that different fields drew down capital in different ways: fields were defined by distinctive laws, policies, and practices.

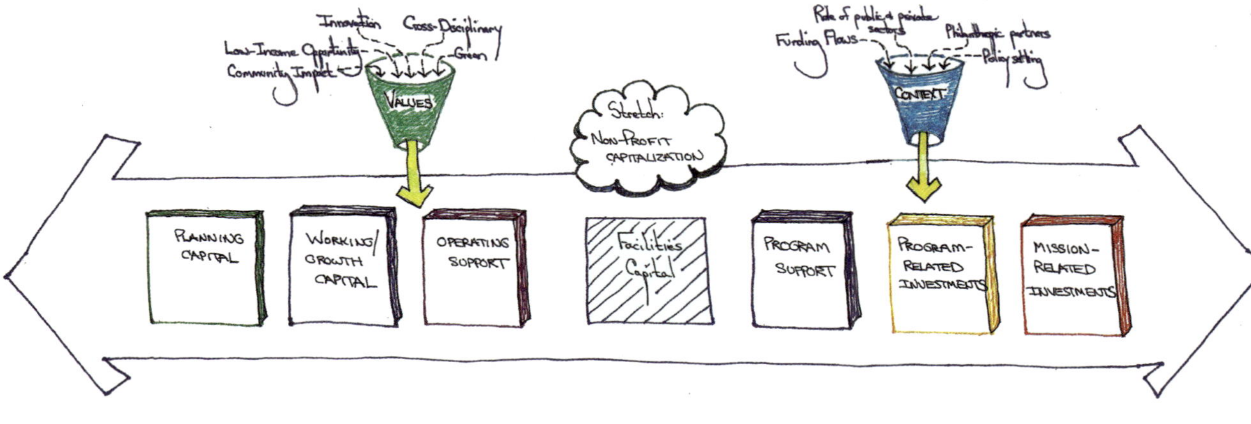

Understanding that context might raise opportunities to contribute to fields beyond contributing to organizations within them.

Most national private foundations had staked out this approach long ago and took it for granted. One look at Guidestar tells you that Ford might be making grants to fortify the field of reproductive rights . . . or MacArthur to creative international diplomacy . . . or Packard to alternative energy . . . or Rockefeller to agricultural research . . . and on and on. The question was, where did it make sense for us to concentrate?

I suggested we start with those fields in which we had a history of grant-making: environment, health, arts and culture, human services, higher education, and community development. That seemingly simple proposition turned out to be more complex than it sounded. Each of those fields was actually an aggregation of multiple subfields; we counted, for example, more than one hundred subfields within the human services field (domestic abuse, foster care, drug treatment, elder care, and on and on). The complexity of the question was, moreover, magnified by Kresge's lack of focused disciplinary expertise within any of those categories, big or small. We knew how quality, successful capital campaigns should be structured; we didn't know how to deliver specific human services most effectively.

It helped someone in one part of the organization to see another part of the organization's evolution depicted on a single piece of paper.

I proposed creating workgroups for each of the six areas, and charging them with identifying two lead "strategies"—priority areas that would guide our grantmaking for both intermediating organizations and the on-the-ground organizations within the field. Throughout the following year, the contours of a preliminary approach did, in fact, crystallize along those lines.

The big-picture plan was for our team leaders to cultivate an expertise in their fields, and to also begin bringing on staff who possessed disciplinary expertise.

There was one more step we'd need to take to complete the outlines of a new Kresge framework. Informed largely by our experiences in Detroit, we explored what it would look like to have both our tiers—capital support for individual organizations and field-specific strategies—land in place. And not just any place, but Detroit, our hometown. That would be our third tier. (See right.)

We emerged from the retreat with a shared sense that what was dubbed "Tiers and Baskets" offered a roadmap for recalibrating the organization's strategic orientation. The subsequent staff retreat followed the same path.

Building out that orientation became the work of the next four years. Beyond agreeing on the strategy, it also entailed retooling the "shop floor." We had to reinvent how we made grants, for example. In the capital challenge grant era, site visits weren't necessary; we simply reviewed financial documents through the lens of a tight algorithm based on an ideally structured fundraising pyramid. That wasn't sufficient when assessing a field-building grant or a grant to advance Detroit's revitalization: we had to visit, talk to people, listen, form judgments.

And as we grew our staff, we needed to develop—from scratch—a capacity for talent management. As we pivoted, we needed to communicate to others the path we were on. As teams emerged with distinct personalities, we had to be intentional about the values and norms that would shape an emerging organizational culture.

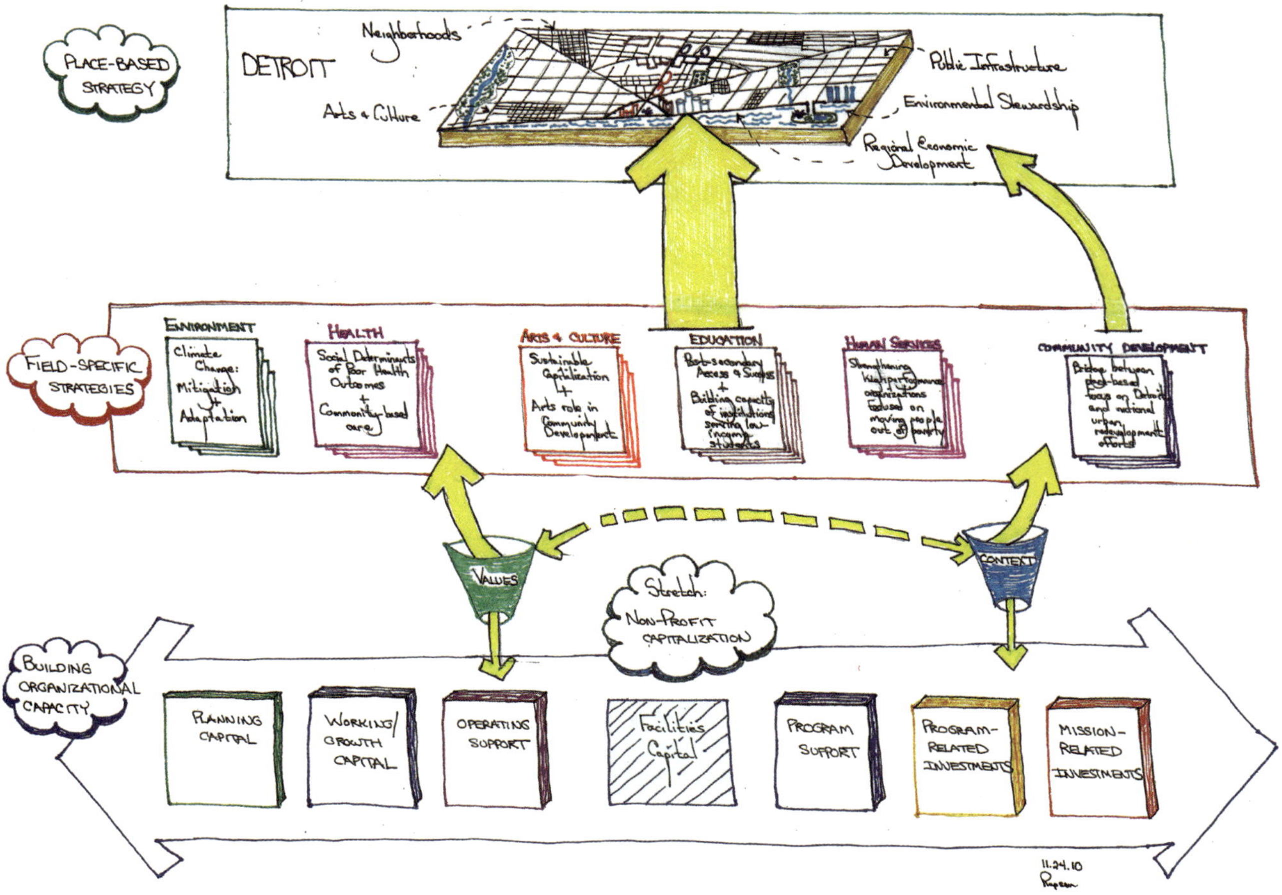

The "Tiers and Baskets" drawing is now in the permanent collection of the Smithsonian Institution's National Museum of American History.

It was dizzying, with multiple efforts moving on parallel paths. We discovered that the visualization process helped ground the staff. It helped someone in one part of the organization to see another part of the organization's evolution depicted on a single piece of paper. That was particularly true for how we proposed to grow and retain our talent.

We applied some of the same visualization methods to our program development, helping the entire organization keep our strategies in clear view. Drawings could never be a substitute for the hard work of thinking through investment and implementation strategies, but they provided a mezzanine-level perspective. And once we settled on an apt depiction of our strategy, we had a descriptive tool that also helped our board understand our purposes and methods.

What was useful for specific strategies also became useful for the organization as a whole.

Five years after adopting the Tiers and Baskets framework in 2006, the board decided to convene a second retreat—in part to assess the progress we'd made in implementing it. We had not only built out each of the three tiers; we'd also created a suite of new operational functions, including communications, human resources, grants management, and social investments (authorizing loans and other financial tools beyond grants).

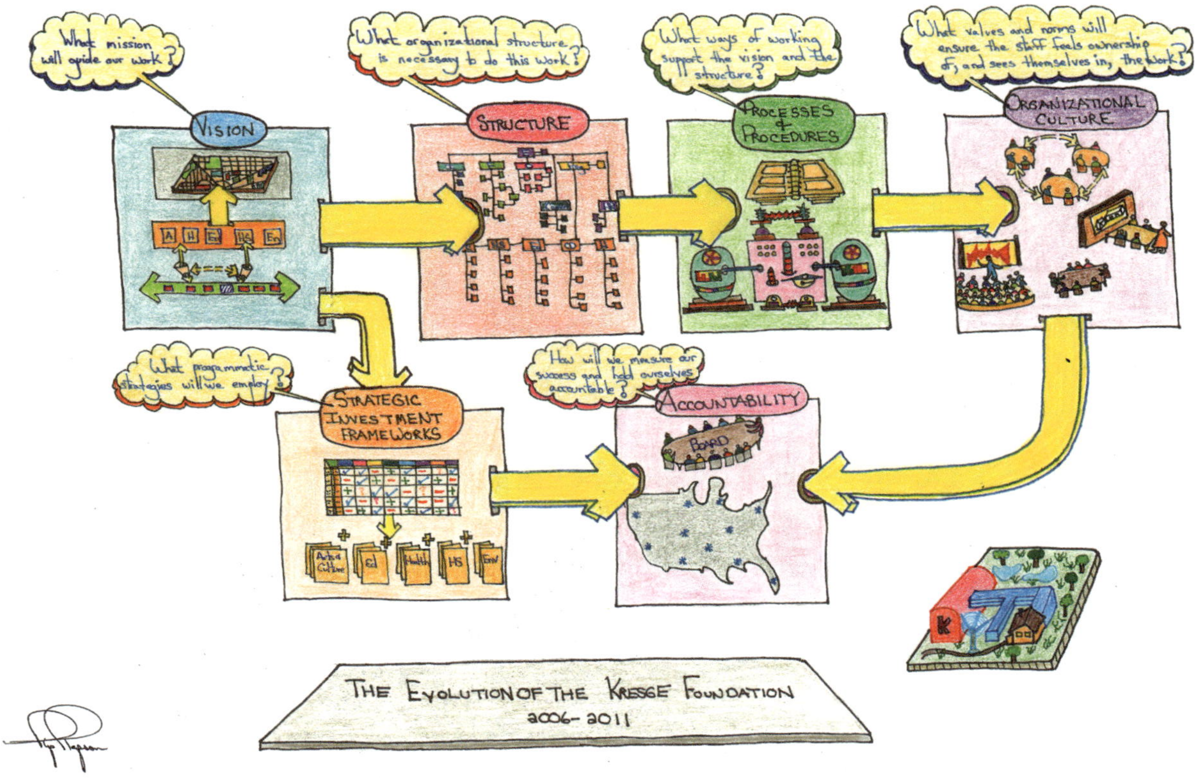

The overarching purpose of the retreat was to review the idea that all six of our program strategies should be oriented toward fortifying the building blocks of economic and social opportunity in American cities. Without that organizing aim, we were simply a holding company of programs that had little relationship with one another. The focus on cities was still broad, but it did serve to construct a fence line outside of which a great many things fell. So too was the focus on the building blocks of opportunity, but that grounded us clearly in seeking to deconstruct, and replace, barriers to equity and justice.

Drawings could never be a substitute for the hard work of thinking through investment and implementation strategies, but they provided a mezzanine-level perspective.

The second-level purpose of the retreat was to clarify and affirm the ways we went about our work, the five methods represented by the columns in the drawing above. Providing field leadership where appropriate. Working across disciplines, rather than in silos. Employing multiple philanthropic tools. Embracing risk-taking. Partnering with others, whether in the public, private, or philanthropic sectors.

The retreat demonstrated that our transition away from the Blue Box was complete. Not that we wouldn't continue to evolve in ways that none of us could predict. But we'd created a philanthropic machinery that was agile and adaptable enough to tackle the issues increasingly confronting our hometown, and in other cities across the country.

Resetting the trajectory of an iconic American city

Detroit.

Perhaps no other place has the power to evoke such powerful negative imagery: of deep and corrosive cycles of financial mismanagement, intense racial polarization and economic segregation, massive blight and abandonment, and paralyzing political dysfunction.

For the past century, the city's identity has been synonymous with the automobile industry, which stretched vertically from the behemoths of General Motors, Chrysler, and Ford to the smallest car dealerships . . . and horizontally across a seemingly infinite supply chain—plastics, glass, rubber, computers, design, fabrication, and more.

But when I arrived in 2006, the auto monoculture that so totally dominated the southeast Michigan economy had slowly and inexorably declined over the last 30 years, reshaping the region in profound ways:

- Shedding 300,000 to 400,000 manufacturing jobs and vacating hulking industrial plants.
- Draining investment from the core city, triggering the flight of Black and white middle-class families alike to the outer edges of the region, in turn blighting the neighborhood landscape with tens of thousands of abandoned residential and commercial structures in Dresden-like scenes of devastation.
- Eviscerating the tax base, leading to the under resourcing and politicizing of essential public services, including safety, public education, parks, and transportation.

The velocity of this death spiral accelerated in 2008 and 2009, when Detroit was drawn into the vortex of a storm of massive proportions and severity. Its already fragile economy was knocked to its knees by the Great Recession. Its weak housing market was destabilized by the foreclosure crisis. Its major employers were pummeled by auto industry bankruptcies. Its political stability imploded in a corruption scandal that landed a charismatic, popular mayor and scores of his coconspirators in jail.

It was as if we were watching our obituary play out on the national stage.

For the Kresge Foundation, the devastating convergence of events called the question of what role a private philanthropic institution could play. Three events hastened our consideration of that question.

First, our board of trustees was increasingly concerned about the nature and magnitude of our grantmaking in Detroit.

Eight of our board members lived outside of Detroit and couldn't help but harbor painful, yet legitimate, questions about what our endgame could possibly be in the face of public and private sector collapse. Our four Detroit-based board members kept the faith, but they, too, needed to know exactly how we could have meaningful impact.

Second, the new president of the Ford Foundation, Luis Ubiñas, had begun to raise similar concerns about Ford's future investments in the town of its birth.

Ubiñas had been a partner in the communications and technology practice at the McKinsey offices in San Francisco before succeeding Susan Beresford, who'd served as Ford's president from 1996 to 2007. Beresford had nurtured Ford's roots in Detroit, including launching a $100 million fund with Kresge and eight other foundations to foster entrepreneurial growth in the city. But Ubiñas, who read the same national media commentaries on Detroit's plight as everyone else, was asking whether the city should remain central to his foundation's urban investment portfolio.

I called him to ask whether I could come visit him in New York to make the case that Detroit was still an investable proposition, and he agreed.

Derek cut right to it. "I just came from a cabinet meeting with the President. He said—his exact words—'I'm not going to let Detroit become the Katrina on my watch.' So, we want to announce something in Detroit."

Walking into the offices of the Ford Foundation's president then felt a bit like entering the inner sanctum of a potentate: passing by ground-floor security, riding a keyed elevator to the eleventh floor, passing another security guard, traversing a long hallway overlooking architect Kevin Roche's magnificent indoor garden courtyard, stopping for two receptionists, walking past the vast board conference room, and finally arriving in Ubiñas's office.

I wasn't sure I was sufficiently steeled for what was to come.

I couldn't have been more mistaken. Coatless with sleeves rolled up, Ubiñas met me at the door with a big smile and a robust handshake. "Welcome to Valhalla," he grinned. "I've been looking forward to this conversation—it's incredibly important."

We spent the next two hours discussing the revitalization of cities. Ubiñas grew up in the Bronx and was passionate about the ability of disinvested places to claw their way back, even when others had given up on them. "But it takes resources, metrics, and leadership," he stated. "I'm not sure I see that in Detroit. Do you?"

I described some of the energies at play in Detroit, including those not being covered by the *New York Times*: The New Economy Initiative's entrepreneurship fund that Ford had jump-started. Efforts by the corporate sector and Kresge to construct a light rail line as the first leg in a regional transit system. The tenacity of community organizations to reclaim abandoned and vacant land through urban farms, mural projects, and restoring community parks. The nascent suite of artist fellowships and operating support grants to bolster the city's vibrant arts and culture ecology.

Ubiñas never took his eyes off me. "So, Rip, how much will philanthropy invest in Detroit in the next year?" Uh-oh, I thought—here comes the McKinsey intervention. I did a quick mental calculation: $30 million from the Community Foundation, Kresge's $25 million, $15 million each from the Ford Foundation and the Skillman Foundation, $10 million each from the Hudson-Webber Foundation and the MacGregor Foundation, and smaller amounts from another dozen.

"I'm thinking $150 million," I suggested. Without missing a beat, Ubiñas replied, "So that means you'll spend $1.5 billion over the next decade in Detroit. That's a substantial investment. What do you propose to buy with that?"

I paused. That was the big question. We had some things in motion, but what else was needed? How did the different actions add up? Would they make a material difference in such an unforgiving environment?

I reiterated that I believed enough investments were being made in enough critical areas by enough of the right people to suggest we had a path forward. Without directly answering Ubiñas's question, I suggested that these areas—these touchpoints—could be seen almost like acupuncture points, capable of radiating more broadly into the civic system than a single pinprick could.

Ubiñas grinned. "Makes sense. You've convinced me that we should stick with the program, at least for the while. But I'd welcome your giving even deeper thought to my question. Let's talk again soon." I left feeling that we had an ally, albeit one who'd be uncompromisingly rigorous. Not a bad result—there was hope.

The third event reinforced further the signals from my board and from Ubiñas that we needed to crystallize just what we proposed to do.

Early in 2009, I answered in disbelief when Denise from the Kresge front desk buzzed me to say that the White House was on the line. I laughed, figuring it was a prank—or someone from Project Veritas trying to trap me into saying something regrettable on right-wing radio. "He says it's important," Denise insisted. "He says he's Derek Douglas, the special assistant to the President on the White House Domestic Policy Council." I knew Douglas by reputation through his work with Governor David Paterson of New York. She put him through.

He cut to the chase. "I just came from a cabinet meeting with the President," Douglas relayed. "The President said—his exact words—'I'm not going to let Detroit become the next Katrina on my watch.' So we want to announce something in Detroit."

"That's terrific! What?" I replied.

"Well, that I don't know. That's why I'm calling," Douglas continued. "We know we'll create an auto task force to address the car companies' struggles. But we're in the dark about what's possible beyond that, given the paralysis in the Detroit economy and the turmoil in its politics. We need someone to provide some ground truth for us and help determine how we can be helpful."

OK. I'd now gotten the message from three angles. The immediate task was clear: identify what's in play that holds promise, elevate the actors outside city hall prepared to exercise leadership, be realistic about what resources are available . . . and synthesize all of that into a coherent picture. I told Douglas that we'd get back to him. Although that probably wasn't the message the special adviser to the president wanted to hear, he was gracious, saying he would welcome my call anytime—as long as it was sooner rather than later. The President was serious.

I spent the next weekend holed up in my office trying to get some traction on the assignment. I started with what I believed was the overarching objective: offer a blueprint for reimagining Detroit. That blueprint had to answer the questions everyone was asking about what we proposed to "buy," what our surest path to progress would be, and who could play what roles in such a dauntingly complex undertaking.

Piecemeal and academic wouldn't do the trick. It had to be comprehensive, anchored in work already underway, led by a sophisticated network of actors, and supported by real financial resources. And it ultimately had to be accountable to the elected leadership of Detroit.

After contemplating more than a dozen possible nodes of substantive action, I narrowed it down. Key initiatives included strengthening the central commercial corridor; nurturing an infrastructure to support small businesses; building a light rail line; fortifying the arts and cultural ecology; pursuing environmental protections in neighborhoods; creating a new nonprofit intermediary to promote educational reform; attacking blight and abandonment through a 21st century land use plan; and supporting the anchoring roles played by Detroit's medical and educational institutions.

I dubbed it "Re-Imagining Detroit 2020." (See fold-out at the start of this chapter.)

The drawing was intended to help me, and our staff, get our internal bearings—and to equip me to share our thinking with the board, with Ubiñas, and with Douglas.

But Doug Stewart, who led Detroit's Fisher Family Foundation, soon saw it in my office and asked if I might share it with Fisher's board. Where I had seen it as largely an internal document, Stewart saw it as a useful tool to help the rest of Detroit's foundation community—or at least one organization within it—understand how they might fit in and contribute.

After I spoke with the Fisher Foundation, word traveled; other foundations asked if I might do the same thing for their boards. It became a reference point for us to compare notes about what we were doing, and how we might reinforce one another's work. Indeed, by rotating the drawing 90 degrees, it could suggest a template for mapping a critical path for each of the nine modules. Taken together, those nine critical paths could become a master workplan that would give coherence to our collective effort.

That coherence began to emerge. A group of foundation, civic, and corporate leaders representing the different workflows began meeting regularly in an attempt to coordinate, and stay abreast of, one another's efforts.

Soon I received another call from Douglas, asking if I could arrange for a meeting with Melody Barnes, head of the White House's Domestic Policy Council, and Shaun Donovan, secretary of the Department of Housing and Urban Development. We convened our group, including others involved in the nine modules of action. Using the Re-Imagining Detroit drawing as a point of departure, we explored where and how the federal government might assist.

Barnes and Donovan focused less on specific policy interventions than on how the federal government might more effectively connect different city departments and agencies to federal counterparts in a position to support them. Donovan, in particular, clearly had something in mind. He took the drawing with him, calling me a few days later. He said he'd be in Detroit a few weeks hence and would like to have dinner. We agreed to meet at the newly renovated historic Westin Book Cadillac Hotel.

Donovan, trained as an architect, had a reputation for deep and wide-ranging intelligence and a dazzling mastery of housing policy, honed during his tenure as commissioner of the New York City Department of Housing Preservation and Development. There he had—

among other things—created the largest municipal affordable housing plan in the nation's history. He had also served in the Clinton administration as deputy assistant secretary for multifamily housing. I accordingly sat down across from him with all appropriate trepidation.

Donovan was intimidating. But he was also uncommonly kind, and deferential to someone he perceived as having a nuanced understanding of an environment he knew only superficially. After comparing stories about life as an architect—or in my case, life with a father who was an architect—we cut to the essence. Donovan described the administration's continuing challenges in finding an appropriate set of landing pads for working with Mayor Bing's administration. "Mayor Bing's staff doesn't seem to have a clear path," he ventured. "We're not sure whom we should engage with on different issues. And it's unclear whether they have adequate capacity to leverage the resources of not only my agency, but other agencies as well. Am I misreading the situation? Where would you suggest we land?"

I paused before finally answering—reluctantly. "At least right now, Mr. Secretary, I think your analysis is correct. I'm just not sure there *is* any logical place for you to land." I reddened as I spoke; the last thing I wanted to do was discourage assistance from a federal agency that *wanted* to help Detroit. "The Bing Administration is stretched too thin, has too little depth, and lacks a systematic or coherent set of revitalization strategies," I said. "They're not ready for your help on housing stabilization, or commercial revitalization, or blight remediation."

Word traveled. The drawing became a reference point for us to compare notes about what we were doing, and how we might reinforce one another's work.

I was starting to feel like Benedict Arnold. But I recalled that Donovan had spoken, at our meeting the prior month, about an idea he'd been formulating to put federal staff on the ground in a handful of places, to demonstrate innovative ways the federal government might support cities. "Could I build on our recent meeting?" I asked. "I don't mean to be presumptuous, but I think Detroit could be the perfect demonstration site for the kind of capacity-boosting activities that you and Melody Barnes talked about. If the city had competent navigators assigned by federal agencies, you might get somewhere."

Donovan nodded. "That's exactly what I've been thinking about: making federal liaisons available for a year or two. And you shouldn't feel bad," he added. "Our engagement with the city has so far been challenging. Good people wanting to do the right thing, but without the kind of systems they need to do it. We've had better luck working with Kresge and the other players in your orbit. But we have to get the city more fully into the game."

The conversation may have been more productive than I thought—even if it simply confirmed what Donovan already sensed and was inclined to do. Indeed, a few months later, he returned to Detroit to launch the Strong Cities Strong Communities, or SC^2, initiative. The Obama Administration would assign a federal liaison to a half-dozen cities, including Detroit, to help local officials bridge more effectively to federal technical, financial, and regulatory assistance. Detroit's liaison would be a Treasury Department official named Don Graves. Graves's role would prove invaluable over years to come, as Detroit began putting its house back in order.

Two years later, the Kresge board traveled to Washington, D.C. for its quarterly board meeting. Secretary Donovan agreed to spend an hour with us. At the end of the conversation, he reached into his briefcase and pulled out a piece of paper: the Re-Imagining Detroit drawing I'd given him in 2010. Looking around the table, he smiled and said, "You probably recognize this. It was something Rip gave me on my first visit to Detroit. I wanted you all to know that it was recently the focal point of a cabinet meeting with Vice President Biden.

"Each of the secretaries talked about how they were assisting Detroit, and we used his 'placemat'—this drawing—as the organizing device. It was a whole lot better than a twenty-page PowerPoint. Having Detroit's complexity distilled onto a single sheet of paper gave us a common point of reference. It was a policy Rorschach test."

"You probably recognize this. It was something Rip gave me on my first visit to Detroit. I wanted you all to know that it was recently the focal point of a cabinet meeting with Vice President Biden."

At a time when Kresge was still discerning what its role might be in Detroit, the cataclysms of 2008-'09 forced us to confront the reality that philanthropy didn't have a failsafe manual for moving a city to higher, more stable ground. But we quickly realized that what we *did* have was the ability to illuminate some key parts of that manual, to suggest their interplay, and to create a three-dimensional narrative to reassure key actors—within and outside of Detroit—that there was reason for hope, even optimism.

Kresge began a profound reenvisioning of the role of philanthropy in Detroit. With sufficient skill, focus, and discipline, we could help build an infrastructure of change whose impact would transform the city. It was the answer to Ubiñas's question of what we would buy with our investments and our reputational equity.

And it was a partial antidote to the belief of some in the city that it simply wasn't possible to take on more than a single large-scale challenge at a time. Or that philanthropy had no legitimate business stepping into territory that should have been the domain of municipal government. We conceived a pathway to progress that could build incrementally on strengths the residents of Detroit knew, but had lost sight of. Our actions affirmed that philanthropy could work, and had an obligation to work, alongside the private, public, nonprofit, and civic sectors to create the city of the future.

20 Streetcar Fandango

Overcoming the Motor City's antipathy to mass transit

The nation's first paved road had come to symbolize the transit graveyard that was southeast Michigan.

Driving up Woodward Avenue from downtown Detroit to visit the Kresge Foundation offices for the first time in 2006, I was struck by the harsh barrenness of the streetscape: eight lanes across almost devoid of cars, buildings set apart from the road by ghastly parking lots, unadorned commercial strips, boarded businesses, no trees.

It shouldn't have been a surprise. If there was ever an environment resistant to mass transit, it was postwar southeastern Michigan, birthplace of the automobile and the home to the Big Three—General Motors, Ford, and Chrysler. In 1909, a mile-long segment of Woodward was paved with concrete, a national first; by 1916, it was paved for 27 miles.

Southeast Michigan in 2006 was inadequately served by two separate bus systems, one city and one suburban. So separate, in fact, that the suburban buses that brought suburban commuters to the city of Detroit were not able to stop for passengers along the route once inside the city limits. And those bus systems were, for all practical purposes, the area's only large-scale public transit. In one way or another, the region had failed more than three dozen times in forty years to adopt a comprehensive, unified system.

One of my first meetings after arriving in Detroit was a lunch arranged by one of Kresge's trustees, Bob Larson, with Roger Penske. Penske was a legendary figure in car racing, owner of an automotive empire, and perhaps Michigan's most respected business leader. Larson had previously told me that Penske had just overseen Detroit's successful hosting of the Super Bowl and was thinking about what his next civic contribution might be. We would be joined by Matt Cullen, a General Motors executive with a deep passion for the city.

When the conversation turned to the future of Detroit, Penske asked about my early impressions and my thoughts on a worthy next civic undertaking. With my initial read of Woodward Avenue still fresh in mind, I suggested that the eight-lane avenue had the feel of a freeway, not of the city's primary commercial and residential artery. I asked the group why it wouldn't make sense to run a light rail line along the avenue, from mile zero at the Detroit River to the city's border eight miles north. Plainly not expecting that, Penske asked me to explain why that would be a priority.

I told Penske that in Minneapolis, the first investment in light rail was along Hiawatha Avenue, a similarly overbuilt avenue radiating from downtown. We had seized on the public right-of-way to create a light rail line connecting downtown to the airport (and Mall of America) to the south, opening a conversation about a comprehensive regional transit system. I said the Detroit situation seemed analogous: nobody would believe regional transit was possible without a first, tangible step. Woodward, like Hiawatha, could be that showcase. Woodward had many more lanes than it needed and, as a state highway, wouldn't present any right-of-way issues; the real estate was there for the repurposing.

Woodward was the region's spinal cord, extending some thirty miles into the northernmost suburbs. A light rail line would connect the scores of churches, arts organizations, medical campuses, and educational institutions along the spine. It would help revivify a swooning commercial corridor—particularly between the downtown core and Midtown, about three miles up the road. This could be an ideal way to get the ball rolling for regional transit, connecting both to the Amtrack line running west to Ann Arbor and Chicago, and to an existing fixed rail line running to the northern job centers of Oakland County.

Penske and Cullen paused before responding. Evidently, Congresswoman Carolyn Cheeks Kilpatrick, who represented Detroit (and incidentally, was the mother of Mayor Kwame Kilpatrick) had been considering an idea like this, but nothing had materialized. Cullen noted that this kind of public infrastructure was so closely tied to federal and state funding sources that it wasn't clear what role private or philanthropic investors could play. But Penske seemed intrigued, and courteously thanked me for giving him something to think about.

In retrospect, I'm glad I didn't have a deeper history with Penske. The audacity of proposing a mass transit strategy to a man who had built a career, fortune, and reputation on cars wasn't top-of-mind at lunch. But he took the conversation with grace and seriousness.

The audacity of proposing a mass transit strategy to a man who had built a career, fortune, and reputation on cars wasn't top-of-mind at lunch.

And he would pick up the conversation in different form a year later. In late 2007, Penske called to ask whether I could join two dozen civic leaders to talk more about the light rail idea. We would be joined by John Hertel, a former state senator and CEO of the Regional Transit Coordinating Council.

Opening the meeting, Penske said he and Hertel had been exploring the feasibility of creating a light rail line along Woodward. He explained that he'd commissioned a series of preliminary engineering studies that had concluded that the idea was viable, and that planning, construction, and vehicle procurement would cost roughly $100 million. That was why we had been invited, Penske said: he wanted to discuss the wisdom of pursuing the idea, and he wanted to explore ideas about how to marshal the necessary resources.

Penske said he was fully confident that he could sell naming rights to a dozen stations along the line for $3 million apiece. And given his expertise with vehicle leasing, he predicted that he could arrange to lease the vehicles, removing another $30 from the total budget. Which left another $35 million to be raised—a big number.

Most people in the room weren't sitting on that kind of capital. With one exception.

Penske looked directly at me and said, "OK, Rip. That's where you come in. This was your idea to begin with. If Kresge is willing to commit $35 million, we can do this."

Cold panic. That's not the way a foundation does business. I didn't even have a discretionary grant pool, let alone a *$35 million* discretionary grant pool. Only once had the Kresge board approved a grant of this magnitude—a $50 million challenge grant to incentivize other donors to help build the Detroit RiverWalk—and it had taken the board years to agree on that. The board would surely need to see additional analysis of the idea's feasibility. But perhaps most importantly, the idea of a foundation being the major underwriter of a private-cum-public infrastructure project like this was crazy.

I knew that the live-action trustee exchanges would likely catapult from the written materials into charged and unpredictable territory. That turned out to be an understatement.

Naturally, I said yes.

I explained that our board would have to deliberate and approve; my assent was in no way final. But I believed the audacious creativity of the aspiration—backed by the person, Penske, advancing it—justified the risk, or so it seemed to me. Most of us left the meeting believing we really might break through southeast Michigan's ossified public transit policy.

I called our board chair, Irene Hirano Inouye, the minute I left the room. Perhaps because I was still in my honeymoon period, she agreed that it was worth a conversation. It wasn't in Hirano's nature to signal enthusiastic affirmation for the idea, and she didn't. But it was in her nature to trust the judgment of the organization's executive. If I believed there was merit to the idea, she said, the board should give it a full airing. We agreed that first, the staff would thoughtfully assess the innumerable pieces that needed to fall into place before the idea could translate into wheels on rails.

To jump-start that due diligence process, the director of our Detroit program, Laura Trudeau, and I approved two planning grants. Each came back validating Penske's assumptions. Hirano gave us the go-ahead to introduce the proposal at the March 2008 meeting.

Trudeau and I spent hours poring through the engineering feasibility, mapping out contingencies, verifying preliminary costs, preparing the arguments, and taking all the other steps one takes to avoid getting fired by one's bosses. I could not have wished for a more skilled partner than Trudeau, who'd come to Kresge after a twenty-five-year career in banking. She was whip smart, passionate about the city, and meticulous with details.

We sent the board supporting materials in advance. But I knew that the live-action trustee exchanges would likely catapult from the written materials into charged and unpredictable territory. That turned out to be an understatement.

I began by reminding the board of the origin story of the concept, and positing that only a private-philanthropic partnership could break through the public sector's inertia on mass transit. Next it was Trudeau's turn.

She was terrified, her hands shaking from the moment she began speaking. But her preparation, her insights, her integrity, her history in Detroit, and her passion made us all forget about her nerves. As the force of Trudeau's arguments became increasingly clear, the change in the trustees' body language was palpable. This wasn't a flight of fancy or an abstract policy conversation—it was tangible, urgent, and compelling. Heads began nodding.

But the questions that followed were brutally direct. Why would we move into a realm best suited to state and municipal government? Did a nongovernmental entity have the credibility or expertise to oversee a public works project? Would Kresge be on the hook for cost overruns? Wouldn't we need approval from state and federal regulators? And so on, for well over an hour.

Trudeau was prepared for all of this and more. She was magnificent. I stepped in to summarize, and to propose that we authorize investing up to $35 million, subject to a string of conditions. I looked to Elaine Rosen, who'd been chosen in December to succeed Hirano as Board chair. In her first formal act as chair, she asked for a motion to approve. She received it, and a second; one by one, the trustees voted to approve. The decision was unanimous.

Armed with Kresge's consensus, Penske and Cullen took the lead in forming a philanthropic-private sector consortium named M-1 RAIL. We assembled a team with the requisite legal, financial, engineering, and project management sophistication. And true to his word, Penske secured $39 million in naming right commitments from hospitals, businesses, universities, and others for each of thirteen stops along the three-mile stretch. We were on our way.

Yet we had no idea just how difficult the next six years would be.

The troubles began with the city of Detroit. The M-1 team knew that Congresswoman Kilpatrick had investigated some form of transit along the corridor. It was not aware, however, that that effort had worked its way into the thinking of her son, the mayor. Indeed, the Kilpatrick administration had been quietly formulating a light rail plan of its own. The plan was based on a "heavy rail" concept that would focus on getting commuters in and out of Detroit with as few stops as possible. It would extend all the way to the city limits at Eight Mile Road. It carried a price tag of nearly a half-billion dollars, to be raised from federal public transit funds.

We had no idea just how difficult the next six years would be.

The mayor was confident of his prospects. He had secured a federal planning grant with the assistance of Congresswoman Kilpatrick: chair of the House Appropriations Subcommittee on Transportation and the powerful head of the Congressional Black Caucus. Mayor Kilpatrick was not keen on sanctioning a rival project, to say the least.

But there were problematic elements of the mayor's approach, including the fact that Detroit was likely dead last on the federal government's list of investable transit projects. The city's proposal had no local match funding. Having failed scores of times to deliver mass transit, Detroit had no track record, so to speak. The Michigan legislature was hostile. And the city would arguably be poorly served by a system that blasted riders into downtown in the morning and sucked them out in the evening, with no attention paid to intermediate stops that could drive residential and economic development.

Reluctantly, city hall realized that the two approaches had to be welded into a single plan reflecting the best elements of both.

It took us two years of maneuvering, but M-1 and the city finally agreed to a hybrid strategy. The portion of the line from the river to Midtown would be designed according to the M-1 objectives of fostering economic development along thirteen stops. The portion from Midtown to the city limits would be shaped by the city's desire to minimize stops, maximize speed, and attract the greatest possible number of commuters. Having linked our fates, both sides felt confident we could tackle issues like tearing up and reconstructing the street, installing new high-speed underground cable, replacing lighting, figuring out how to pass under bridges, and countless other engineering challenges.

Enter the federal government.

The entire project depended on competing successfully for federal transit dollars—particularly so-called "New Start" funds. Although the Obama Administration supported efforts to help Detroit navigate through the Great Recession and the attendant automotive bankruptcies, it couldn't work miracles. Before the M-1 project was birthed, Detroit was likely 435th on the federal government's list of 435 New Start priority projects—something the Federal Transit Administration didn't try to hide.

In summer 2009, I'd sat next to the Secretary of Transportation, Ray LaHood, at the dedication of a new bus terminal in Detroit. I mentioned the M-1 effort, and he peppered me with questions. His department would welcome the chance to explore such an innovative three-way partnership among the public, private, and philanthropic sectors, he said. "But there's always the small matter of our having to fund directly elected bodies, not private entities. Think you can work something out with the city?" LaHood asked. I told him we had every intention of doing exactly that.

The administrator of the Federal Transit Administration followed up several days later. Peter Rogoff was a play-it-by-the-book kind of administrator. Rogoff conveyed his skepticism about the M-1 approach in his earliest conversations with us. In his view, public accountability could be undermined if the M-1 coalition were to step into the shoes of a municipality. The enterprise risked inviting ambiguity about who was really in charge. All legitimate questions. But all could be addressed. Or so we thought.

We realized an early victory when the department awarded the project a discretionary $25 million TIGER (Transportation Investment Generating Economic Recovery) grant designed to recognize transportation innovation—an astounding vote of confidence. The secretary and the administrator flew to Michigan in December 2011 to announce the award.

Unfortunately, they weren't happy with what they found.

Unlike M-1's privately funded plan for the river-to-Midtown segment, the city had predicated its Midtown-to-Eight Mile portion of the plan on issuing bonds. Rogoff and LaHood's teams had discovered that those bonds were built on fumes: the city, in fact, could not support that bonding. Inveterately opaque, the director of the city project, Norm White, had gotten too far over his skis and hadn't chosen to let the feds know.

I woke up early the next morning to a call from Roger Penske. "Have you seen the newspaper? Take a look at the lead story. LaHood has cancelled the TIGER grant to the city and given it to Governor Snyder to build bus rapid transit. Mayor Bing [who'd replaced the indicted Kwame Kilpatrick] is not contesting the decision," Penske said. "We're cooked, Rip. We need those TIGER dollars to meet our budget. We can't do battle with the secretary, the transit administrator, the governor, and the mayor."

Silence in the face of cataclysm wasn't a good look. But we held back to see what he was cooking.

Within minutes I got a second call, this one from Jared Fleisher, of the Washington, D.C. law firm Patton & Boggs, whom Kresge had put on retainer for his expertise on federal transportation policy. "Don't make any public statement, Rip," Fleisher advised. "We have one final card to play: see if you can't get the M-1 representatives to hold their comments." Fleisher was a political wizard, but this seemed a reach; silence in the face of cataclysm wasn't a good look. But we held back to see what he was cooking.

Fleisher proposed seeking a meeting with LaHood, Rogoff, the governor, the mayor, both

Michigan senators, the four congressional members who represented a portion of the region, the Wayne County executive, and the lead representatives of M-1. The purpose would be to convince the feds that the M-1 portion of the project was still viable. It would not be open to the press. I relayed the idea to Penske and Cullen, who now worked for Dan Gilbert, the founder of Quicken Loans, who'd recently moved Quicken's headquarters downtown and become a significant investor in the M-1 project. We agreed it was worth a try.

The meeting was set for January 6, 2012, in the Mayor's conference room. Penske, Gilbert, Cullen, and I would represent M-1. Not only did all the principals come, but they brought gaggles of staff. The room was filled to the gills.

The governor and mayor welcomed us, then turned matters over to Senators Carl Levin and Debbie Stabenow. The senators told the group that they had already made an unrequited appeal to the secretary to reverse the TIGER reallocation. LaHood simply nodded. Congressman John Dingell followed with an impassioned appeal for reconsideration. LaHood nodded again. Gilbert and I then made short statements. Yet more noncommittal nodding from the secretary.

It was Penske's turn. His stature, gravitas, and expertise immediately altered the energy in the room. LaHood straightened up, and he and Penske locked eyes. The congressional representatives had made a moral case. Gilbert had made a technical feasibility case. I had made a community development case. Now Penske made the business case.

Penske reminded LaHood that the federal government risked leaving $100 million of privately raised capital on the table were they to abandon the M-1 project in favor of busways. The M-1 consortium had done something that, to his knowledge, no U.S. community had done: engage the private and philanthropic sectors to help address a transportation void left by a municipality too resource-strapped and poorly equipped to deliver an essential public good. This was innovation serving the long-term interest of the region. LaHood was nodding again, but this time in agreement.

"Mr. Secretary, we're not asking for an open-ended commitment from your office. I'm a businessman, and I don't work that way," Penske continued, as if he and LaHood were the only two people in the room. "I'd instead ask you to give the M-1 team ninety days to show we can accomplish our part of the plan. Maybe the city's portion can come later. But we can deliver the original plan: a streetcar line from the river to Midtown, funded without the City's bonding capacity.

"We'll meet any and all engineering, financial, environmental, and political conditions that the Federal Transit Authority believes it appropriate to impose and we will do it within the time period I've suggested."

Calm, decisive, powerful.

LaHood leaned over to the governor, whispered something, and looked back directly at Penske, and nobody else.

"Mr. Penske, I have the most enormous respect for you, and for what you and your team are attempting," LaHood began. "In fact, I believe that the M-1 effort is among the most creative, audacious, and important transit projects I've seen." Transit Administrator Rogoff started to fidget, but LaHood took no notice.

"I take you at your word," he continued. "If you can actually meet all the preconditions that Administrator Rogoff believes are necessary, I'll find another $25 million somewhere in my department's budget for you." Looking at the governor, he said slyly, "You can keep your TIGER grant for your bus system."

A woman sitting immediately behind LaHood jumped to her feet and said in a panicked voice, "Mr. Secretary, you cannot make that commitment. Legally, I mean." She was, it turns out, the department's attorney. And by all appearances, she was about to have heart failure.

LaHood turned toward his counsel and offered his now-familiar nod. Then he looked back at Penske and said, very deliberately, "Mr. Penske, I commit to you that I will find $25 million in the federal budget if you meet the conditions we set forth. You have your ninety days." LaHood rose, thanked the participants, and left with his entourage.

Sure enough, the FTA followed up shortly thereafter with its list of ninety preconditions. We swallowed hard. One a day? Mandated environmental assessments. Project management requirements. Additional contingency funds. And, significantly, a requirement that the legislature pass—and the governor sign—legislation creating an authority to manage a regional transit system. It was a heavy, heavy lift. Heavier than any of us could have anticipated.

I tasked Laura Trudeau to work full-time with teams from the Penske Corporation, Quicken, and the M-1 staff to start chipping away at the list. They quickly picked off the smaller, less complex items. Since even the FTA agreed that certain requirements would require more than ninety days to complete, they gave us more time. Steadily—almost miraculously—within six months, the M-1 group had checked off eighty-nine of the ninety issues the federal government had dictated.

A woman sitting immediately behind LaHood jumped to her feet and said in a panicked voice, "Mr. Secretary, you cannot make that commitment. Legally, I mean."

The hanging chad was the legislative package.

The caveat that LaHood's $25 million depended on Michigan enacting legislation authorizing regional transit was the steepest of all the mountains M-1 had to scale. The Michigan Legislature had tried and failed twenty-four times in the past half century to accomplish this. Not once. Not four times. Not fourteen. But twenty-four.

LaHood knew that, so threw himself into the effort. With Administrator Rogoff and the M-1 team, he worked with the governor to ensure the state could satisfy this condition. And as a former Republican congressman, he wasn't afraid to mix it up with political colleagues. He traveled to Michigan several times to advocate publicly—and in private conversation with legislators—for the creation of a regional transit governance authority.

We also had a powerful ally in the Michigan Department of Transportation. MDOT had agreed to bear the cost, and potential risks, of repaving the length of Woodward, including reconstruction of a bridge over an east-west freeway running under the road. The department's commitment was no small matter: much of the water, sewer, gas, and electrical infrastructure buried under the road was close to a century old. No one knew what the construction crews would find once they started excavating.

The requisite legislative authority was not a single bill, but eight separate pieces of legislation. Getting eight separate but related bills drafted—one creating the regional authority, one stipulating the terms of county referenda approving a plan, one authorizing funding, and others—was legally complex, but logistically straightforward. Shepherding those bills through the Republican-controlled chambers was something else altogether. Enthusiasm for passing complex and even controversial legislation intended to benefit disproportionately the Democratic strongholds of Detroit and its inner suburbs was less than overwhelming.

The Michigan Legislature had tried and failed twenty-four times in the past half century create a regional transit system.

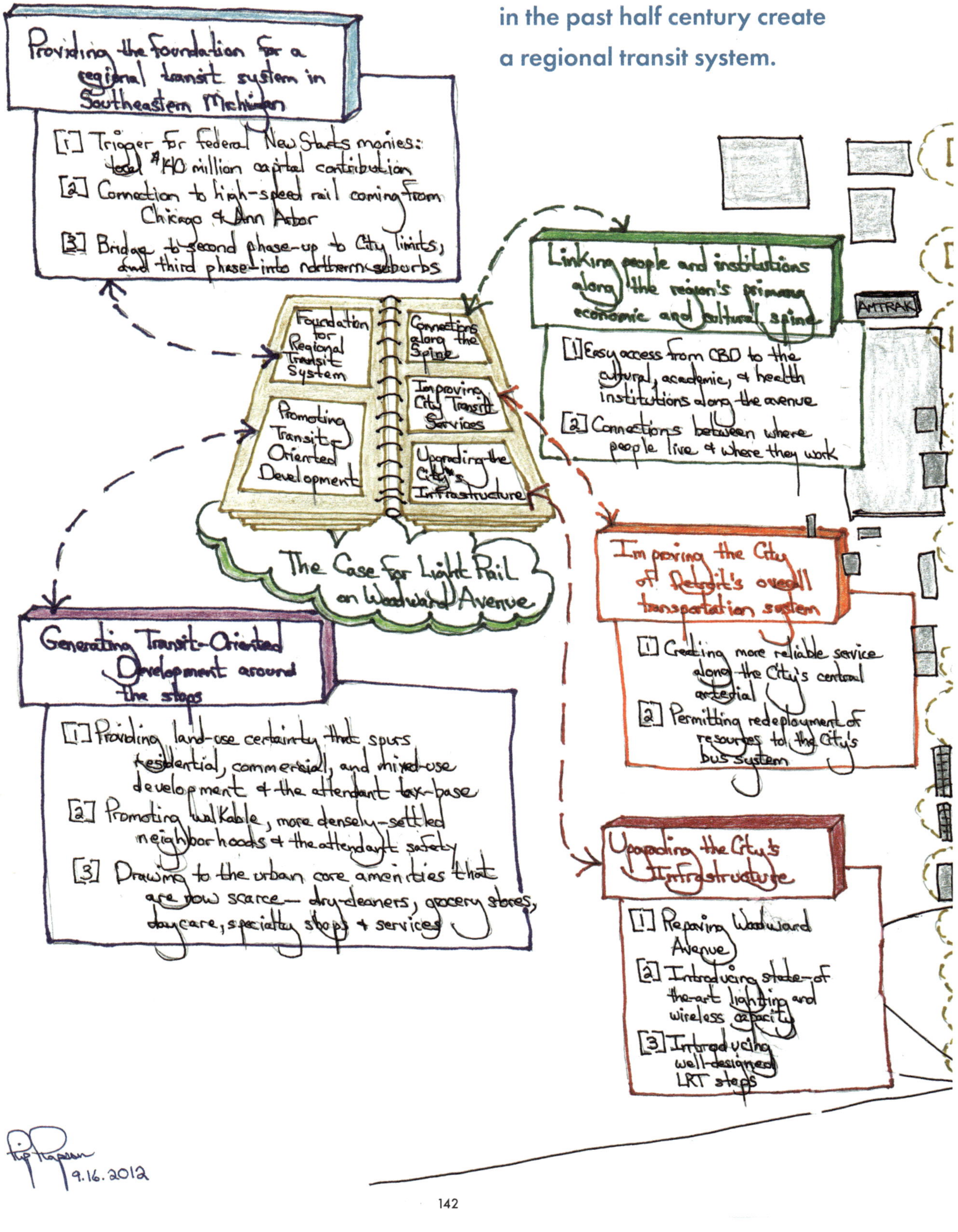

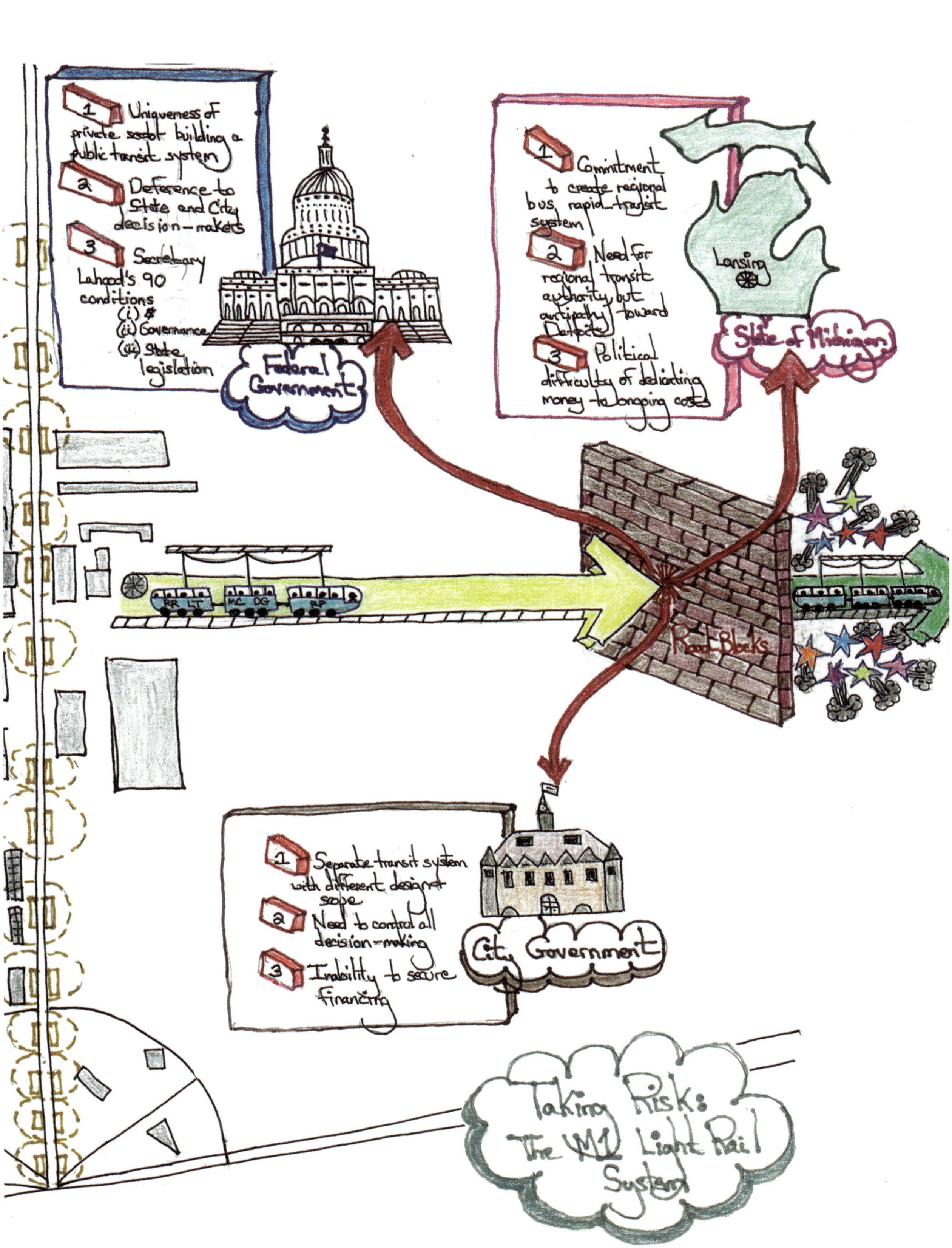

1 Uniqueness of private sector building a public transit system
2 Deference to State and City decision-makers
3 Secretary Lahood's 90 conditions
(i) $
(ii) Governance
(iii) State legislation
Federal Government
1 Commitment to create regional bus rapid transit system
2 Need for regional transit authority but antipathy toward Detroit
3 Political difficulty of dedicating money to ongoing costs
Lansing
State of Michigan
RR LT MC DG RP
Road Blocks
1 Separate transit system with different design scope
2 Need to control all decision-making
3 Inability to secure financing
City Government
Taking Risk: The M1 Light Rail System

With the legislative package drafted, Kresge's influence had come to an end; federal law forbade us to advocate for specific legislation. The burden fell directly on our private sector partners. They assembled a coalition to persuade reluctant legislators; the alliance included Secretary LaHood; leaders of the Department of Transportation; plus Penske, Gilbert, and Cullen, three of Michigan's most widely known and respected corporate leaders. The group coordinated closely with Governor Snyder to build a strategy for dislodging the bills from committee and moving them to the House and Senate floors.

Governor Snyder made clear that the legislation was important to him. He made several behind-the-scenes assurances to his caucus in return for their support—and the final vote came in the waning hours of the 2012 legislative session. Snyder signed Public Act 387 into law on December 19. LaHood promptly scheduled a trip to Detroit to announce that he had found the promised $25 million.

The M-1 board still had work to do. Faced with increased project costs, it had to raise additional philanthropic, private sector, and federal dollars—including another $15 million from Kresge. It had to renegotiate the New Markets Tax Credits the project had earlier secured. It had to replace the firm that had contracted to build the six streetcars. It had to steer through four years of uncertainty, as efforts to pass regional transit referenda fell just short. It had to weather the turbulence of the nation's largest municipal bankruptcy.

But the M-1 effort had assumed a "little-engine-that-could" persona, and it climbed one hill after another until the first rider boarded the line in May 2017.

As with the Itasca Project in Minneapolis more than a decade earlier, each of the sectors involved had stepped into unfamiliar, uncomfortable roles, extending their brands into territory that carried tangible institutional risk. A foundation becoming the largest underwriter of a streetcar line. Corporate leaders filling a void created by failures of municipal leadership. The federal government bending its protocols to support a transit governance structure decidedly outside its experience.

It's tempting to conclude that this recalibration of traditional roles was possible only in the free-fall years following Detroit's most difficult period. And although that conclusion would contain elements of truth, it would miss the larger point: a crisis-induced distortion field doesn't necessarily preclude the players from recognizing the need to step out of their traditional comfort zones, to stretch beyond them.

These sectors were, and are, evolving, pulled by societal pressures to redefine themselves. To renegotiate their roles in relationship to one another. To measure their collective effort against the long-term horizon line of serving the public interest. A recalibration that began, in Detroit, with a situational imperative ultimately showed that it's possible for sectors to make more far-reaching and long-lasting changes of norms, methods, and risk appetites.

A sectoral fandango that is not a one time or one-place proposition, but instead a fundamental reimagining of how sectors situate themselves in the ever-changing and challenging landscape of American cities.

Recasting the challenges of blighted and abandoned land

"I may have gone too far," Detroit Mayor Dave Bing admitted to me on the phone one day in 2010.

Bing had been elected in 2009. He took office following one of the most tumultuous periods of Detroit's political history, during which Mayor Kwame Kilpatrick resigned after being charged with perjury, misconduct in office, and obstruction of justice. The president of the city council, Kenneth Cockrel Jr., stepped into the seat. Months later Cockrel lost to Bing in a special election. And months after that, Bing won a full term in a general election.

An NBA legend with the Detroit Pistons and then founder and chief executive of one of Michigan's largest steel processing firms, Bing had run on a platform of returning decency and integrity to city hall and tackling physical blight and building abandonment. When he took office, more than 75,000 of Detroit's 380,000 individual land parcels were vacant or blighted—a landmass the size of San Francisco. Blight consumed more than fifty percent of the land in some neighborhoods. Not only did the Dresden-like images so fetishized by national photojournalistic essays make reclamation seem impossible, but the blight fostered a poisonous concoction of criminal activity, health risks, and economic instability that drained neighborhood life.

The challenges were compounded by population decline. Detroit's population, which peaked at 1.85 million souls in the 1950s, had fallen to 700,000 people. Those residents were distributed over 140 square miles—an area large enough to fit San Francisco, Boston, and Manhattan, with room left over for St. Paul. Bing understood, and spoke honestly about, the fact that there simply wasn't enough tax base to spread high-quality municipal services equally across that expanse.

The mix of blight and depopulation led Bing to announce during the campaign his intention to essentially shrink the city's footprint by concentrating city services in still-healthy neighborhoods. The reaction was scorching: many residents were livid at the idea they could find their neighborhood deprived of basic services, or that they might be forced to move. Hence, the mayor's call to me, conceding that he may have gone too far. "I really touched a nerve," Bing admitted.

A political third rail.

"I've come to realize that we need a plan to help us understand how we can convert all this blight into something more productive. My staff isn't adequately equipped to do that; they're overwhelmed and don't have the background to take on something that big," he continued. "But I understand that you've worked a long time in urban planning and might know who can help. I'm hoping you and Kresge could identify a world-class planner to prepare a master plan for the city."

I suggested to Mayor Bing that preparing another city plan—Detroit had seen scores of them in recent decades—was perhaps not the best option. I noted that New Orleans had faced something of a similar challenge in the post-Katrina period and had, after two less-than-successful attempts at master planning, decided on a more incremental path: blending professional planning with unprecedentedly expansive community engagement.

I asked Bing if he could give us a month. We'd send a team to New Orleans, understand more fully what had and hadn't worked, and come back with some recommendations for his team. After a long pause, he said, "Well I can't afford that."

I replied, "That's why you called us. We're honored to bear the costs."

Working closely with the administration's planning director, Warren Palmer (whose experience lay largely in overseeing parking structure construction), we spent four weeks studying New Orleans and preparing recommendations. Though detailed, they were simple: engage the community in a meaningful way to identify needs and ideas, and enlist planning experts to craft a plan rooted in those needs and desires. Not an academic master plan but a community-driven planning process supported by world-class expertise.

Palmer was enthusiastic, but expressed the same concern as the mayor had: his department didn't have the capacity to undertake something quite this nuanced and complex. I reiterated that Kresge was prepared to help.

"The plan must be rooted in equity and justice. It has to be tied to real people living in a real place: I'm not going to sign up for a paper exercise."

I put out feelers in the community development field for people who might fit the bill. I soon got an email from a longtime friend and community organizer in the Washington, D.C. area, Bill Potapchuk. Potapchuk said he had worked with someone who might be perfect. A brilliant Harvard Graduate School of Design-trained architect and planner named Toni Griffin was just wrapping up a stint as director of community development for Mayor Cory Booker of Newark. She'd previously delivered the Anacostia Plan for District of Columbia Mayor Tony Williams. And Griffin knew the city: she had begun her career as an architect with Skidmore, Owings and Merrill when that firm had been engaged to help overcome the design flaws in Detroit's Renaissance Center complex.

Potapchuk arranged an introduction, and Griffin was open to a discussion. I flew to New York City to meet her for dinner in Midtown. Griffin was, indeed, closing out her engagement with Mayor Booker. She did indeed feel a connection to Detroit. And she did have thoughts about what kind of process would be best under the circumstances. I was thrilled. "So, you'd be interested in coming to Detroit to take this on?" I asked.

Griffin gave me an up-and-down look as if to say, you may not fully understand what you're asking. "I'd need some assurances," she began. "First, that you, as president of Kresge, will have my back—at all times and in all circumstances. I will work on behalf of the city, but I can assure you based on extensive experience that there will be times I'll need you as a buffer and backup.

"Second, I'll need to be sure that city hall wants me. I have no business presupposing that I'm the right person to take this on; they need to agree to my role before I start. I'll need to be sure that the planning director and the mayor feel comfortable having me lead something of this visibility and magnitude. And I'll need to have direct access to both of them," Griffin continued.

"Third, I'll need to build a team. Someone in charge of community engagement. Technical advisory teams for seven or eight bodies of work—housing, economic development, water, transportation, and others. It won't be cheap, but it's essential.

"And fourth, the plan must be rooted in equity and justice. The process has to respect the dignity of Detroit residents, their past as well as their future. It has to be tied to real people living in a real place: I'm not going to sign up for a paper exercise," Griffin concluded.

The town hall had turned interminable, hostile, and utterly unproductive.

I hesitated for three-quarters of a heartbeat, at most, before responding. "Yes to all four. When can we get you to Detroit?" Griffin had loose ends to attend to in Newark, but we set a time for her to meet Mayor Bing and Warren Palmer.

Those meetings were cordial, welcoming, and appreciative. We all agreed that Griffin would start as soon as her obligations to Mayor Booker were fulfilled. Griffin would be housed at city hall so she could forge connections with the planning department, the mayor's senior staff, and other key department actors. She would brief the mayor regularly.

It started splendidly. Griffin began assembling her teams, and enlisted Potapchuk to plan the community's introduction to the process. She spent countless hours with Laura Trudeau, the head of Kresge's Detroit program, to learn more about the state of community politics.

But flares went up quickly in city hall. A handful of the highest ranking women in the administration began asking—usually, but not always, behind closed doors—why "that woman from Harvard" was being imported to lead this effort despite the availability of capable, hardworking city employees who were already here. It didn't help that Griffin started to refer to them as the "mean girls of city hall." It seemed petty and marginal at first; later we would understand that it was a dire mistake to underestimate just how corrosive that resistance culture would become.

As promised, Griffin launched parallel paths of community engagement and technical analysis. The latter went smoothly, as she enlisted a half-dozen teams from around the world to assess water and soil resources, housing patterns, clustered economic development, transportation, and countless other dimensions of city life. The former, not so much—at least initially. The first community meetings in fall 2010 were a disaster.

The plan was to create large venues in which residents could voice their hopes for vibrant, healthy neighborhoods of the future. The team got the large venues part right. But they got the hopeful commentary part quite wrong. In the very first session, attended by hundreds of residents, the mayor, Griffin, and Griffin's community engagement team began describing their objectives. But the train quickly veered off the track when they then opened the floor for comments and questions.

Not that providing the space for community input was a bad idea; it was essential. But once in possession of the roaming microphone, residents wouldn't let go until they'd vented frustrations that had been compounding over many years. Those included but weren't limited to the inadequacy of garbage pickup, the vermin infesting the abandoned house next door, the woeful underfunding of local schools, the pervasive failure of streetlights, and more. That attendees were expected to go along with a bunch of consultants who lived elsewhere added insult to injury. The town hall had turned interminable, hostile, and utterly unproductive, at least from the perspective of beginning a constructive visioning process.

The mayor was mortified. It was like a political campaign of one's nightmares—only worse. The "mean girls" were in high gear. Griffin was beside herself; she hadn't encountered blowback this powerful in either Newark or Anacostia.

We recalibrated immediately. As skilled as Potapchuk's community organizers were, they didn't have the knowledge of Detroit needed to surmount these kinds of speed bumps. We needed a direct, trusted groundwire to the community, one who could elicit the kind of constructive commentary necessary to advance Griffin's process.

One of the original naysayers was now the planning director.

Dan Pitera, director of the Detroit Collaborative Design Center and a member of the University of Detroit Mercy architectural faculty, fit that bill. Pitera had been a mainstay of resident organizing and planning in Detroit for twenty years. He was widely known and respected. He played well with others. And, he and Griffin were sympatico. The only question was whether he'd agree to put his reputation—and that of the Center—on the line. The process could go very wrong, and this was, after all, his hometown.

Without hesitating, Pitera agreed to step in. His role would prove transformational.

Pitera designed and implemented the most extensive community engagement process Detroit had ever seen, using every conceivable method to tap community insights and ideas: social media, email, text, phone calls, targeted door-knocking, gatherings in public spaces and residents' homes and places of worship. The entire process engaged more than 100,000 residents, businesses, and other stakeholders.

Pitera and Griffin enlisted a cadre of twenty-five citizens to lead geographically oriented pods of residents. These pod leaders would regularly feed back to Pitera and Griffin issues that needed more attention: where technical experts needed to connect more fully to residents, what changes might enhance community buy-in, how to bring ever-broader circles of people and organizations into the fold.

Those energies, ideas, and ground truths were exactly what Griffin's technical teams needed. Their technical analyses needed to be complemented—and sometimes modified—by community memory, knowledge, and values. The community knew where the clandestine dump had been; the technical team knew what groundwater contamination markers to look for. Residents knew how people traveled to get to local businesses or places of worship; the technical team knew how to adapt public transit routes to enhance those patterns. The residents knew why certain parts of the neighborhood had fallen prey to drug houses; the technical team knew how it might be possible to introduce remedial zoning and regulatory responses. This give-and-take created a labor-intensive, time-consuming, yet invaluable virtuous loop.

Just as the process began to gain momentum—or perhaps, *because* the process had picked up momentum—the early city hall warning flares burst into full view. The people around Mayor Bing who'd initially expressed displeasure at an outsider being placed in control had picked up new adherents and added traction. One of the original naysayers was now the planning director. Another, the communications director. They began pouring poison into the mayor's ear about Griffin being a prima donna . . . an outsider tone-deaf to the real aspirations of Detroiters . . . an elitist who would substitute arcane academic analyses from international "experts" for commonsense, homegrown solutions. They told the mayor that he had to regain control of the process before it was too late. Get rid of Griffin.

Mayor Bing was a profoundly kind and decent man who never acted precipitously. But his Iagos finally wore him down. He realized that the breakdown in working relationships between what had come to be known as "Detroit Works" and his inner circle had become so intense and paralyzing that it was untenable to carry on. He called me with his decision. We had to bring the project to a close.

Two years of community inputs. Two years of unassailable technical analysis. Thousands of hours of time from all quarters. Discarding that struck me as out of the question. But this was always the mayor's initiative—we were caught between Scylla and Charybdis.

I sat with Griffin to test a third possibility. "Could you continue the work outside city hall?" I asked. "So much of the community engagement has been done. Could you carry on with the community resident leadership structure while you finish synthesizing the work of your expert teams?" Griffin thought a long time. "Yes. We're far enough along that I could still create a work product that would have integrity—and value."

Of course, it was one thing for Griffin and me to agree. It was another to ensure that the community leaders would be willing to, for all practical purposes, take ownership of the project from the city. And we'd have to secure the support of the Kellogg and Ford Foundations, who had helped underwrite the community engagement process.

Most everyone involved agreed that the work that had been done couldn't be abandoned. Griffin would disengage from the city, synthesize what she and Pitera had gathered, secure from her consultants whatever else she needed, and pull all of it together into a final framework we'd call—instead of "Detroit Works"—"Detroit Future City." Trudeau and I would continue to have Griffin's back, as she'd requested at our first meeting; just in a more direct way.

Pitera designed and implemented the most extensive community engagement process Detroit had ever seen. The entire process engaged more than 100,000 residents, businesses, and other stakeholders.

It took more than a year, but the strategy worked. In January 2013, the Detroit Future City framework document was ready for its public unveiling—all 354 pages of it, complete with thousands of pages of underlying technical appendices. It was divided into six broad chapters: Landuse and Economic Development; Employment Districts; Residential Neighborhoods; Public Lands; City Systems; and Ecological and Productive Landscapes.

Mayor Bing attended the press conference. But the focus was on the twenty-five community leads. One after another, they took the stage to describe their pride in "owning" a plan of their own making. Indeed, Hester Wheeler, one of the cochairs of the process and then-head of the Detroit NAACP, spoke directly to the mayor and said, "We are indebted to you, mayor, for having the vision to launch this process. But it has become something larger than your—or any—administration. This is the People's Plan."

The other cochair, Alice Johnson, the deeply respected head of a large local nonprofit serving Detroit families, echoed the sentiment. Johnson said it was the first time in her

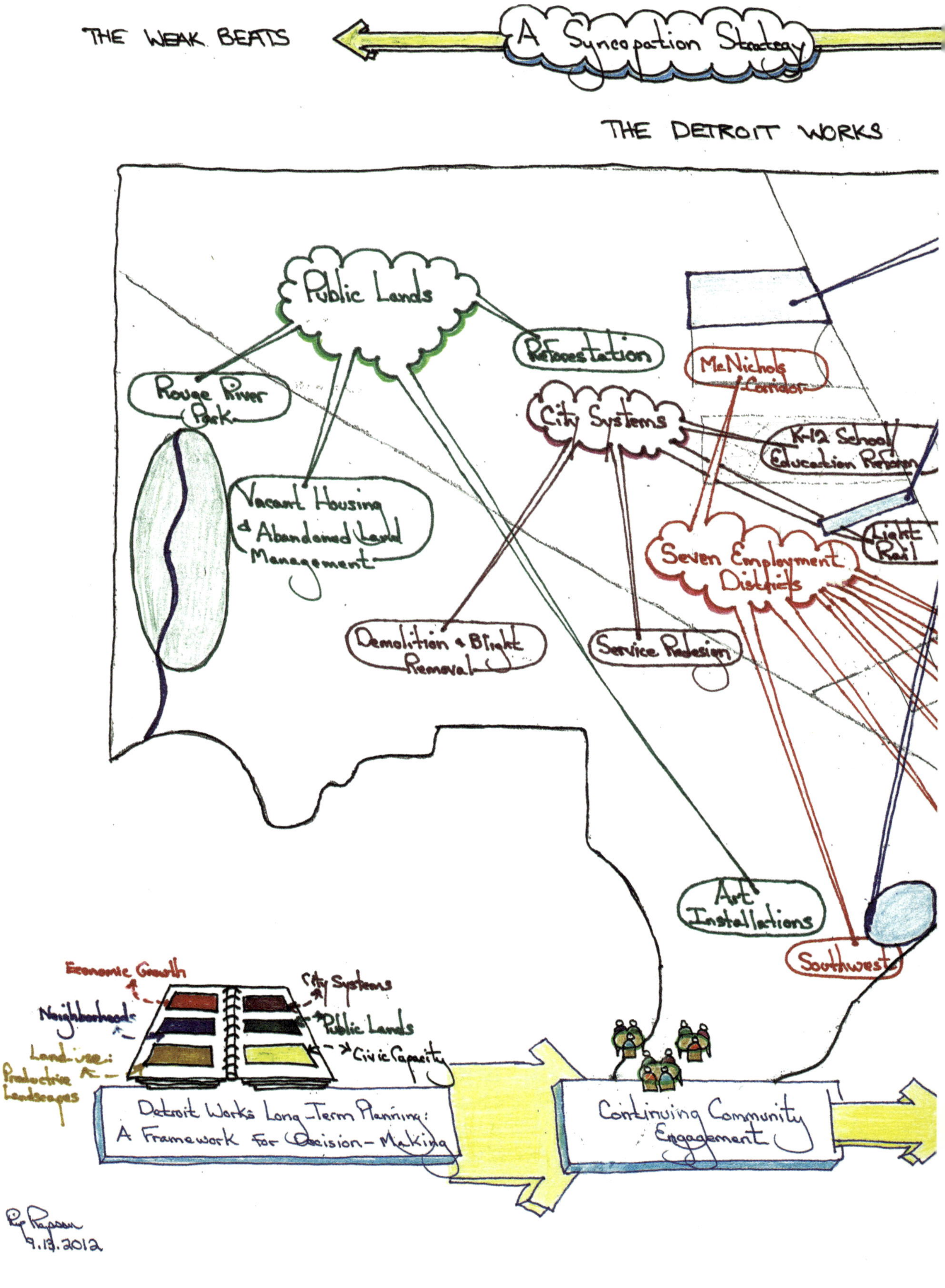
THE WEAK BEATS
A Syncopation Strategy
THE DETROIT WORKS
Public Lands
Reforestation
Rouge River Park
Vacant Housing & Abandoned Land Management
McNichols Corridor
City Systems
K-12 School Education Reform
Light Rail
Seven Employment Districts
Demolition & Blight Removal
Service Redesign
Art Installations
Southwest
Economic Growth
Neighborhoods
Land use: Productive Landscapes
City Systems
Public Lands
Civic Capacity
Detroit Works Long-Term Planning: A Framework for Decision-Making
Continuing Community Engagement
Rip Rapson
9.13.2012

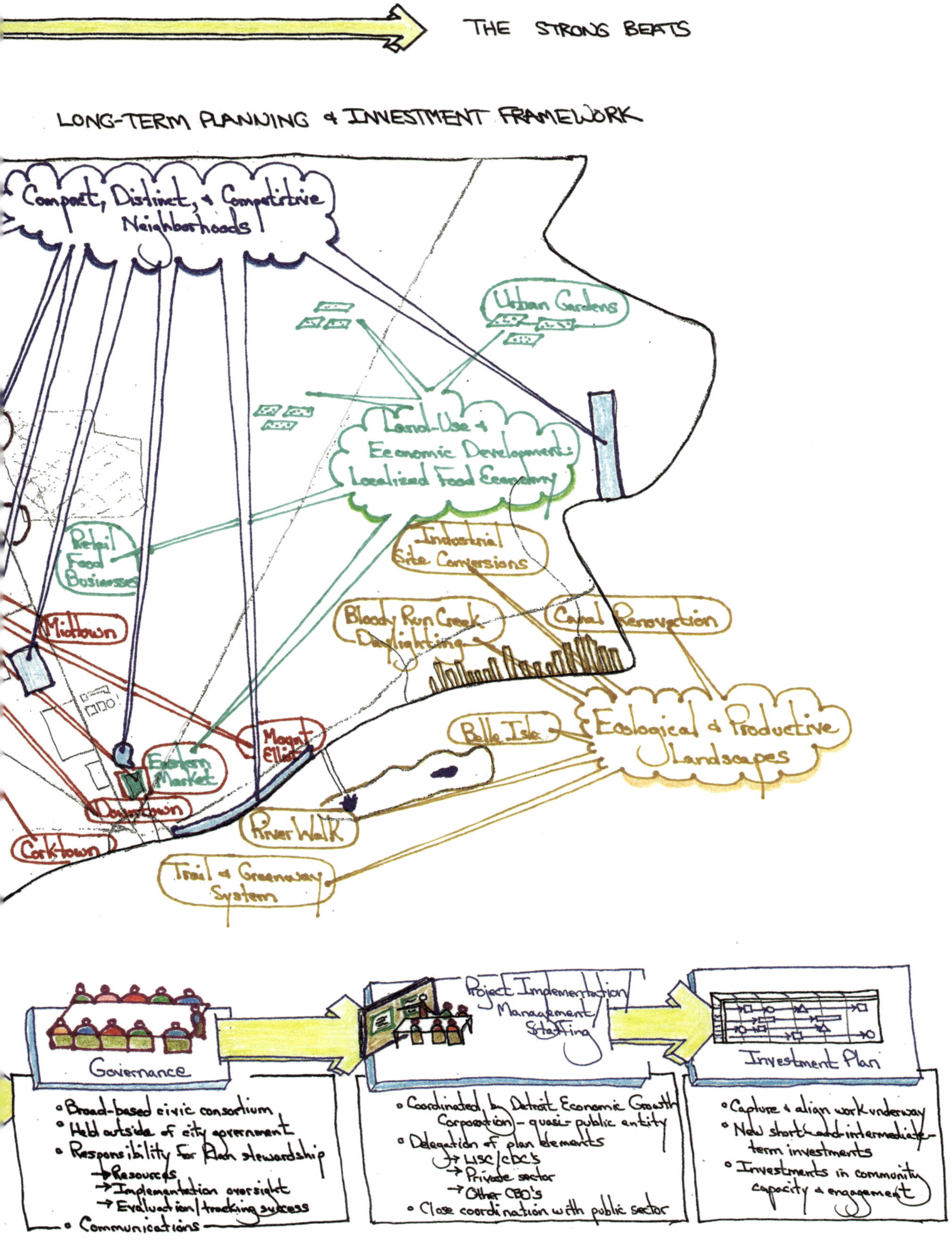

THE STRONG BEATS
LONG-TERM PLANNING & INVESTMENT FRAMEWORK
Compact, Distinct, & Competitive Neighborhoods
Urban Gardens
Land-Use & Economic Development: Localized Food Economy
Retail Food Businesses
Industrial Site Conversions
Bloody Run Creek Daylighting
Canal Renovation
Midtown
Eastern Market
Mount Elliott
Downtown
Corktown
Belle Isle
Ecological & Productive Landscapes
River Walk
Trail & Greenway System
Governance
Project Implementation/ Management/ Staffing
Investment Plan
• Broad-based civic consortium
• Held outside of city government
• Responsibility for Plan stewardship
→ Resources
→ Implementation oversight
→ Evaluation/tracking success
• Communications
• Coordinated by Detroit Economic Growth Corporation – quasi-public entity
• Delegation of plan elements
→ LISC/CDC's
→ Private sector
→ Other CBO's
• Close coordination with public sector
• Capture & align work underway
• New short- and intermediate-term investments
• Investments in community capacity & engagement

very long memory that there was a roadmap for decision-making and investment that was infused with equity, legitimacy, and staying power.

Mayor Bing stood proudly on the podium, recognizing that by removing the planning process from the heat of his administration's internal rivalries, he had given the community the opportunity to create a collective visioning document that transcended partisanship and parochialism.

When Mayor Mike Duggan took office a year later, his administration placed the plan at the core of its efforts to stabilize and rebuild the health of Detroit neighborhoods. The Duggan Administration's head of economic development, Tom Lewand, repeatedly observed that it would be his department's "Bible." Lewand said it would serve as the city's investment and decision-making framework for every dimension of community life: where the city might prioritize investments in commercial corridors and emerging job centers. How it might pursue new mixed-use, mixed-income neighborhoods of choice. How it might adjust transit service. How it could test ideas for urban farming, reforestation, innovative stormwater management, and more.

Meta technical analysis had met micro community voice in the middle to produce a powerful synthesis. The mezzo zone had proved a powerful crucible.

It had offered a space in which community members, equipped with the expertise of technical experts, felt a sense of agency in helping shape the city's future. It had modeled the kind of processes necessary to draw citizens fully and meaningfully into the public decision making process, infusing public policy options with greater insight, legitimacy, and staying power. And like the Minneapolis Neighborhood Revitalization Program (Chapter 12), it focused on practicality, differentiating what can be achieved now and what will need sighting against a more distant horizon line.

"It has become larger than your—or any—administration. This is the People's Plan."

It would have been relatively simple to fold the Detroit Future City plan into the city's planning department and declare a wrap. But doing that would have squandered the opportunity to make it something more than a one-time investment plan. Doing that would have diminished its long-term vitality as it became caught up in the inevitable conflicts over quality and control just like it had encountered during its formation. And doing that would have diminished its relevance as it became subject to the vagaries of political election cycles.

We accordingly made a different choice. The community advisory board, and Kresge, decided to create an implementation office that would stand independent of the city. There, the plan could serve as a roadmap for ongoing community engagement, a platform of strategies to be continually refreshed and renewed, a point of departure for ongoing assessment of progress against the initial report's objectives.

We chose L. Ken Cockrel Jr., the former city council president and interim mayor, as the first director, and assembled funding for Cockrel to hire staff and create an office. The enterprise started slowly with a host of small projects that fit neatly into the plan's landuse principles: a handbook for creating side-gardens; deeper analysis of what steps could activate each of the chapters; community listening sessions about small-scale neighborhood projects that could have outsized impact.

Over the next decade, however, under the leadership of a former Local Initiatives Support Corporation executive and longtime Detroit resident, Anika Goss, Detroit Future

City would take on even greater ambition, becoming a full-blown nonprofit that, in the organization's characterization, was "a think tank, a policy advocate, and an innovation engine developing data-driven strategies to create a more equitable and sustainable future for Detroit." It has become the go-to Detroit institution for analysis of the next-generation issues shaping Detroit's future: water management, housing supply and affordability, barriers to small business development, and countless others.

The genesis of the Detroit Future City process had been completely situational; a response to the immediate needs of a mayor seeking to take on the gnarliest issue facing the city. But it became something beyond that—and much of its value came from the fact that it worked outside the vicissitudes of city hall.

The pull of transactions that generate tax base or convey political efficacy can threaten that kind of long-term view.

It held the possibility of stewarding a long-term perspective toward growth and prosperity capable of placing discrete transactions into the context of a larger set of core principles. Government at its best aspires to that, of course. But the pull of transactions that generate tax base or convey political efficacy can threaten that kind of long-term view.

It strikes me that this kind of external think/do mechanism does triple duty in cities. It can elevate the power of shared, long-term community values above transactions that offer only short-term advantage. It can create a form of accountability by which to gauge whether public and private sector actors are delivering on their promise to honor those values. And it can be tremendously useful to a public sector that doesn't always have the resources, or inclination, to assess the impact of its community development efforts.

Foundations step up to help resolve the nation's largest municipal bankruptcy

Detroit had been declared dead before, but this time, there was every evidence that the diagnosis was correct.

Detroiters had long prided themselves on their resilience. Maybe it grew from the great fire of 1805, when Detroiters came together to rebuild their homes and businesses and birthed their motto: "We hope for better things; it shall rise from the ashes." It was an act of civic defiance against the destructive power of nature and humanity. Detroiters laid down a marker that day: "We're not going anywhere." And they didn't.

That resilience was the formative matter that made the Detroit of the early- and mid-20th century a haven for tens of thousands of Americans seeking respite from the plantations and coal mines—people looking to fulfill their own share of the American Dream and become part of the burgeoning middle class. And that resilience was manifest as Detroit became the assembly line for the "Arsenal of Democracy" during World War II.

Indeed, in 1960—just six decades ago—Detroit was the richest city in the U.S. Not New York. Not Chicago. Detroit.

But sixty years can be an eternity in the life of a city. And so it has been in Detroit, as the city endured ever deeper and more corrosive cycles of disinvestment and financial mismanagement, racial polarization and economic segregation, political dysfunction, and educational atrophy.

Fifteen years ago, this noxious brew grew even more toxic as Detroit was drawn into a storm of unfathomable proportions and severity. The Great Recession knocked an already fragile economy to its knees. The housing foreclosure crisis crushed the economic and emotional lives of countless families. The automobile industry stared into the abyss of corporate bankruptcies. An all-consuming corruption scandal landed a charismatic, popular mayor and scores of his coconspirators in jail.

This confluence of crises exposed and widened the underlying fault lines that had already made Detroit synonymous with urban devastation, dysfunction, and despair. The city narrative read like a municipal obituary.

Indeed, many Americans appeared to embrace the insidious proposition that equity and justice simply were not possible in Detroit. The market had failed low-income people: starving neighborhoods of living-wage jobs, creating food deserts, withholding the capital that neighborhood businesses needed to survive and grow, leaving scores of individuals and families struggling at the economic margins. Detroit's 2013 entry into bankruptcy was the tragic and inevitable consummation of those forces.

The paths leading a city to the doorstep of financial calamity—there have been several since 2008, though Detroit remains the largest U.S. city to have done so—vary substantially. Each city has to travel a unique road to reverse their circumstance. And yet, Detroit's situation seemed by far the most intractable.

And, "intractable" doesn't adequately convey the sense of pessimism and fatalism that attended Detroit's bankruptcy filing: words like impossible, hopeless, irreversible, and fatal were increasingly invoked both locally and nationally. The numbers were jaw-dropping: the city's debt was estimated at $18 billion, and within ten years, some two-thirds of the city's budget was projected to be consumed by the payment of retiree benefits alone. The city was cannibalizing funds for essential municipal services just to pay interest on bonds and loans. It was running an annual deficit to the tune of $350 million.

Although cities exist as extensions of state authority, it's the cities themselves that are expected to manage their finances. But as Detroit failed to bring its costs and revenues into balance, Governor Rick Snyder's hand was forced. He possessed the authority to remove financial management authority from the city's elected officials. Loathe to invoke it, however, he sought to give the city both the mandate, and the opportunity, to chart a path to solvency.

The governor and the mayor's office agreed that the first move would be for the mayor to submit, and the governor to approve, a blueprint for balancing the budget and managing long-term debt. After several good faith attempts on both sides, however, it became clear that this couldn't be done through normal political processes: the numbers were too big, the structural impediments too deep, and the politics too fraught.

"Intractable" doesn't adequately convey the sense of pessimism and fatalism that attended Detroit's bankruptcy filing: words like impossible, hopeless, irreversible, and fatal were increasingly invoked both locally and nationally. The numbers were jaw-dropping.

Snyder had no choice but to take a painful next step, announcing in March 2013 that he would appoint an emergency financial manager armed with extraordinary powers to accomplish what the elected officials had shown they couldn't. That decision would be criticized as an unforgivable assault on democracy: decisions affecting the lives of Detroit residents would now be made by someone without an election certificate.

The governor knew full well that he couldn't sidestep that criticism. But he also knew that there was probably only one person on the planet who could both blunt it—at least partially—and do the job.

Kevyn Orr, a partner with the Cleveland-based law firm Jones Day, was widely recognized as one of the most brilliant, creative, and tenacious bankruptcy lawyers in the country. Orr knew the auto economy, having helped Chrysler work its way through bankruptcy four years before. His father was an A.M.E. minister who had marched in Civil Rights protests in the '60s, and his mother had been an educator for the Broward, Florida public school district.

Orr spent his first four months trying to put Detroit's financial house in order. But even armed with the extraordinary superseding authorities of an emergency financial manager, he couldn't do it. In July, Orr recommended that Detroit file for Chapter 9 bankruptcy. It would be the largest municipal bankruptcy in U.S. history. The case was assigned to Chief Bankruptcy Judge Stephen Rhodes, who ruled that the bankruptcy could move forward.

Rhodes was not about to launch a proceeding of such unprecedented complexity and gravity without first seeking to find a consensual path forward—or, at least, to narrow the issues. He sought a mediator to work alongside Orr. As Orr worked to assemble a package to bring the city's annual spending and revenue books into balance, the mediator would attempt to resolve the outstanding creditor and bondholder claims.

Either pension reductions or the sale of the art would effectively sign Detroit's death certificate.

Rhodes's choice was unorthodox: he selected the person who was, technically, his boss: Judge Gerald Rosen, the chief judge of the United States District Court for the Eastern District of Michigan. Rosen had been appointed to the federal bench in 1990 by President George H.W. Bush and had served as chief judge since 2009.

Rosen didn't have much room in which to mediate. The city's $18 billion in obligations was spread across underfunded pension obligations, underfunded retiree healthcare obligations, and bond payment obligations. The city simply didn't possess assets sufficient to meet those obligations.

Rosen was on a tightrope: either pension payments and retiree healthcare benefits had to be sharply reduced or bondholders had to agree to pennies on the dollar of repayment. Or, city assets worth billions of dollars had to be liquidated to meet the pension and creditor claims. Or, some combination of these scenarios.

Rosen understood that he would have to land in the "combination of the above" option. No single solution alone would resolve the situation. The complexity of the proposition made it a seemingly impossible task.

The pensions were perhaps the most sensitive issue to be confronted. An average Detroit pensioner received roughly $20,000 per year; for police and fire retirees, the number was $30,000 a year. Hardly a gilded retirement in either case. Without new revenue and concessions from the creditors, it was likely that these would have to be cut by 40 or 50 percent. Rosen realized that his charge carried no higher imperative than preventing that outcome; it was unthinkable that a retired city employee could survive her pension being reduced to $10,000 a year.

The creditors were represented by experienced and tenacious lawyers who'd look to every possible asset to satisfy their claims. But their choices were actually more limited than it first appeared. They knew that although they could go after the pension funds, satisfying corporate interests at the expense of devastating the retirement of working-class people living on modest pensions wasn't a stellar PR move.

The asset that seemed more promising was the world-class art collection held by the Detroit Institute of Arts. In a peculiarly rare arrangement among American cities, the city of Detroit owned the Institute and its collection. Knowing the paintings, sculptures, textiles, and other works were likely worth many billions of dollars, the creditors reasoned this was a sensible first line of attack.

Rosen knew that either pension reductions or sale of the art would plunge the city into a purgatory of litigation that would drag on for a decade, effectively signing Detroit's death certificate.

On one hand, Michigan's constitution prohibited the impairment of public pension obligations, the state would argue. The creditors would then argue that federal bankruptcy law preempted the state's constitutional provisions. Endless trials and appeals would follow, with the ultimate disposition being made by the U.S. Supreme Court.

On the other hand, the Institute's collection could be seen as held in a public trust, removing it from the reach of the creditors. As with the federal preemption issue, the argument would be battled out endlessly in court including probate courts who might have jurisdiction over gifts made by private individuals to the collection. Again, it was almost certain to be resolved only after wending its way to the nation's highest court.

Rosen recognized that the challenge was not just legal. Even if state constitutional constraints could be breached, impairing pension obligations by 50 or 60 percent would cause unspeakable hardships for thousands of retirees. And even if the public trust argument failed, auctioning the DIA's Van Goghs, Bruegels, Riveras, and other masterworks in a fire sale would deal a devastating blow to Detroit's cultural history, identity, and dignity.

Auctioning the DIA's Van Goghs, Bruegels, Riveras, and other masterworks in a fire sale would deal a devastating blow to Detroit's cultural history, identity, and dignity.

Time was of the essence. Orr had no choice but to put both pension reductions and art sales on the table as he began assembling the building blocks of what would become the "plan of adjustment" that would signal to Judge Rhodes that the debts were satisfied. Acting independently—but in consultation with Orr—Rosen sought a different route.

Rosen hadn't been chosen by mistake; he was a brilliant mediator with a steel-trap mind capable of seeing possibilities others would never have dreamt of.

I should have remembered that before accepting a dinner invitation from him.

Rosen and I had been tennis buddies in Washington D.C. almost thirty years before. He worked for Michigan Senator Robert Griffin when I worked for Minneapolis Representative Donald Fraser. We would sneak off during the lunch hours to a secret tennis court at the U.S. Navy Yards and exchange forehands for an hour. After we both left Congress to pursue legal careers, though, we fell out of touch. I was delighted to read of Rosen's appointment as mediator. He possessed all the skills, and the perfect temperament, for the job. And in late 2012, he called to ask if Gail and I would join his wife and him for drinks and dinner.

I had expected to open the visit with the customary gentle, meandering path to reacquaintance—how careers had evolved, how we had connected with our spouses, how kids were making life more complex. And it did . . . for about seven minutes. Rosen then redirected the conversation. "Let's spend dinner talking about our families—I really want to hear more about how you and Gail have been. But Rip, I've got an idea, and I want to test it out on you."

I actually knew that that was the purpose of the dinner. Rosen intended to convene a meeting at the end of the week of Michigan's foundation community to discuss his idea. Because I was scheduled to travel overseas and couldn't attend, he wanted to be sure he ran it by me before sharing it with the group.

"Nothing in what I'm planning to propose will work without you and Kresge agreeing to it," he said. "I need to know whether you're willing to entertain it." I put down my glass of wine: this was evidently going to require concentration—and sobriety.

Neither selling the art collection nor decimating the pensions was something Rosen said he could live with, or that the city could recover from. But in the absence of other assets that could meaningfully placate the creditors, he needed to convert the art into a very different kind of asset capable of salvaging the pensions.

"The only way I can even hope to open a conversation with the creditors is to identify a new asset outside the city's control," Rosen explained. I had begun to see where this was going.

"I sketched out a pretty simple idea on a small piece of paper when I was out west working on the case," Rosen continued. "It's just a couple of boxes and arrows, but I think it might do the trick. The central box is called the Art Trust. If we can raise enough money to essentially buy the art from the city and place the proceeds in that trust, the city could use the trust dollars to prevent serious cuts to the pensions.

"Without that infusion, Orr will have no choice but to get serious about selling off the art. With it, though, we can freeze the attacks on the pensions and art, freeing me to negotiate on a different playing field with the creditors. What do you think?" Rosen concluded. He smiled broadly, and his eyes danced; he was justifiably delighted with his idea.

"Fascinating," I replied. "How much would be required for this to work? Isn't this an $18 billion problem?" Rosen shook his head vigorously. "No, no, we don't need that much—and it would be impossible to raise. We just need enough to pay fair market value for the art. That will enable me to convince the creditors that because we won't raid the art or pensions, they'll have to swallow a deep discount on their debts; probably 10-20 cents on the dollar. It's not that simple, I admit, but I'll have enough leverage to negotiate differentially from creditor to creditor; how we approach health care benefits will differ from how we approach bond obligations, for instance."

Rosen was on a roll. But it made him only that much more charming—and persuasive. "It's a reasonable amount, I assure you. Well within the capacity of this enormously generous and well-resourced foundation community."

I hadn't heard a number. "Judge, you're dancing around the question," I joked. "What's your bottom line?"

Rosen was on a roll. But it made him only that much more charming—and persuasive. "It's a reasonable amount, I assure you. Well within the capacity of this enormously generous and well-resourced foundation community. But again, that assumes that you—that Kresge—takes the lead," he smiled.

"And so . . . the magic number is?" I persisted, against all my better instincts. I realized I was becoming complicit.

"Between $500 and $800 million," he replied.

It's one thing to fear an answer. It's another to be stupefied by it. It seemed a good time to break the flow with another long drink of wine. The judge held my stare, unblinking. "That is a very, very large number for a foundation to consider," I managed, trying to get my equilibrium. Rosen quickly replied. "Oh, I'm not asking you to do it alone. It needs to be *all* our foundations. Divide it up and it doesn't seem out of the question."

It dawned on me that he was both right and wrong. There were perhaps a dozen foundations who might contribute—though many were small and would struggle to contribute even $10 million to a pool. Rosen had to know that, but I said anyway, "You realize, of course, that Kresge and the Ford Foundation are the only two Detroit-focused foundations even remotely capable of contributing the kind of sums that would bring you within range."

Rosen was unfazed. "Yup, that's why I started with you. Without you, it doesn't work." Pause. "That's why the first conversation is the one we're having."

We agreed to take a breath and drive to dinner. I tried to ask about the Rosen family, the judge's passion for Winston Churchill, or anything else I could think of to buy myself time to sort through the questions. I admired his solution, but the commitments he had in mind from Kresge and Ford—he imagined that $250 million from the two of us would be necessary—seemed to be hallucinatory.

It's one thing to fear an answer. It's another to be stupefied by it.

My delay tactics were unsuccessful. There was no chit-chatting about our family life at dinner; Rosen wasn't about to let me off the hook. Over salad, he explained the process Orr would use to formulate the plan of adjustment. Over linguini, he scrolled through what each creditor class believed they would ultimately need and how the money would help him convince them that they needed only a fraction of that.

I settled on chipping at the edges before coming to the core question.

I started by suggesting that his first step might be to drop the nomenclature of the "Art Trust." "You can't have this grand scheme be seen as simply a way of protecting artwork—your approach has to convey just how brutal and raw the bankruptcy is to Detroiters, particularly pensioners facing the threat of life-altering cuts to their livelihoods," I said. "Given a choice between protecting a bunch of centuries-old canvases or enabling retired public works employees to pay their water bills, people won't be faulted for choosing the latter.

"On the other hand, you can't frame it entirely in terms of pension protection either," I continued. "Foundations will have a really hard time seeing their way to bailing out public pensions . . . we could be asked to do that in every city in America. Maybe it's best to avoid either characterization and describe it as the only way to resolve the bankruptcy—the only way to avoid unending, debilitating litigation," I mused.

"That enables a foundation—or anyone else who might contribute to the pool—to argue that all the work we've done over the last six years to restabilize Detroit and lay the groundwork for forward progress will be for naught if we don't resolve the bankruptcy quickly and by agreement. Dedicating the money unlocks the bankruptcy. Full stop."

Rosen became more animated. "You're absolutely right. The overall package is what counts, not its parts." But he knew how to close a deal. "If we did it that way, would you be willing to be the first dollars in?"

I had to take a deep breath.

"Given the frame I've just concocted, the answer has to be yes. But everything depends on the details," I said. Although I was about to leave on an overseas trip, I offered to send a Kresge board member to Rosen's upcoming presentation. "You can certainly mention that we've talked and that I've encouraged you to carry the conversation forward. After I get back to town early next week, I'll go to work on this. My first call will have to be to my board chair, and then I'll give Darren Walker, the new president of Ford, a call."

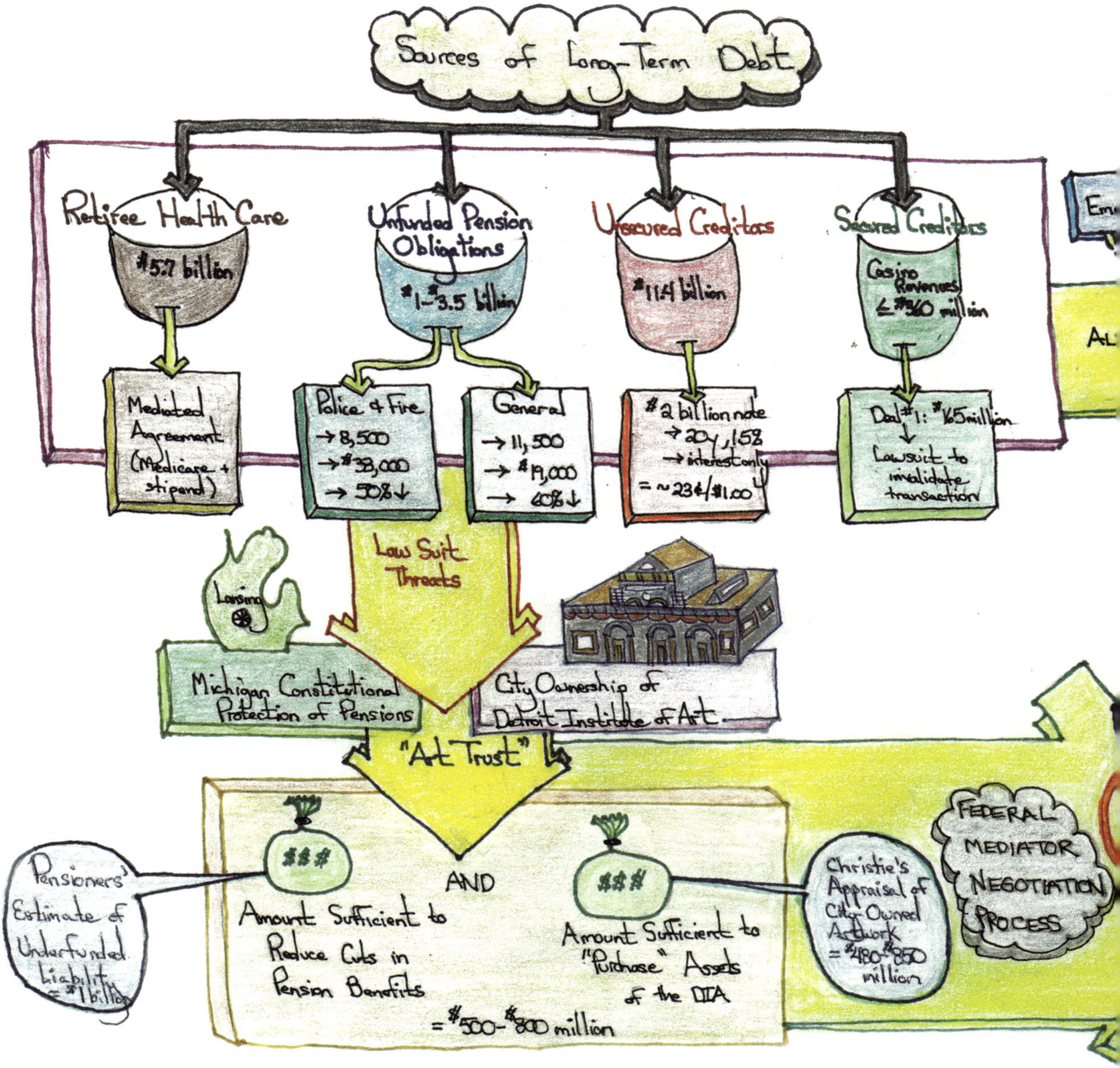

ADJUSTING LONG-TERM DEBT: THE BANKRUPTCY

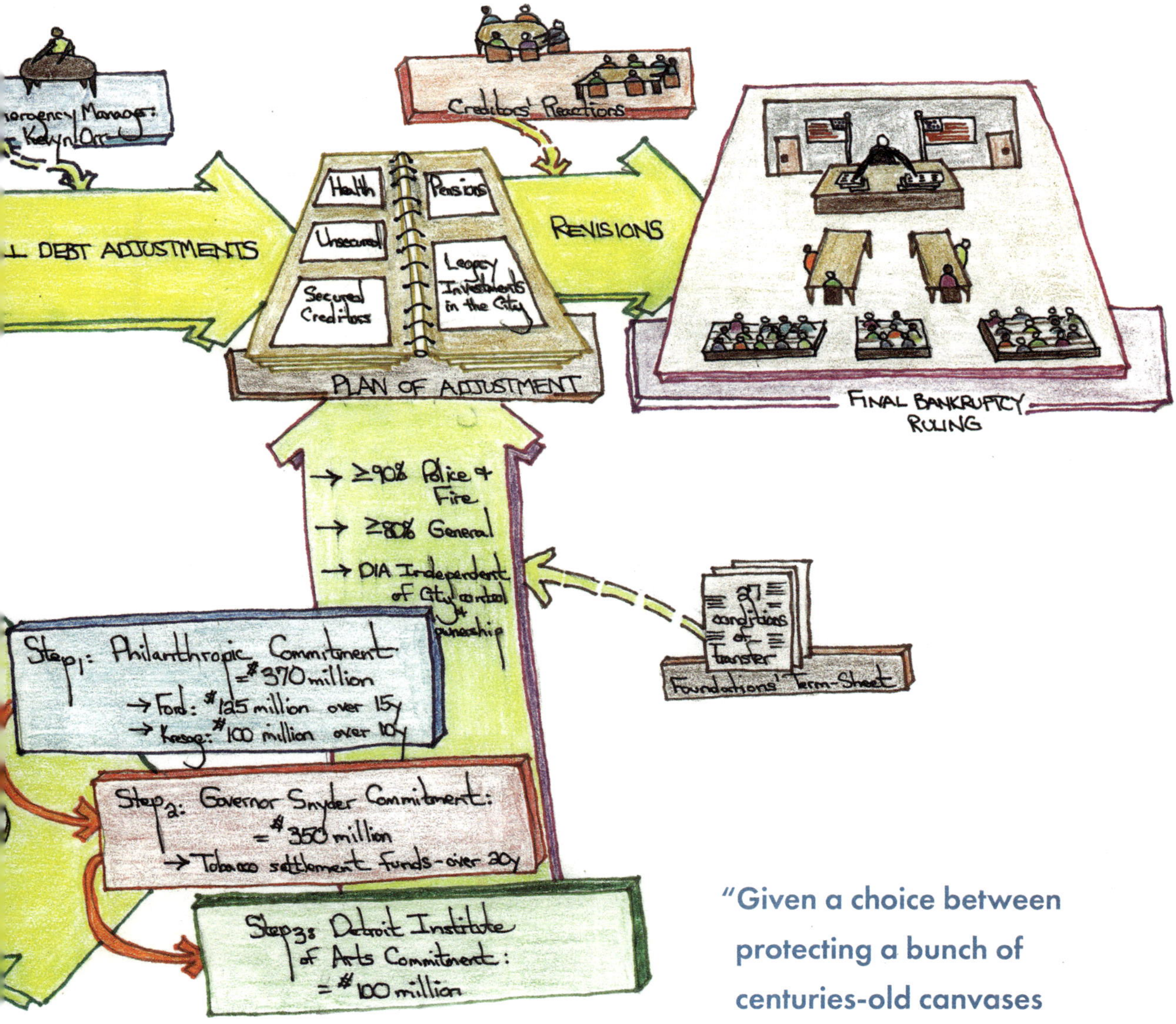

"Given a choice between protecting a bunch of centuries-old canvases or enabling retired public works employees to pay their water bills, people won't be faulted for choosing the latter."

Rosen left our dinner a happy man. I left more an uncertain one. I'd made a commitment in principle to a strategic construction of indeterminate shape, size, and viability. Even if the initial response from other foundation representatives was positive, it would almost certainly fall to Kresge and Ford to take the lead: making large dollar commitments, hammering out the conditions of our participation, managing communications, and so much else. And there was the small matter of ensuring that our governing boards would agree to such an unprecedented dive into the pool of municipal finance.

After my trip, I learned from Paul Hillegonds—the board member who had represented Kresge at Rosen's meeting—that the reception had been lukewarm. The numbers were just too big, and the ambiguities of debt mediation too complex, for anybody to immediately commit. Or even express serious interest. Indeed, for at least a week afterward, there was only radio silence.

"You just can't leave $370 million on the table."

The only good news—which would emerge publicly only much later—was in a cab-ride back from a dinner after the judge's presentation. Alberto Ibarguen, the president of the Knight Foundation, and Darren Walker of Ford, agreed that if the Rosen plan were to succeed, it would require lead gifts in the neighborhood of $100 million from the big fish—Kresge and Ford. That they were discussing it in these terms in the immediate aftermath of the meeting indicated the seeds of potential buy-in.

I called Walker to gauge his impressions. He said Rosen and his mediation team had made a compelling case. But Walker also affirmed that the overall mood was deep skepticism. "This is not what foundations do," he said. "I'm prepared to advocate for our participation, but I'm not sure I can get my board to go along. Setting aside the art, it will be a challenge convincing them that a foundation should invest in saving public pensions."

I suggested that we think about a form of indispensable mutuality: Kresge couldn't commit without commensurate support from the nation's largest philanthropy connected to Detroit, and Ford couldn't commit without the city's largest funder. Neither of us could go it alone. "Let me see what we can do at our end to keep the possibilities open," he said. "What level of commitment were you imagining?"

I replied that only a commitment in the neighborhood of $100 million from both foundations could make this happen. It would approach half of the minimum the judge had indicated he needed, sending an unequivocal message to our peers that we all needed to participate. Walker agreed.

Each of us then went back to float that proposition with our boards.

In a stroke of remarkable good fortune, we shared a board member of uncommon integrity and skill named Irene Hirano Inouye. The founder of the Japanese American Museum in Los Angeles, a member of dozens of national nonprofit boards, and the spouse of Senator Daniel Inouye of Hawaii, Hirano had served on the Kresge board since my 2006 arrival and was chair during my first two years. And Hirano was the current board chair at the Ford Foundation.

Hirano advocated passionately for our two organizations to see their fates as inextricably linked. Detroit was Kresge's hometown and Ford's place of origin. The city's fate had never been more dire—and the potential impact of philanthropy never clearer.

As Hirano worked both sides of the equation, the on-ramps to agreement came into brighter relief. Both organizations would commit at the levels Walker and I discussed, with

Ford coming in at $125 million, commensurate with its nearly $10 billion in assets, and Kresge anteing up $100 million from its $3.5 billion endowment. That gave us the confidence we needed to reconvene the region's foundations at the Kresge offices.

No other foundations had announced any commitments, so we jump-started the conversation by declaring Ford and Kresge's intent to contribute to the fund. Silence . . . I was taken aback. But then-Stuart Mott Foundation President William White, who was on the phone, opened the gates, telling the group, "OK, we're from Flint. But I'll open the bidding at $10 million." Others soon followed: the Knight Foundation at $30 million (which was later increased to 40). The William Davidson Foundation at $25 million. The Hudson Webber Foundation at $10 million. The Community Foundation of Southeast Michigan at $10 million. In the ensuing weeks, the total rose to $370 million.

It wasn't as much as Rosen wanted, but he had another card to play, and our pool of commitments gave him the opening he needed to play it. He paid a call on Governor Snyder to remind him that the state was constitutionally bound to prevent the impairment of pensions; they had an obligation to step into the vortex. When the governor seemed to balk, Rosen pulled out a handwritten list of the foundation commitments. "You just can't leave $370 million on the table," he urged.

The governor picked up Rosen's paper and gave it a long look. He shook his head and a smile emerged.

Silence . . . I was taken aback. But then-Stuart Mott Foundation President William White opened the gates: "OK, we're from Flint. But I'll open the bidding at $10 million." Others soon followed.

"You're right, judge," Snyder replied. He committed to finding a path to matching, with state funding, what philanthropy had raised: $350 million. Rosen's pot was now well within range of what he had hoped to assemble.

Somewhere along the way, Rosen had come up with the campaign moniker of "The Grand Bargain." But he wasn't quite through. Even though the Detroit Institute of Arts—like the pensioners—was an unwilling pawn in the bankruptcy chess game, being freed from creditor claims made contributing essential. The only question was how much.

Early expectations pegged that amount at $25 million; not an inconsiderable sum given the institution's modest endowment of around $100 million. In my conversations with Rosen, however, we realized that the figure had to be higher—much higher. It wasn't just the optics of the gulf between the value the DIA stood to receive and its proposed contribution, though that mattered. More important was the appraisal of the collection that Kevyn Orr had secured from Christie's auction house.

Christie's had opined that the heart of the DIA's collection (some 40 or 50 works of its 65,000) could command somewhere between $450 million and $866 million. Although that struck the creditors (and many art experts) as low by a factor of four or five, it gave Rosen what he needed to complete his calculus. And the appraisal underscored the need for the DIA to help supplement the $730 million in hand. Led by their board chair, Gene Gargaro, the institute promised to raise $100 million to support the fund.

The contours of the bargain had crystallized. The $830 million would go to the emergency manager to "purchase" the DIA's art and transfer it to a nonprofit outside the creditors' reach. That money would buffer the pensions from sharp decreases.

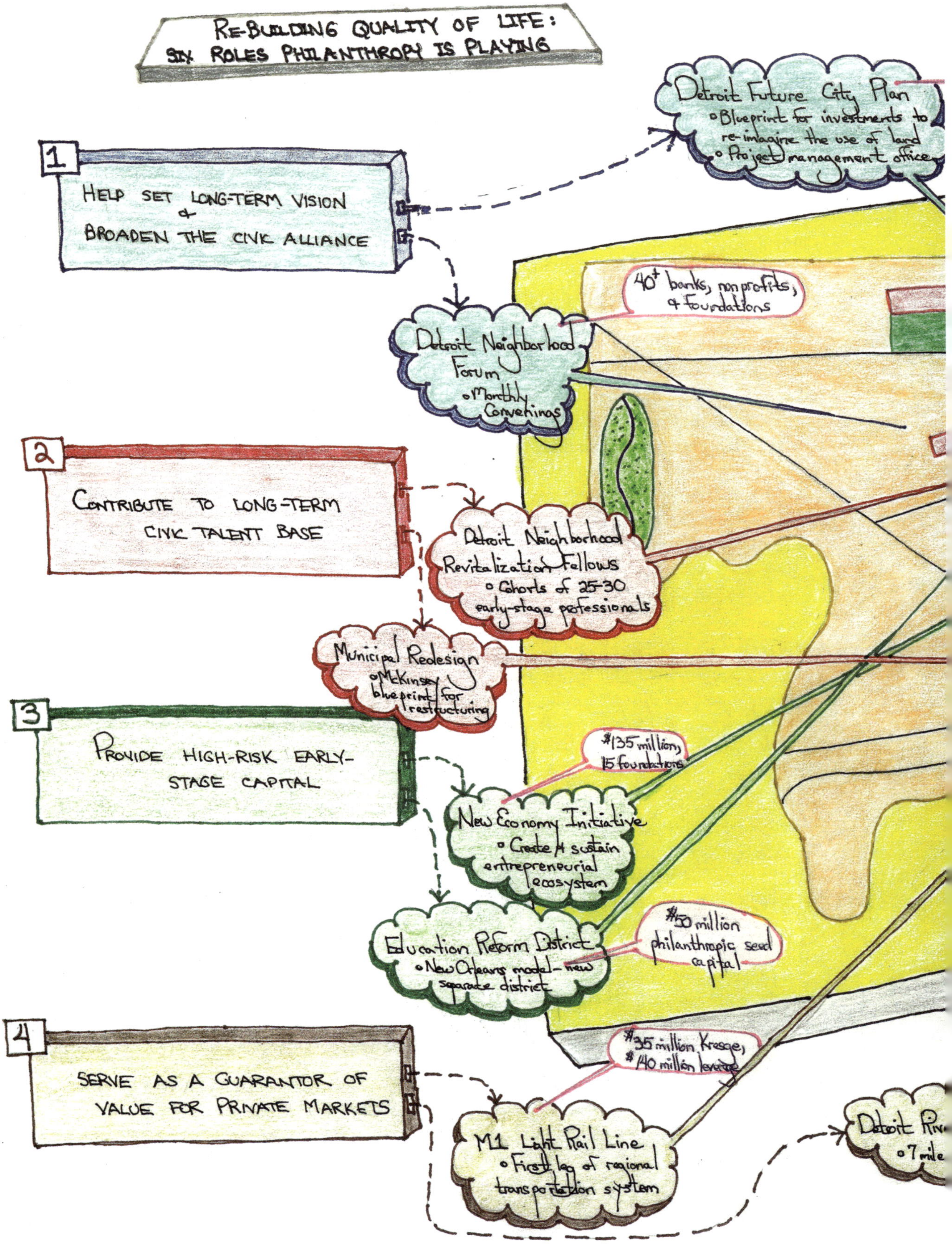
RE-BUILDING QUALITY OF LIFE:
SIX ROLES PHILANTHROPY IS PLAYING
1
HELP SET LONG-TERM VISION & BROADEN THE CIVIC ALLIANCE
Detroit Future City Plan
◦ Blueprint for investments to re-imagine the use of land
◦ Project management office
Detroit Neighborhood Forum
◦ Monthly Convenings
40+ banks, nonprofits, & foundations
2
CONTRIBUTE TO LONG-TERM CIVIC TALENT BASE
Detroit Neighborhood Revitalization Fellows
◦ Cohorts of 25-30 early-stage professionals
Municipal Redesign
◦ McKinsey blueprint for restructuring
3
PROVIDE HIGH-RISK EARLY-STAGE CAPITAL
$135 million, 15 foundations
New Economy Initiative
◦ Create & sustain entrepreneurial ecosystem
Education Reform District
◦ New Orleans model - new separate district
$50 million philanthropic seed capital
4
SERVE AS A GUARANTOR OF VALUE FOR PRIVATE MARKETS
$35 million Kresge, $140 million leverage
M1 Light Rail Line
◦ First leg of regional transportation system

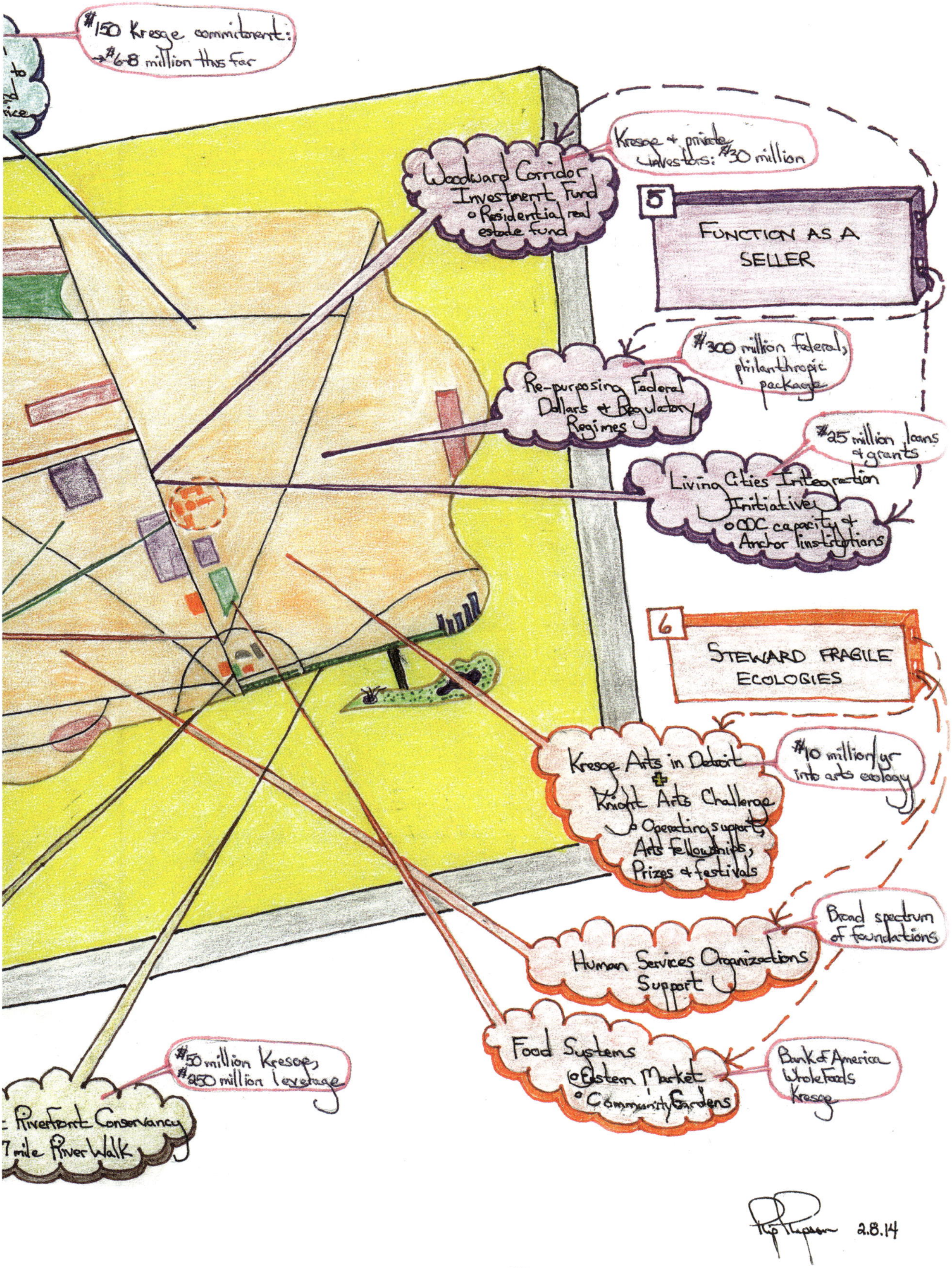
$150 Kresge commitment:
→$6-8 million thus far
Woodward Corridor Investment Fund
○ Residential real estate fund
Kresge + private investors: $30 million
5
FUNCTION AS A SELLER
$300 million federal, philanthropic package
Re-purposing Federal Dollars + Regulatory Regimes
$25 million loans + grants
Living Cities Integration Initiative
○ CDC capacity + Anchor institutions
6
STEWARD FRAGILE ECOLOGIES
Kresge Arts in Detroit
+
Knight Arts Challenge
○ Operating support, Arts fellowships, Prizes + festivals
$10 million/yr into arts ecology
Broad spectrum of foundations
Human Services Organizations Support
Food Systems
○ Eastern Market
○ Community Gardens
Bank of America
Whole Foods
Kresge
$50 million Kresge,
$250 million leverage
Riverfront Conservancy
7 mile River Walk
2.8.14

Even with the terms of that exchange solidified, the enormity and complexity of what Rosen would yet need to accomplish can't be overstated. His charge as mediator was to orchestrate a consensual resolution of all claims. That meant endless, exhaustive negotiations among all the creditors to convince them to relinquish claims to the art, forgo deep raids into the pensions, and accept 10-20 cents on the dollar in yet undetermined physical assets from the city. And Rosen also needed the philanthropic community to agree on the terms of its gifts.

Ford and Kresge took the lead in setting terms for the transfer of philanthropic dollars. Ford general counsel Ricardo Castro, Kresge chief investment officer Rob Manilla, and Kresge program director Laura Trudeau formed the team that would hammer out what came to be known as the "term sheet." The state of Michigan had to make good on its commitment to contribute. The pensioners had to vote to approve the ultimate bargain terms, including the provision that the funds would be parked at the Community Foundation for Southeast Michigan for distribution into the pension funds over a twenty-year period. And release of the funds would be subject to an oversight board, on which the foundations would be represented.

Judge Rhodes took it all in. He even allowed my drawing to be entered into evidence.

Perhaps most importantly, we agreed that the court had to approve the plan of adjustment proposed by the emergency manager; the bankruptcy in its entirety needed to be brought to resolution before the dollars would flow. We would not make our investments in a situation of unresolved, continuing litigation.

Throughout Rosen's shuttle diplomacy and the foundations' forging of the term sheet, Judge Rhodes had been moving the bankruptcy trial forward, taking testimony from community members, creditors, pensioners, and anyone else who wanted a say. It would fall to him to approve a plan—whether based on a consensual package predicated on the Grand Bargain or a set of terms imposed on unwilling parties. He needed to be thorough to a fault, transparent beyond critique, and fair in every dimension.

After Rhodes was convinced that the financial components of the litigation had fallen into place through Rosen and Orr's handiwork, he turned to the final puzzle piece. Rhodes conveyed that he would not approve a plan to close the bankruptcy only to have the city fall back into insolvency within a few years because it didn't have the community supports in place to rebuild the tax base and public services.

He sought testimony from three community representatives who had contributed to Detroit's stabilization over the previous five years, to determine whether their commitment to the city and its revitalization remained strong: Roger Penske, the corporate leader who had spearheaded the M-1 Light Rail effort; Dan Gilbert, who'd moved the Quicken Loans headquarters into downtown Detroit three years earlier; and me.

Penske and Gilbert testified forcefully to their continuing commitment. I then echoed their sentiments, testifying that the roles Kresge had played before the bankruptcy were the same roles we intended to play following bankruptcy. For years, we had used different tools to address a range of the city's challenges. I pledged that Kresge would continue to deploy those tools—tied to a different set of problems—once Detroit emerged from bankruptcy and the public and private sectors reassumed their proper roles. Our commitments included:

- Acting as a neutral convenor to facilitate conversations in which the community could address "third-rail" issues such as land use and blight remediation.
- Helping build a new generation of community problem-solving capacity, as we had by creating the New Economy Initiative to help foster and sustain entrepreneurship.
- Serving as social venture capital by peeling back the first layer of financial risk on community development transactions, as we'd done in enticing private markets to invest in multiple commercial projects that contributed to the revitalization of the Woodward Corridor.
- Investing in public spaces and infrastructure that would show the private sector that essential quality-of-life building blocks were in place, as we had in the reclamation of the Riverfront, the conversion of a barren downtown intersection into a vibrant public park, and the introduction of a light rail line along the city's main arterial.
- Serving as ambassadors to spur the infusion of talent and money into Detroit, as we had when encouraging other foundations to invest in Detroit pre-bankruptcy.
- Helping safeguard nonprofit and community organizations working at the knife's edge of survival, as we had done with arts and culture organizations, human service providers, and the city's nascent food economy.

Judge Rhodes took it all in. He even allowed my drawing to be entered into evidence.

In December 2014, the judge approved the plan of adjustment, releasing the city of Detroit from bankruptcy.

The skill—brilliance—with which Rosen, Orr, and Rhodes had executed their roles is even more striking in retrospect. The city had shed 40 percent of its $18 billion debt, restructured another 17 percent on more favorable terms, and embraced a multiyear $1.7 billion plan to revitalize city services and operations. The creditors had agreed to the package, accepting the transfer of multiple real estate parcels with future development value. The pensioners had made very real sacrifices, but emerged with the least possible reduction to their pensions. The art had been preserved and transferred into a nonprofit entity that would be free from future claims.

That Detroit had emerged from its nightmare consensually, and in under eighteen months, foretold a new era in the city's trajectory. The ignominy of being the largest municipal bankruptcy in American history was replaced by a sense of rising from the ashes. The city was ready to begin its renewal in earnest. The Grand Bargain was key to it all.

The ignominy of being the largest municipal bankruptcy in American history was replaced by a sense of rising from the ashes.

Indeed, it would be easy to come away with the conclusion that the financial transaction itself was the central innovation. After all, if philanthropy hadn't assembled its $366 million contribution, none of the rest would have been possible. But aggregating capital—at least not in isolation—is not necessarily a prescription for resolving other municipal bankruptcies. The more significant and replicable process innovation was demonstrating that the public, private, and philanthropic sectors—by redistributing resources and the responsibilities of their traditional roles—could illuminate an ingenious path forward.

How that innovation played out was unique to one place at a unique moment in time, fueled by a unique interplay of community actors and relationships. And yet in some form, it has applicability to any city where different sectors join forces to creatively redeploy resources—whether financial, material, organizational, or managerial.

The Detroit bankruptcy underscores philanthropy's ability to engage a community's most intractable challenges. Not just at the moment the Grand Bargain was forged, but also in the years leading up to the bankruptcy. Working with the private and public sectors, philanthropy helped construct a scaffolding necessary to stabilize a city in extremis. Light rail. Land use. Parks and open space. Small business development. Commercial corridor revitalization. Arts and cultural activity. Social services. Essential ingredients for a federal bankruptcy judge to conclude that Detroit would emerge from bankruptcy equipped to begin its long-term renewal.

Joining forces with the federal government to jump-start Detroit's recovery

"We can't forgive your bonds. And heaven knows we can't get anything through the Congress. But the President wants to find some way to help."

The call from Gene Sperling, head of the Council on Economic Advisers for President Barack Obama, came at the beginning of the Detroit bankruptcy. Sperling went on to explain that representatives of the Administration wanted to come to Detroit and "figure something out."

I encouraged him not to do that. Getting who-knows-how-many people together to talk about a federal response in the middle of the bankruptcy would, I suggested, be a dumpster fire. It would encourage an assumption that Detroit City Hall was the focal point for solving the problem, when in fact its hands were tied because of the bankruptcy-imposed limbo.

And it would be impossible to construct a manageable guest list: too many disparate interests would be jockeying for advantage. Without adequate preparation defining the meeting's scope, purpose, and methods, it would be impossible to actually accomplish anything. And then there was the politics: word would get out and it would become a media feeding frenzy.

"There will be a time and place for your team to come to Detroit. But I would narrow the scope first," I said.

Sperling was taken aback. "Well, we've got to do something," he countered. This was true. "What would you suggest?"

I suggested our philanthropic community might first lay some foundation. "We could identify five or six of the city's most pressing priorities, then match that up against available federal funding flows, the policies we think would be most helpful, and areas in which the administration might have some discretion. We could then send that off to you as a way of getting started," I proposed.

"Sounds good, but this can't be a prolonged, academic exercise. I can't wait months," Sperling replied. "How fast can you turn something like that around?" I asked for two weeks.

Kresge staffer Laura Trudeau quickly took the lead in synthesizing analyses of potential federal channels of help in housing, commercial blight, public safety, transportation, and information technology. We sent the summary to Sperling. Shortly thereafter, Sperling called me again.

"It's great! Just what we needed—a perfect working document," he said. "We're circulating it among some of our departments and agencies for their reactions. Could you organize a group of folks who know enough about these issues to keep pushing this forward, and bring them to D.C.?"

We assembled a team of people who'd been working on the issues our white paper had identified, including Dan Gilbert, CEO of Quicken Loans; Matt Cullen, head of the M-1 Rail board; Nancy Schlichting, CEO of the Henry Ford Health System; former Mayor Dennis Archer; and Debbie Dingell, then a lobbyist (later to become John Dingell's successor in the House of Representatives). And me. Days later, our Detroit contingent was ushered into the spacious Roosevelt Conference Room off the Oval Office. We expected to see Sperling and perhaps two or three aides.

We were flabbergasted to see almost the entire Cabinet—and then some—sitting at the conference table.

We were flabbergasted to see almost the entire Cabinet—and then some—sitting at the conference table: Valerie Jarrett, the President's special adviser; Cecilia Munoz, head of the Domestic Policy Council; Attorney General Eric Holder; HUD Secretary Shaun Donovan; Todd Park, chief technology officer; and numerous secretaries and assistant secretaries from Commerce, Treasury, and other departments and agencies.

Everyone present was well acquainted with the analysis we'd forwarded, Sperling explained, so we could jump right into discussing what the departments felt they might be able to do.

We started with housing. The white paper had suggested four or five federal programs that could help remediate blighted and abandoned properties and encourage improvements in public housing. Before the administration representatives could say anything, Dan Gilbert declared: "We need to eliminate every blighted house in the city. All 90,000 of them." He pounded the table for emphasis. Secretary Donovan—familiar with the scope and complexity of such a vast undertaking—smiled.

"You think that's possible?" Donovan asked Gilbert.

"It damn well better be," Gilbert replied. Donovan proceeded to ask if Gilbert would then be willing to head up a Blight Task Force to accomplish that if the administration could find federal resources to help. "Done," Gilbert said. He committed to putting the full weight of his company behind the task force.

The task force was created immediately after our return. The effort mapped every blighted parcel in the city (roughly 370,000 of them) into a database organized by Quicken. A hundred two-person teams of young people armed with smartphones would drive the city's streets and beam photos of each property back into Quicken's "war room," which became command central. Armed with the expertise of one of the nation's largest housing lenders, staff in that war room would ask the photographers to zoom in on a home's foundation or get a wider angle shot of the roof.

Those data were combined with almost two dozen other public data sources—records of electrical or water shut-offs, delinquent taxes, titles of ownership, 911 calls, and the like—to create a composite, comprehensive depiction of that parcel. Times 370,000. It took six months, but it became the bedrock of the city's comprehensive plan to attack blight.

Back in the Roosevelt room, the meeting's second topic was transit. Our efforts to move the M-1 rail project forward were being stalled by a particularly thorny set of federal transportation regulations governing labor relations. After Matt Cullen laid out the situation, Deputy Secretary of Transportation John Porcari said the matter would be resolved without further delay. Indeed, a written order lifting the roadblock was in our inboxes by the time we returned to Detroit that evening.

Next up, public safety. Attorney General Holder said he believed he could identify public safety funding that hadn't been used in other cities—including dedicated funds for community-oriented policing and the purchase of protective police gear—and could be redirected to Detroit.

The conversation continued to move around the room for more than three hours. As it wound to a close, Chief Technology Officer Todd Park quietly apologized that he didn't have a budget to offer up. "But I *can* invite the chief technology officers of Google, Microsoft, and other major tech firms to do an audit of what you have."

Park was true to his word. That audit of Detroit's 19th century technology capacities, right down to hand-written index cards containing tax records, generated an ambitious, far-reaching plan that would enable the city over the next three years to leapfrog an entire generation of technological advances and create state-of-the-art 21st century capacities. (One of the members of Park's audit team, Beth Niblock, chief technology officer for the city of Louisville, was recruited to that role in Detroit a year later by Mayor Mike Duggan.)

We left the White House with Sperling's assurance that he would further workshop the ideas we'd discussed.

And he delivered on that promise, assembling cross-agency working groups for each of Detroit's top priorities and tasking them with delivering specific, actionable or investable next steps.

The audit of Detroit's 19th century technology capacities—right down to tax records hand-written on index cards—generated a plan that would enable the city to leapfrog an entire generation of technology and create state-of-the-art practices.

Weeks later, I got another call from him. It was vintage Sperling. "We've got something, Rip. It's big. We've got a clear bead on what we can do from our end. But we'll need a little bit of help from you and the other members of the foundation community," he said. "I'll send you what we have, but you'll have to keep it under your hat—if it's leaked out before we're ready, it could blow up in our faces." He then told me to watch my email.

Minutes later, a new and greatly enhanced version of our white paper arrived in my inbox. It was indeed "big": a $300 million assistance package. With just one catch: it hinged on a $50 million commitment from Detroit philanthropy, to demonstrate that we had skin in the game.

True to the Roosevelt Room meeting, it contained funding for residential demolition ... unprecedented permission to use Community Development Block Grant funds for commercial demolition ... reallocation of unused funding from other cities for bus purchase and repair ... transfer of law enforcement equipment and money for community policing efforts ... official notice that the Department of Transportation would waive the regulatory obstacles impeding the M-1 light rail project ... acknowledgement of Park's IT audit.

Contingent, of course, on the $50 million from Detroit foundations. Kresge pulled in Ford, Skillman, and other foundation partners to calculate how we could meet Sperling's commitment threshold. He'd let us know that the optics were as important as the dollar levels: we could count grants we had in the pipeline or had already budgeted for.

Philanthropy met the $50 million bar.

Soon thereafter, a group of Obama Administration representatives led by Sperling came to Detroit to unveil the package. It was a stunning affirmation of the work that Emergency Finance Manager Kevyn Orr and Mayor Mike Duggan were doing to stabilize funding for essential services. Indeed, the package was consistent with, and dramatically accelerated, implementation of the Plan of Adjustment that the federal bankruptcy court approved months later.

The Obama Administration had been full throated in its support of Detroit from the outset. From the initial call from Derek Douglas four years earlier . . . to the launch of the Smart Cities Smart Communities initiative . . . to Secretary LaHood's embrace of the M-1 light rail project . . . to the assignment of a Treasury Department executive in Detroit to serve as a liaison to Washington . . . to the announcement of the Sperling package . . . the administration showed up for the city in a steady and substantive way. It was an astounding level of sustained commitment.

Not every city could command this kind of attention, of course. But in the process of addressing the exceptional case, the federal commitment modeled a very different way of working with cities. It was like capillary action: by establishing new mechanisms of receptivity to innovation and local knowledge, the federal government enabled the Detroit community's framing of issues and strategies to scale the wall of federal policy and funding. The interactions between national and local actors created the kind of trust and cohesion to yield stunning progress.

The interactions between national and local actors created the kind of trust and cohesion to yield stunning progress.

That progress wasn't *bestowed* on Detroit—the city was an equal partner in creating it. Despite the immense complexities of the bankruptcy, Detroit had deployed its collective intellect, creativity, and spirit in a systematic, methodical way. It was muscle memory that would be called into play many years later, when President Joe Biden's administration challenged communities across the country to summon the ideas and capacities necessary to land federal American Relief Act, Infrastructure, and Inflation Reduction Act funds.

24 Immaculate Conception

Transforming a college closure into an unprecedented model of educational promise

Elizabeth Burns didn't ask to be president of Marygrove College, a century-old Catholic progressive college in Northwestern Detroit, but now she was and had no good options.

The Sisters of the Immaculate Heart of Mary had opened the 53-acre, bucolic campus in 1927 to train teachers. Over the ensuing ninety years, the college had educated generations of teachers, artists, and social workers, drawing extensively from the surrounding Black, predominantly working-class neighborhoods and rooting the school's mission deeply in the Order's tenets of social justice.

Located a mile to the west of the University of Detroit Mercy, Marygrove had also become an anchoring presence in the Livernois-Six Mile Road neighborhood. Marygrove was a stone's throw from some of the most stable middle-class Black neighborhoods in the city and the historic "Avenue of Fashion" along Livernois Avenue, a 1960s Black retail mecca that had—like the city itself—suffered flight and disinvestment in the subsequent decades.

Marygrove had been afflicted by the same dwindling funding and declining enrollment dogging many other independent colleges, including Catholic colleges, throughout the country over the last twenty years. In an effort to raise money for building maintenance and program expansion, President David Fike had encouraged the Sisters to deed the land to the college, which had in turn pledged the land as collateral for a variety of loans, which could be paid off by projected expanded enrollment. In 2013, Fike had also relaxed the college's admissions standards in an attempt to boost enrollment.

Neither of these stratagems worked: the college wasn't able to adequately serve the higher student numbers, and the retention rate took a nosedive from about 70 percent in 2012 to 40 percent by 2017, while enrollment sank from 1,041 students to 667. At those levels, the enrollment couldn't begin to produce revenues equal to the debt obligations.

When the board took full account of just how dire the situation was, it moved to replace its administration. Fike left to lead a university on the West Coast; two subsequent interim presidents revolved out quickly.

In 2015, the board asked one of its most respected members, Beth Burns, to move into the president's role. A Marygrove alum who had been a medical college administrator following a pediatric practice, the straight-as-an-arrow Burns was passionate about the college's mission of serving the residents of Detroit. Shortly after she took the reins, Burns called me at Kresge.

She explained that the college was in a difficult financial situation, but had developed a blueprint for renewal. Knowing of Kresge's deep investments in the Livernois/Six Mile neighborhood, she asked if I would arrange a meeting of Detroit foundations in which she could share the college's plans and test the waters for potential support. About two weeks later, we gathered a dozen foundations in the large conference room of the College's grand Madame Cadillac building.

Burns told the group that Marygrove was running a $5 million annual shortfall on its $20 million annual budget. She walked us through a presentation that suggested balancing the budget through a dramatic increase in online education and draconian cuts in spending. An infusion from philanthropy was essential to underwrite these changes and to bridge to a balanced budget, Burns explained. Without that, Marygrove would have to close.

It was inconceivable that a campus that had anchored the community for almost a century might shutter just as revitalization in the neighborhood was gaining momentum.

Although a few of the foundations showed openness to helping with the short-term cash crunch, there was less enthusiasm for underwriting the larger bailout package. I suggested that Burns open the college's books and give us a few weeks to excavate the underlying finances and assess the package's viability.

Somewhat surprisingly, she hesitated: clearly there were issues she hadn't shared with the group. But Burns quickly recognized that there was no alternative.

Kresge commissioned an external forensic audit, and I tasked Aaron Seybert of Kresge's staff with monitoring its progress. A former banker at J.P. Morgan Chase who'd been charged with delivering some of Detroit's most complex financial transactions, Seybert had recently joined the foundation's social investments practice. He was ideally suited to manage a thorough and accurate audit.

We soon understood why Burns had hesitated in wanting to subject the college's finances, data systems, and academic practices to outside view. The audit laid bare fiscal opacity, mismanagement, and perhaps even malfeasance. Indeed, it revealed landmines far beyond what Burns and her board had suspected.

In addition to disturbingly high faculty compensation, extremely low professor-to-student classroom ratios, and staggering levels of deferred maintenance, the audit exposed the depth the financial hole the college had dug. A bank loan of $7.5 million was due at the end of 2016. The college was in default on a $500,000 loan from Wayne County for renovating of the former Immaculata High School building. The United States Department of Education would likely require Marygrove to post a $7 million letter of credit to backstop the extension of $15 million in financial aid. The prospects for meaningfully expanding enrollment through online courses seemed remote at best.

Then there was the small matter of the Sisters having pledged as collateral almost $10 million of their pensions to support the college's operations. It was unthinkable that they'd seek repayment if that came at the cost of Marygrove having to shutter. And yet, the pledge was a moral obligation somebody had to recognize.

Having tracked each detail of the audit's findings, Seybert was convinced that the scope of the interventions necessary to rescue the institution was insurmountable—at least, for Kresge.

First and foremost, the money needed simply to stave off creditors could approach $15 to $20 million—and that would merely serve to buy time.

Second, there were students, faculty, staff, operations, and community ties that required a longer-term solution if Marygrove were to continue operating.

And third, giving the college even just a fighting chance of survival would require a complex suite of non-monetary assistance—skill in financial negotiation, expertise in debt restructuring, capacities to formulate crisis communications, competence to pursue program redesign, and a great deal more.

Seybert's advice to me was accordingly succinct and forthright: "It would be too much for one foundation to take on, and with no guarantee of success. Let the entire house of cards collapse. We can still catch it on the bounce before the creditors swoop in. We'll just start over." This, I thought, is why we have brilliant financial brains on our staff.

On the other hand, maybe brilliant financial brains could take the analysis only so far.

It seemed unfathomable that Marygrove's 90-year legacy as a progressive educational force might come to an end. And it was inconceivable that a campus that had anchored the community for almost a century might shutter just as revitalization in the neighborhood was gaining momentum. Without philanthropic help, the college would either wind up dismembered by creditors in a bankruptcy—or be immobilized for years in a stream of lawsuits.

I told Seybert that although his analysis was impeccable and deeply appreciated, we needed to employ the full spectrum of our resources and wade in. Declining to intervene simply wasn't an option. Nor was waiting on multiple foundations to sort out the situation at their customary speed of continental drift.

I asked Seybert to identify what strategies Kresge could pull from its toolbox to address each element of debt the audit had surfaced. We needed to *ju jitsu* each to enable Burns's administration and the Sisters to find a way forward. Even though it was their path to choose, not ours, Kresge would have to undergird them with money, advice, and technical support.

I asked Seybert to identify what strategies Kresge could pull from its toolbox to address each element of debt. We needed to *ju jitsu* each to enable a way forward.

Seybert turned on a dime, quickly surfacing ideas for helping the college navigate away from the immediate threats. Among his ideas: negotiating with the bank to write down their loan; urging forbearance from the county until the situation sorted itself out; opening a line of communication with the Department of Education to gauge whether we could reduce the size of the letter of credit required to free student loans to Marygrove's students. All this while simultaneously keeping Marygrove's educational programming intact.

This would be just the beginning of a stabilization and rescue effort, Seybert explained. After those short-term interventions, we'd have to work with the administration to explore hard decisions about how to recalibrate the college's cost structure to carry it into the next academic year. And finally, we'd have to develop a long-term plan.

From undertaking the forensics, to assembling a stabilization package, to pivoting toward reimagination: distinct competencies within a single undertaking. It would be a tall order. "What are our odds," I asked? "I'm not sure, but they're pretty long," Seybert replied with his customary directness. "We'll have to get a bit lucky. And it will be really hard and really expensive, no matter how lucky we are."

Over the next 18 months, Kresge stood with, and gave support to, Marygrove's administration as they made exceedingly difficult decisions to move toward short-term stabilization. Declaring "financial exigency"—the academic equivalent of bankruptcy—they cut administrative staff, reduced course offerings, pierced the guarantees of faculty tenure, and finally, pulled the plug on their undergraduate programs to reposition the college as a graduate-level and certificate-granting institution only.

The pain points along the way were excruciating. Seybert used all the tricks of his long deal-making career to ease the pressure by restructuring the college's most pressing debts. Kresge took over—and assumed the risk for—the college's loans. We issued a letter of credit to satisfy the Department of Education, paid off the Wayne County loan, and made grants to maintain academic and campus operations. We created stipends to enable undergraduates to transfer to other colleges, provided two semesters of salary for faculty and staff, and made grants to stabilize and upgrade the physical plant. And we transferred the campus to a conservancy, beyond the reach of creditors, that would be governed by a community board led by Sister Jane Herb, head of the order.

The pain points along the way were excruciating.

All told, the stabilization package amounted to nearly $20 million.

Even as Marygrove closed out one chapter of its history, we opened a conversation with the sisters and Burns about how to preserve Marygrove's educational and community-centered legacy while retaining the campus's centrality to neighborhood life. The Sisters were, throughout, the key voice. Nobody would have moved in a direction they didn't support. And they staunchly supported any solution that preserved the mission of serving the community.

We quickly seized on the idea of converting the campus into a "cradle to career" campus in which we could colocate an early childhood center, a high school, some elements of college or graduate programming, community programming, and perhaps novel revenue-generating activities.

The concept became a magnet for interesting ideas. Some were sensible but financially unfeasible; for instance, a Catholic high school proposed expanding onto campus if Kresge provided millions of dollars of subsidies. Some were not quite so sensible, but tempting; for example, a private company suggesting that it locate its workforce training programs on campus. And some were eminently worth pursuing: such as creating a Detroit satellite campus for a university without a presence in the city.

Then a deeply serious, compelling, and brilliant idea walked in the door.

Elizabeth Moje, dean of the University of Michigan's College of Education, had been evolving a theory that a medical school residency model might work for teacher training. Rather than the century-old practice of injecting education graduates into a classroom after a few months of student teaching experience, Moje proposed stretching out the training period over a teacher's first three years on the job—as we do with aspiring physicians—and providing them with ongoing supervision and training.

Moje believed that a University of Michigan-sponsored K-12 school on the Marygrove campus might be the perfect vehicle to test the idea. Education students, whether undergraduates or graduate students, would complete their student teaching at the school under the guidance of high school administrators, veteran teachers, and university professors. They would then stay on for three years as salaried "residents" teaching in the classrooms—again, with the guidance of experienced colleagues.

Moje's vision was that once the program was up and running, two-thirds of the school's teachers would be veteran teachers, and one-third residents. As the residents improved their teaching skills, they would in turn help mentor those following behind. Once a teacher completed the three-year residency, they could stay at the school, if openings were available, or transfer to another school.

And then, a deeply serious, compelling, and brilliant idea walked in the door.

Moje's idea intrigued Nikolai Vitti, the newly arrived head of the Detroit Public Schools Community District. Kresge agreed to broker conversations between Vitti, Moje, and University of Michigan President Mark Schlissel to explore the concept further. Schlissel was keen to establish a flagship program that would demonstrate the University's commitment to the city of Detroit. The university operated scores of small programs in the city, but nothing with the visibility that the Marygrove project promised. Vitti was excited about the possibility of a new school model that could appeal to students and parents who might otherwise look for school options outside the district.

The next puzzle piece was a preschool.

Kresge, along with the Kellogg Foundation, had launched an effort a few years prior to strengthen the city's early childhood development system. Called "Hope Starts Here," the initiative envisioned creating a handful of state-of-the-art early childhood centers bringing preschool, health, and community services together at a single site. Were we successful in establishing a University of Michigan-Detroit Public Schools high school on the Marygrove campus, one of those early childhood centers could be built right next door on open space in the campus's eastern quadrant.

The potential synergies would be powerful. One could imagine a continuum in which a neighborhood child started in the early childhood program, moved through the primary grades and high school, and received early admission preference to the University of Michigan. The University expressed willingness to extend its training, research, and evaluation programs into the preschool. And the center could become a resource for early childhood care providers in the neighborhood.

Working with Detroit's premier early childhood care provider, Starfish Family Services, Kresge committed to building the center.

As the first center of its kind to be built in the city, it needed to convey excellence in every dimension of its design and programming. We contracted with Marlon Blackwell Associates, an Arkansas architectural firm whose broad body of work would subsequently earn the American Institute of Architects' prestigious Gold Medal. The center's exterior would need to blend with the turn-of-the-last-century campus buildings, yet convey a 21st century aesthetic—something Blackwell accomplished with a daring multicolored terra cotta façade. The open layout placed a premium on natural light through extensive use of glass, skylights, playful colors, and fluid connection of spaces. And I pushed Blackwell to integrate the indoors and outdoors by creating interior courtyards that would provide direct

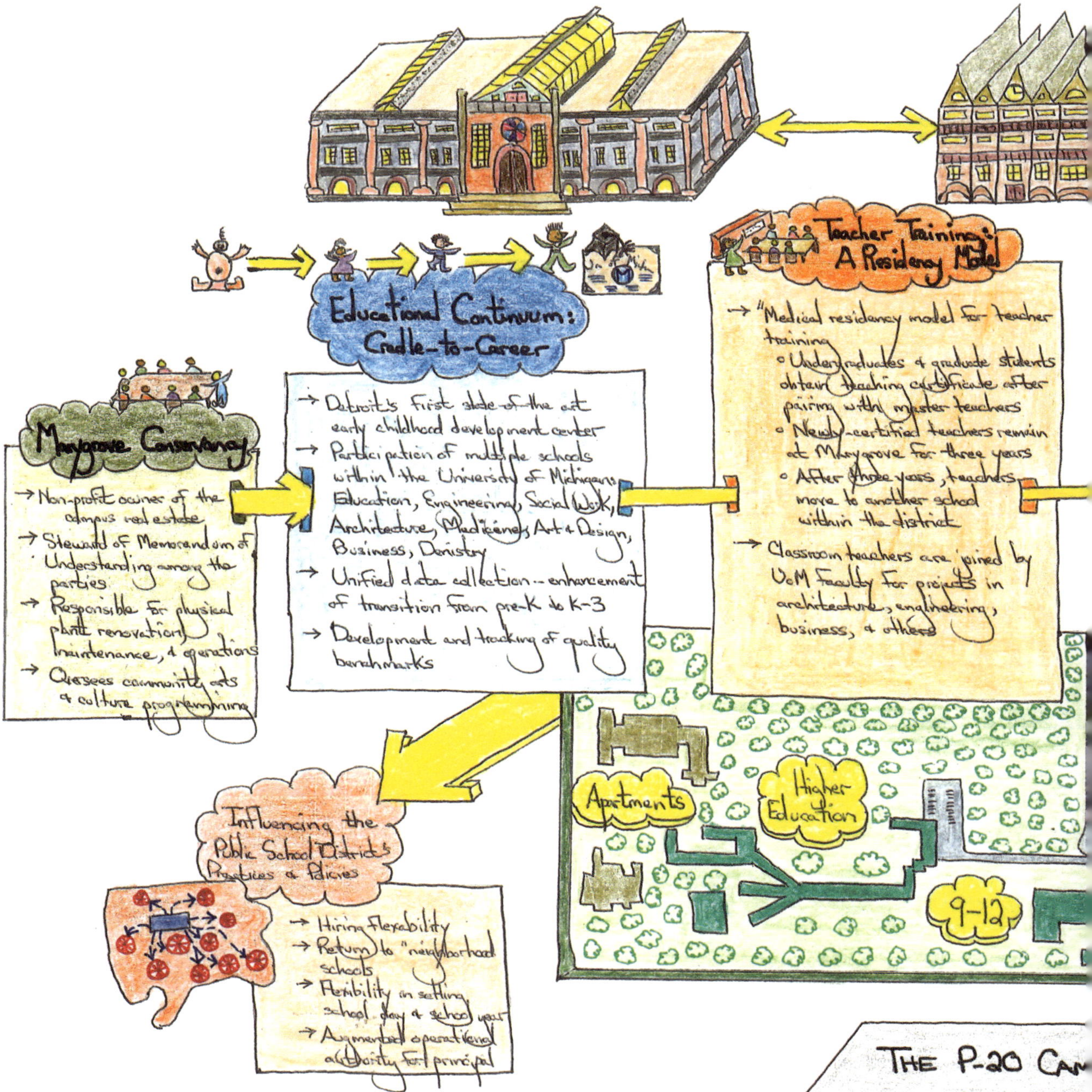

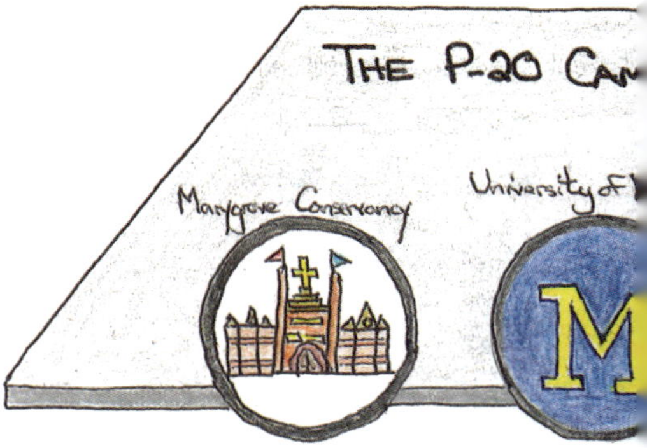

The potential synergies would be powerful. Imagine a neighborhood child starting in the early childhood program, moving through the primary grades and high school, and receiving early admission preference to the University of Michigan.

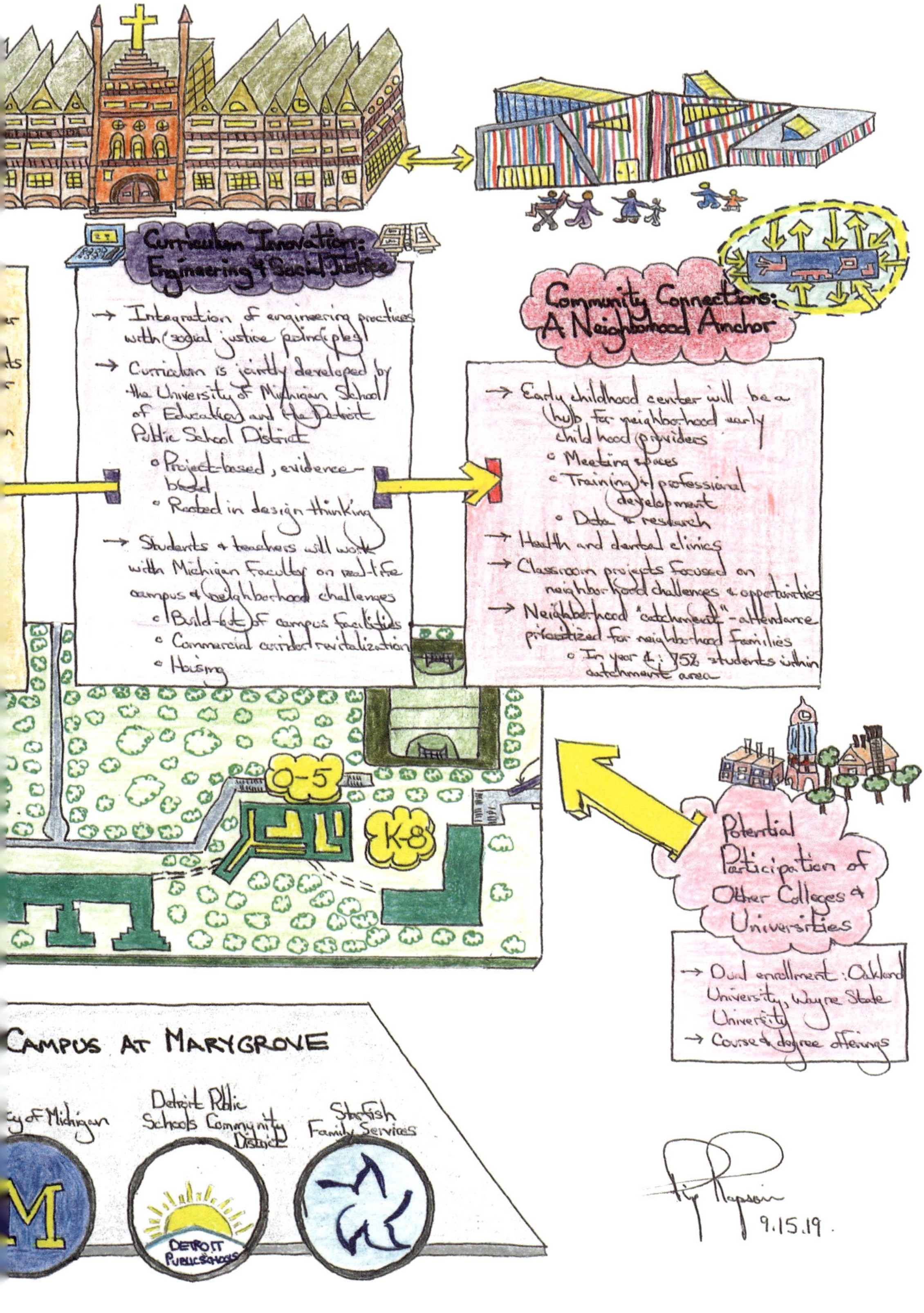

Curriculum Innovation: Engineering & Social Justice
→ Integration of engineering practices with social justice principles
→ Curriculum is jointly developed by the University of Michigan School of Education and the Detroit Public School District
◦ Project-based, evidence-based
◦ Rooted in design thinking
→ Students & teachers will work with Michigan Faculty on real-life campus & neighborhood challenges
◦ Build-out of campus facilities
◦ Commercial corridor revitalization
◦ Housing
Community Connections: A Neighborhood Anchor
→ Early childhood center will be a hub for neighborhood early childhood providers
◦ Meeting spaces
◦ Training & professional development
◦ Data & research
→ Health and dental clinics
→ Classroom projects focused on neighborhood challenges & opportunities
→ Neighborhood "catchment" - attendance prioritized for neighborhood families
◦ In year 1: 75% students within catchment area
0-5
K-8
Potential Participation of Other Colleges & Universities
→ Dual enrollment: Oakland University, Wayne State University
→ Course & degree offerings
CAMPUS AT MARYGROVE
y of Michigan
Detroit Public Schools Community District
Starfish Family Services
M
DETROIT PUBLIC SCHOOLS
9.15.19.

lines of sight, and access, to the site's existing grove of mature oak trees and its naturally landscaped playground.

As the plans for the center proceeded, Schlissel and Moje worked with Vitti to fashion a high school focused on applied engineering, design, and social justice that would serve more than a thousand students. They committed to enlisting other University units to provide wraparound services and additional programming on the campus, including the schools of architecture, urban planning, business, dentistry, nursing, engineering, social work, and pharmacy.

Vitti managed to convince the board of education to waive some of the district's customary policy constraints. The board agreed to reserve 80 percent of the K-8 seats to families within a two-mile area; give all eighth-grade graduates automatic enrollment into the high school; substitute a new hands-on engineering curriculum for the district's standard curriculum; allow the principal to be hired outside the confines of the normal union contract provisions; and exempt the school from certain collective bargaining rules around recruitment, retention, and development of the school's teachers.

The open layout placed a premium on natural light through extensive use of glass, skylights, playful colors, and fluid connection of spaces.

By the time the memorandum of understanding was signed in 2018 among the university, the school district, Starfish, the Marygrove Conservancy, and Kresge, our foundation had committed an additional $50 million to the spectrum of components on campus: building renovations; the conservancy's operating budget; and construction and operation of the early childhood center. Together with the $20 million Kresge had already invested in stabilizing the college, the sum was the second largest commitment in Kresge's history—second only to the Grand Bargain. And it was the largest philanthropic investment ever to a single neighborhood revitalization effort in Detroit.

The School at Marygrove saw its full high school open in 2023, together with the K-2 grades of the elementary school—with the remaining grades to be phased in over subsequent years. The school has drawn more than 60 percent of its students from the surrounding neighborhoods, 97 percent from Detroit, and 50 percent from students previously attending suburban districts and charter schools.

The Early Childhood Center opened its doors in fall 2021 to 150 children, offering both subsidized and full-pay preschool as well as a health clinic, wraparound social services, a library, and community meeting spaces for daycare providers in the neighborhood.

The Marygrove Conservancy has renovated the campus's buildings to house the school and office space for local nonprofits. The campus has become the neighborhood's arts and cultural hub, complete with a performing arts auditorium, artist workspaces, an art gallery, a sprung-floor equipped dance studio, and rehearsal rooms. Where once the inescapable outcome seemed to be a beautiful and historic campus going dark and being sold off in pieces, there is now a multipurpose campus standing at the heart of the district's efforts to revitalize its housing stock, create new open space, and breathe new life into its commercial corridors.

Along with the Grand Bargain, Marygrove recalibrated the community's expectations of how each sector could participate in civic problem-solving. Faced with challenges of such extraordinary magnitude and complexity, no single sector could crack the code alone. The public sector's command-and-control structure can be too rigid, one-dimensional, and limited in vision. The private sector's sensitivitities to market imperatives can delimit the nature of the challenges it's willing to engage. The academic sector's focus on research and analysis, however valuable, can constrain the range of its engagement.

What grew up on the Marygrove campus was a form of social reverse-engineering. Once there was an agreed-upon articulation of the challenge, each of the involved sectors had to identify the most suitable tools from its toolbox and negotiate with one another how best to mix and match those tools, determine the proper dose and sequence of their deployment, and reach consensus on the pacing of the joint activities.

It was a form of distributive leadership in which the unique qualities of each sector are accentuated or subordinated at various points in the process as different institutions take the lead, over time, on different issues.

It's important to acknowledge that the weightier and more complex the problem, the harder it can be to assemble, maintain, and fortify a coherent collective effort. Public officials can't afford to take their eyes off the politics, which may become uncertain and fraught. Private actors can become hamstrung when working outside the lane of short-term market objectives. Academic players can't ignore the magnetic fields of institutional constraints grounded in research and funding. And foundations incline toward a default assumption that their fundamental purpose is making grants.

And yet. Despite the difficulties of comprehending a challenge in its full magnitude when faced with a multitude of short term pressures, consider setting your sights against a distant horizon . . . calibrating your appetite for risk without sacrificing your passion for the audacious . . . resisting splitting apart elements that are fundamentally interconnected. Sometimes grabbing the web by its intricate whole is the only way out.

"Message delivered. Message not necessarily received."

Dan Gilbert, the founder of Quicken Loans, is fond of using the phrase to remind his employees of the limitations inherent in communicating your thoughts and beliefs to others. I imagine that the same could be said of my two dozen stories ranging in weight, complexity, and consequence. Lots of messages being delivered. I hope at least a few of them have been received.

The protagonists throughout these chapters have illuminated, in various ways, the rich and expansive potential of principled leadership to improve the ebbs and flows, the rhythms, the contours of contemporary life.

And "principled" is necessarily a contextual construct.

Even armed with an ironclad conviction of what's right and what's wrong, in one instance it bends to the imperative to compromise, as with Bud Heinselman's decision on the Boundary Waters.

In another, it's unyielding, as with Ralph Rapson's subversion of Tyrone Guthrie's explicit demands about theater design.

And in yet another, it grows into a willingness to subject strongly held beliefs to rigorous analysis and adaptive resolution, as with Gary Payne's consent to the herbicide mediation.

Leadership can also look different in different contexts.

It may entail creatively refashioning methods of problem-solving within the confines of established decision-making channels—as with the neighborhood revitalization program, the CultureTalks project, the Lake Street paving project, or Detroit's Grand Bargain.

In other cases, it begs openness to stepping outside those channels to create something entirely new—as with the Itasca project, the M-1 Light Rail line, or the Marygrove educational campus.

And sometimes, it shows up as a willingness to begin within the constraints of one system before migrating into another, as with the garbage transfer station's metamorphosis into the Green Institute, the Minneapolis Armory's escape from demolition, or the Detroit Future City plan's evolution to an independent civic institution.

A readiness to adjust, refashion, or even abandon established decision-making expectations or authorities when seeking to crack difficult challenges can, of course, be perceived as incendiary or confrontational. Recall the reaction of Mayor Sayles Belton's administration to the Minneapolis Center for Neighborhoods, or Governor Pawlenty's response to Itasca, or the county commission's answer to suggested reuse of the armory. But challenging that reflexive response is important, I believe. Constructively questioning, informing, enriching, or complementing public decision-making can widen the aperture of problem-solving possibilities.

We tend to presume that the authority that comes with an election certificate is inviolable. And when individuals or groups move outside of it, concerns arise—appropriately—about an absence of accountability, an undermining of public legitimacy, or a removal of prescriptive guardrails that guide democratic decision-making norms. But that process may end up injecting even more expansively democratic dynamics, more creatively adaptive methods, more fully transformational outcomes into the equation.

Henry Cisneros—businessman, former mayor of San Antonio, and former Secretary of the U.S. Department of Housing and Urban Development—told me he likes to think of "mayor" as a verb. He believes there are instances in which individuals, groups of people, or institutions assume some of the essential functions we commonly assume are the exclusive domain of a city government executive.

The totality of a city comprises too many civic functions for one person to hold full responsibility for them all. Command-and-control structures, Cisneros says, need to be complemented by a form of distributed (and distributive) leadership. More people taking the opportunity—and the responsibility—for weaving a part of the civic fabric is a good thing.

Itasca and M-1 Rail show that the private sector can step into this role. The garbage transfer station, the herbicide mediation, and the Whittier neighborhood's revitalization plan are examples of citizens doing the same.

And as the Detroit Future City, Marygrove campus, and West Wing intermediations illustrate, philanthropy can do this as well.

So I agree with Cisneros: it's possible to "mayor" even if that isn't one's title. Not only does that expand the problem-solving capacity of the commonwealth; it also injects dynamism into public discourse, policy, and practice.

I agree with Cisneros: It's possible "to mayor," as a verb, even if that isn't one's title.

"Mayoring" from multiple corners of community also recognizes not only that the public sector doesn't have a monopoly on ideas, and in fact that its administrative machinery works under very real implementaiton constraints. Help from outside city hall may be needed.

The private sector's capacities for marketing, lobbying, and public relations introduced a dimension to comprehensive transportation reform in Minneapolis-St. Paul that couldn't have come from anywhere else. A private-philanthropic consortium's ability to tackle transit outside the public sector's usual scope of motion gave birth to Detroit's light rail system. Philanthropy's ability to deploy a huge pool of discretionary capital made the Grand Bargain possible. And the Kresge Foundation's deep toolbox of grants, loans, guarantees, community engagement, and conservancy-creation strategies enabled a historic college to be transformed instead of carved up and sold to creditors.

Whether substituting fresh ideas for stale ones or creating innovative implementation channels in place of ossified ones, the process is less about leaping into someone else's proprietary lane than it is about blurring expected boundaries, reimagining the universe of possible solutions.

The same skills that foster a new calculus of decision-making across sectors can apply to thinking across disciplines generally. There are no walls separating environmental protection, public safety, arts and culture, historic preservation, land use and urban form, education, politics, community development.

Climate change, for example, is a public health issue, a safety issue, a community development issue—and more. Arts and culture can shape and reflect community aspiration, energize community revitalization, promote healing in the face of violence.

Seeing these interrelationships impels a form of "reverse engineering" in which a challenge, once defined, is broken down in ways that reveal the right strategies, in the right doses, in the right sequence, at the right pace.

There are no walls separating environmental protection, public safety, arts and culture, historic preservation, land-use and urban form, education, politics, community development.

I've wondered whether these observations would reverberate in any way to my 18-year-old self, the young man who was asked to step into the maelstrom of John B. Davis's world of 1968. Or whether they could reverberate in the world of today's 18-year-olds who aspire to be—or already are!—the leaders of the future.

So many of the concerns of a half-century ago are utterly different from those of today. The imperatives of social, gender, and racial justice. The urgent, burning platform of climate change. The deepening fissures of income and wealth inequality. The list goes on. As new crises emerge, and old ones mutate, the principles of leadership must adapt, evolve, and be transformed.

And yet, there is a great deal to be said for a 21st century leader—whether young, mid-career, or matured—understanding lessons from the past.

Calls to transform policing strongly evoke Mayor Fraser's community-oriented safety strategies of thirty years ago.

Ensuring that citizens can access the technical resources they need to challenge professionals determined to tear up a neighborhood for the sake of increasing traffic flow—or to use their neighborhood as a garbage dump—is no less imperative now than it was in Minneapolis decades ago.

Current efforts to incorporate neighborhood resident visioning and planning processes into municipal priorities and budgeting mirror work done by Minneapolis residents in the '90s to guide their neighborhood revitalization program. And more recently, 500 miles to the east, work by Detroiters that yielded the Detroit Future City framework.

The polarized political climate today might suggest that compromise is a quaint anachronism. Indeed, Bud Heinselman's concessions in the name of long-term environmental stewardship may seem to pale in the glare of current debates over critical race theory, abortion, LGBTQ+ rights, or anything refracted through the prism of current partisan ideology.

But the specifics of Heinselman's situation shouldn't obscure the basic truth that he understood that the only way to advance a cause that would ripple through successive generations was to find common ground.

The Sisters of the Immaculate Heart of Mary were loath to give up on a Marygrove College one hundred years in the making, but they recognized that a new entity embracing the spirit of community service would honor their legacy into the future.

And there may be something to be said for embracing collaboration with sectors that at first blush appear poorly aligned, antagonistic, or even ethically flawed. Organizing vigorously, refusing to sell out to crass transactional incentives, advocating loudly over long periods, and deploying Alinsky tactics to break resistance are all essential tools of the trade of young—and not so young—leaders of principle.

But there may come a time when broad-brush assumptions about the inherent flaws of those perceived to be the enemy, or about the intrinsic inability of certain groups or institutions to act beyond self-interest, must yield to a more nuanced perspective about how deep, abiding change can be realized.

There may be times when a corporate entity, or public official, or foundation possesses an intellectual, reputational, or financial asset that can advance the goal at stake. The alliance need not be permanent. And it needn't be compromising, provided one's goals and methods are rooted in integrity and commitment to the greater good.

I hope these stories have suggested just how varied the opportunities for leadership are. And the virtually endless forms it can take. Leadership is contextual. It is personal. It can be fleeting—but its impact can be enduring.

Perhaps most importantly, it is cumulative. Acts of principled leadership compound. Our communities—whether defined by group identity, common challenges, shared environments, or collective values—will progress toward the kind of just, equitable, opportunity-rich, and healthful future to which we aspire only when our individual acts of leadership are combined into an alchemy of shared purpose.

The times demand it. It's tempting to conclude that this is no truer today than it has been in the past. But that simply isn't the case. With each passing decade, our challenges become more multifaceted, interconnected, and intractable. To break the cycle, to set a different trajectory, requires that we learn from where we have traveled. I hope that this book has expanded your view of how we can do that.

Acknowledgments

From conception to execution to refinement, **Elwood Hopkins** has been the animating force behind this memoir. He urged me forward when the stories seemed too small or idiosyncratic, when the leadership themes needed sharpening, when the threads to the present day were insufficiently clear. He read and reread and reread again—each time clarifying, humanizing, and enlivening. It's not possible to express adequately my appreciation for his guidance, and for his confidence that this was a project worth doing.

Elwood was the reviewer-in-chief, but others were generous with their time and thoughts in reacting to the storylines and ideas.

Amanda Storey tested the stories against her exuberant passion for working the difficult channels of community change.

Russ Kavalhuna used his extraordinary experiences as a prosecutor, airline pilot, and college president to help crystalize how lessons of leadership might be conveyed without becoming saccharine and trite.

Beth Brockmann dissected every detail with the experienced eye and sensibility honed by a successful banking career.

Glenn Wilson sized up each account through the lens of an urban community development professional who knows fluff and overstatement when he sees it.

Angelique Power offered early assurance that events of some fifty years ago could reverberate today.

Bill Morrish generously agreed to share examples of his drawings, the brilliance of which I could ever hope to realize in my own.

Although he doesn't know it, **Andres Duany** provided the inspiration for the name of the publisher: Transect Press. Andres used the term to describe an urban planning model in which a community's density transitions from the urban core to the suburban to the rural to the natural. The notion of a synchronist continuum somehow seemed an apt description of the book's intention.

There was only one person I contemplated as being able to provide the right sense of design balance to a book at once filled with words, yet animated by visuals. **Kristi Anderson** of Two Spruce Design was a joy to watch work, as she sought to create a book both serious in its purpose and playful in its execution. I can't say enough about her creativity, humor, and profound professionalism.

Susan Maas describes herself as an "eagle-eyed copy editor," which doesn't begin to do justice to her skills. She invariably read as much for content as she did for grammatical accuracy. She became a wonderful partner in making sure each sentence was not only clear, but important.

Paul Maravelas did a masterful job in indexing a book filled with more names, places, and things than I thought could be indexed.

And finally, my wife, **Gail**, and children, **Avery** and **Anna**, were always the people for whom this book was primarily intended. They were curious, patient, and supportive over many years as I turned inward and to the computer for long periods of time. I hope the book will help them understand a husband and father just a bit better.

Index